FRANZ ROSENZWEIG'S PHILOSOPHY OF EXISTENCE

Studies in Philosophy and Religion

Volume I

FRANZ ROSENZWEIG'S PHILOSOPHY OF EXISTENCE

AN ANALYSIS OF
THE STAR OF REDEMPTION

by

ELSE-RAHEL FREUND

1979

MARTINUS NIJHOFF

THE HAGUE/BOSTON/LONDON

Originally published in German.
First edition, Leipzig: Felix Meiner, 1933.
Second edition, Hamburg: Felix Meiner, 1959.

Translated into Hebrew by Yehoshua Amir (Tel-Aviv: Shocken Publishing House Ltd., 1972).

Translated into English from the German revised edition by Stephen L. Weinstein and Robert Israel. Edited by Paul R. Mendes-Flohr.

The distribution of this book is handled by the following team of publishers:

for the United States and Canada

Kluwer Boston, Inc.
160 Old Derby Street
Higham, MA 02043
USA

for all other countries

Kluwer Academic Publishers Group
P.O. Box 322
3300 AH Dordrecht
The Netherlands

ISBN 90 247 2091 5

PRINTED IN THE NETHERLANDS

In memory of my dear son
SHLOMOH-GABRIEL FREUND
fallen on 4 Iyar 5708 (13 May 1948) in Kfar Etzion
in the fight for Jerusalem, the eternal city.

The author wishes to express her gratitude to the William and Olga Lakritz Endowment Fund in Martin Buber Studies, U.S.A., for providing a subsidy towards this book's publication.

CONTENTS

III. Faith Thinking or the Synthesis 160

INTRODUCTION

INTRODUCTION

The Star of Redemption,* which presents Franz Rosenzweig's system of philosophy, begins with the sentence "from death, (*vom Tode*), from the fear of death, originates all cognition of the All" and concludes with the words "into life." This beginning and this conclusion of the book signify more than the first and last words of philosophical books usually do. Taken together – "from death into life" – they comprise the entire meaning of Rosenzweig's philosophy. The leitmotif of this philosophy is the life and death of the human being and not the I of philosophical idealism, where man ultimately signifies "for ethics" no more than ". . . a point to which it (ethics) relates its problems, as for science also he (man) is only a particular case of its general laws."[1] Rosenzweig deals with the individual's actual existence, that which is terminated by death; he speaks of the individual's *hic et nunc*, of his actions and decisions in the realm of concrete reality. This philosophy is not an exposition of theoretical principles. It is not concerned with man in general in abstract time, but rather with the individual human being, designated by a proper name, living in his particular time.** Human existence in its finiteness and temporalness forms the focus in which Rosenzweig's motif can be gathered together. This does not mean that Rosenzweig wishes to explain the world through the medium of human existence – this would merely be an I – philosophy on an expanded basis, a reduction to the living I instead of to the thinking I, and Rosenzweig explicitly rejects all forms of reduction. For Rosenzweig human existence determines the point of departure, method and aim of philosophizing.

---

[1] Hermann Cohen, *Religion of Reason out of the Sources of Judaism* (New York: Frederick Ungar, 1972), p. 168.

* Franz Rosenzweig, *The Star of Redemption*, translated from the second edition (1930) by William W. Hallo, (New York, Chicago, San Francisco: Holt, Rinehart and Winston, 1970). The following quotations are from this translation and are designated by page number only.

** Martin Heidegger also turns against the I of idealism in reproaching Descartes for not having analyzed the nature of existence (*die Seinsweise*) of the I am (*sum*) in his *cogito ergo sum*. Cf. M. Heidegger, *Sein und Zeit*, (Halle: M. Niemeyer, 1927), p. 24. Similarly, Martin Buber refers to the abstract and consciously capitalized I as "the shame of the world spirit that has been debased to mere spirituality." M. Buber, *I and Thou*, translated by W. Kaufmann, (New York: Charles Scribner's Sons, 1970), p. 115.

Death, of which Rosenzweig had concrete experience in World War One through witnessing the fall of thousands, is the decisive point of departure leading Rosenzweig to an estrangement from idealism, to an undeniable certainty in a reality beyond thought, a certainty impervious to any argument of idealistic reasoning. Death effects "the experience of factuality that precedes all facts of actual experience."* In this sense of an existentially real end death also assumes within actual experience a dividing function and – since it becomes necessary to overcome the division – also a driving function. Death discloses the end of creation and hence forecasts its regeneration in revelation.[2] The death of creation demands the love of revelation which is as strong as death and can overcome it. Death also demarcates the boundaries between revelation and redemption, for only the latter signifies the final defeat of death. "Death plunges into the Nought in the face of this triumphal shout of eternity. Life becomes immortal in redemption's eternal hymn of praise."[3] Through redemption's act of love the "Other," the one that death consummates as solitary and lonely, is transformed from its rigid objectiveness (*Gegenstaendlichkeit*) into the "Thou" and thus quickened to life. Revelation still wrestles with death; again and again death must be encountered and fought, for only in redemption is death decisively negated.

Thus in the sequence of experienced realities of faith (*Glaubenswirklichkeiten*) – creation, revelation and redemption – death assumes a role similar to that of negation in Hegel's dialectic process. And if one transfers the terms creation, revelation and redemption to the three parts of the system, as Rosenzweig does, death acquires an unequivocal dialectic meaning. It separates thesis, antithesis and synthesis. Since, however, death signifies not merely conceptual but existential negation, the thesis which it negates is also not a postulate of reason, but a mode of existence, while the synthesis, as a reestablishment of the thesis at a higher level, is each time a new kind of existence. This same existential advantage ensures that progress is brought about not through thought operating on its own power, but through an act of the human being, an act of freedom. *The Star of Redemption* in its entirety as a philosophy of existence is *the negation of idealism*, a negation implemented by an overturning of the presuppositions of idealism, by the free act of the thinker Rosenzweig himself. Within Rosenzweig's system, which in its tri-

[2] 155.
[3] 253.

* Franz Rosenzweig, "Das neue Denken," *Kleinere Schriften*, (Berlin: Schocken, 1937), p. 397. *Kleinere Schriften* incorporates the anthology *Zweistromland* (1926) and many additional essays either printed in sundry periodicals or previouslu unpublished. Henceforth it is referred to as *Kl. Sch.*

partite division is a well-balanced structure deftly designed, overturning generates a gradation of modes of existence similar to the dialectical structure of Hegel's system, as we shall subsequently see.

The three parts of *The Star* treat three modes of human existence: the solitary human being, the human being before God, and the human being in community. From a methodological standpoint they answer the questions "How is existence to be conceived, how is it to be experienced, and how is it to be envisioned (*schauen*)?" These modes of perception also stand in dialectic relationship among themselves, for vision cancels and elevates thinking by bringing about a new consolidation of experience while nevertheless incorporating within itself the multiplicity of experience. Each of the three parts is in turn divided into three books and repeats the division of the whole. The first part, the thesis, provides the conceptual basis for the system, while its second book, the metalogic, deals with the problems of logic in particular. The second part, the antithesis, represents within the system the position of faith, of experienced revelation. From its perspective the first part, i.e., thinking, appears as creation and the third part, i.e., vision, as redemption, while its second book is concerned with the specific revelation. The third part, faith thinking, occupies the stage of synthesis in the system and is illustrated in the image of the Star of David, which is the "star of redemption." It is not until the third book of this part that faith thinking is brought to its final expression, with the entire structure thereby attaining its culmination. Thus human existence passes in these modes through increasingly higher stages. Regarding that which comes before, each stage appears as an enhancement, while regarding that which follows it is both foundation and limitation.

As important as death and the free act might be for the structure, however, they are merely preparation for the modes of existence. The stress is on these modes of existence themselves. Rosenzweig's first experience of death, as encountered in the First World War, only led him to a conception of the realistic All.* This realism as such in its relation to idealism will now be briefly considered. Idealism had also made the claim to perceive reality; it was the very lawfulness of thinking that was to guarantee reality. Strictly speaking, however, this was possible only because reality was produced by thinking itself, as with Hegel, or at least was established with thinking's decisive assistance, as with Kant. This reality of thinking, which seems to proceed

---

* The All, or the One, is a pre-Socratic concept denoting the ultimate unity that embraces the multiplicity of being. This unity is generally understood to be grounded in God. (Cf. Xenophanes, Stobaeus, *Ecol.*, I, 60). German idealism, which is Rosenzweig's reference, also speaks of the All. Hegel held that philosophy is nothing but the study that seeks to comprehend the All (editor's note).

without presuppositions, in fact has for its basis the pretentious presupposition that the All is conceivable. Now, as soon as a fact (an event) falls
outside the bounds of the conceivable All – a fact that refuses to be the product
of thinking or to submit itself to thinking's rule, as indeed is the case with the
fact of human life and death, the basic presupposition of idealism is shaken.
Personal life is the "indigestible actuality outside of the great intellectually
mastered factual wealth of the cognitive world."[4] The basic concept of this
world, the All, is thereby dethroned.[5] The thinking which based its claim to
authority on the All must tolerate other ways of cognition (*Erkenntnis-
methode*) besides itself. Experience can enlist thinking into its own service and
with its help can found a new All. That a new All does again come into being
indicates the significance idealism nevertheless had in Rosenzweig's thinking.
Within the graded structure of the system idealism has the same importance
as the conceived existence of idealism has vis-à-vis actually experienced existence. Idealism is the thesis the negation of which gives rise to the new thesis of
Rosenzweig's system. Idealism is cancelled by realism, yet in spite of its
negation it has a hand in achieving the new thesis.

The idealism contained in *The Star of Redemption* as a foundation and as a
presupposition always remains the idealism of Hegel. Rosenzweig considered
this to be the most consistent and the most complete form of idealism,
whereas Hermann Cohen, with whom Rosenzweig had a close relationship, served as a guide through those very ideas which were no longer
entirely idealistic. One such influential idea, for example, is the logic of
origins, the begetting of elements out of the differential, that Cohen approp-
riated from his study of calculus. Instead of creating from a pure and
universal Nought,* Cohen takes for his basis the Nought of magnitude, that
is, a particular, no longer purely formal Nought.[6] Another of Cohen's ideas,
one which in Rosenzweig's opinion was decisive in leading Cohen away from
idealism, had an even stronger effect on Rosenzweig: namely, the foundation
of religion upon a concept of relation in place of a concept of generation.
God, instead of being the object of an idea, confronts sinful man as forgiving

---

[4] 11.

[5] Cf. *ibid.*

[6] Cf. 20–21.

* The Nought (*das Nichts, nihil,* non-ens): absolute opposite of something existent, the Aught
– that which possesses content or substance. Christian Wolff (1679–1754) summarizes this
conception of the Nought thus: "what neither is – nor is possible – one designates as the
Nought." For theology this conception of the Nought is crucial; the sovereignty of God is
exemplified in the *creatio ex nihilo.* According to Hegel the Nought is absorbed into and
reconciled to pure Being in the process of reality's becoming (editor's note).

God. It is upon this real correlation that the methodological independence of religion, even though within the limits of reason, is grounded.

The extent to which the idealism of Hegel, which Rosenzweig overcomes dialectically by means of his system as a whole, nevertheless determined the dialectics within this system is best demonstrated by a look at Heidegger's philosophy of existence and the different roles performed by death in the thought of Heidegger and Rosenzweig. Heidegger also views death, the termination of existence (*Dasein*), as being constitutive of this existence. Being is "existing unto death (*Sein zum Tode*)."[7] But for Heidegger death has no driving force. Existence as determined by death is human existence in general and is the object of an ontological interpretation guided by the phenomenological method. To be sure, death for Rosenzweig is also initially the experience of an Aught, leading to a consciousness of existence in general. Rosenzweig, however, does not limit his analysis to this dimension of existence. In the incessant recurrence of death ever-new stages of existence are formed. Death is each time overcome by action, until the last stage brings the realistic All as the highest form of being.

In this succession of modes of existence, the experienced reality of the second part of *The Star* receives a greater accent than the merely conceived reality of the first part, in keeping with the importance actual human existence has from the very beginning. Indeed, here in the book of revelation the heartbeat of the entire system is discernible. Here the subject dealt with is the existence of the living human being, confronting the living God and the living world. The experience of revelation justifies creation and is the basis for redemption – within the system these are also the first and third parts – so that human existence is the living core of the entire structure. That real human existence is grounded in experienced revelation, in other words, the theological turn, becomes evident from the central position which human existence also occupies in theology. The human being in the solitude and uncertainty of his actual existence, in the distress of his life and in his dilemma of conscience, has always been the subject of theology. Both philosophy of existence and theology occupy themselves with the "center of life of the human being."[8] Philosophy, whenever it has been concerned with being in reality, has always had to employ the personal God. This was the case with Kant, albeit in the framework of a theology of ethics, yet in order to guarantee the realization of the moral idea in life. This was also the case with Schelling when he moved from conceived existence to actual existence. Conversely, medieval theology

---

[7] M. Heidegger, *Sein und Zeit*, p. 245.

[8] Karl Heim, "Ontologie und Theologie," *Zeitschrift fuer Theologie und Kirche*, Vol. 11, no. 5 (1930), p. 328.

could make use of Aristotle's philosophy of existence, while Kierkegaard fastened on to Schelling's positive philosophy. The great interest which present-day theology takes in Heidegger's philosophy, as well as Heidegger's theologically-hued expressions, such as *guilt* and *conscience, existing unto death*, being in *degeneration*, can be explained in terms of the identity of the subject matter. A philosophy of existence such as Rosenzweig's which seeks not merely to understand existence as such, but to evaluate and to mark off against eache other the various modes of existence, almost of necessity trespasses on the realm of theology, to which the distinction between true and untrue existence is peculiar.

Man, upon hearing God's call, awakens to true existence. His I is fashioned in the presence of God's Thou. Through the relation to God he is transformed from a closed self to one beloved by God, a soul capable of passing on this love to other human beings and there by making them into neighbors (*Naechsten*), into human Thous. That which man receives as revelation he passes on as redemption. He turns the relation between God and himself into a relation between himself and the world. It is only through both relations that he reaches true humanity. Man's real existence in its totality is thus faith existence. "The root word I-Thou can only be spoken by the entire being."[9] "The concentration and fusion into a whole being can never be accomplished by me, can never be accomplished without me. I require a Thou to become; becoming I, I say Thou."[10] In this way relation constitutes the real living human being in his totality,and it therefore is made the basic concept of *The Star*'s second part.*

Only the relation and not God, world and man themselves can be experienced; otherwise they would become a matter for dogmatic empiricism. Only the actions of these three elements, their effects on each other, can be experienced. They themselves remain as conceived substances (*gedachte Wesenheiten*) in the background of this experience, an experience which is not theoretical. Rather, just as the objects of experience are acts of freedom so too is the experience itself an act of freedom, a turning. On the other hand, it is again only

[9] M. Buber, *I and Thou*, pp. 54, 62.
[10] *Ibid.*, p. 62.

* Nahum Glatzer proposes the name "co-existentialism" for Rosenzweig's philosophy, since man exists together with God and the world. Cf. the introduction to Franz Rosenzweig, *Understanding the Sick and the Healthy*, (New York: Noonday Press, 1953), p. 15. Philosophy of existence, however, always refers to *human* existence. That God and the world are present at the side of man as factualities assumes significance only for man, insofar as through his relation to these factualities a level of human existence, namely existence in faith, is constituted. Man remains the concern of Rosenzweig's philosophy even in his stance vis-à-vis God and the world. Hence the term "co-existentialism" is likely to lead to confusion.

experience that is capable of mastering relation, for the distinguishing mark of every relation is the "and," that is, the premise that both sides will preserve their autonomy as two equal beings. The relation *between* these beings can only be described by experience. Thinking always must say "essentially," since it aims at standardization through *sub*-ordination. Pure *a priori* thinking is always exclusive and domineering; its culminating point – with Kant the unity of consciousness, with Hegel the absolute spirit – is always merely a unity that has conquered multiplicity, indeed conquered it absolutely. Correlation can not possibly be a basic concept of an idealism which is consistent in its quest for unity. Rather it is a sign of the critical strain which experience introduces to pure thinking. The discussion between Heinrich Rickert and Richard Kroner on heterothesis and synthesis[12] is characteristic of this difficulty of "and" and "essentially" even within idealism. Kroner, an exponent of Hegel's idealism – according to Rosenzweig's interpretation the most consistent form of idealism – does not consider Rickert's heterothesis admissible in the realm of pure thought, since it stems from experience, even though in this case from theoretical experience.

Strictly speaking, it is revelation alone which is that experienced relation establishing the total existence of the human being. Man's reality is certainly already grounded in the first relationship of God to the world, that is in creation, but it is precisely his creatureliness which man leaves behind him in revelation. Creatureliness is only the *basis* of man's total existence, a basis on top of which the revelation of God is built. Reality in the full sense arises solely out of the relation to God and to the neighbor. With this binding together of creation, but it is precisely his creatureliness which man leaves behind him in fraternal relationship between the new thinking and theology of experience. Human existence embraces thinking as well as faith, and just as faith discerns in thinking creation, so it discerns in creating revelation. Both thinking and faith should not be left unrelated to each other. There is no truth of reason independent of a truth of faith; both need and complement one another.

Rosenzweig's conception of revelation as relation between God and man is to be distinguished from all theories of revelation which disparage man as recipient of the revelation, such as the dialectic theology of Barth and Gogarten.[13] His conception should also be distinguished from all religion of feeling such as that of Schleiermacher, which projects God into the experience of the

---

[11] Cf. F. Rosenzweig, "Einleitung in die Akademieausgabe der Juedischen Schriften Hermann Cohens," *Kl. Sch.*, pp. 335, 338.

[12] Cf. R. Kroner, "Anschauen und Denken," *Logos*, Vol. 13 (1925), p. 90.

[13] Cf. S. Marck, *Die Dialektik in der Philosophie der Gegenwart*, Vol. 1 (Tuebingen: Mohr, 1929), pp. 99 ff. and p. 104 ff.

human being. In Rosenzweig's case, both poles, God and man, are upheld equally; both are needed precisely in their autonomy in order to make revelation possible.

Inasmuch as the decisive concept for existence is a concept of relation, the spirit is something that is between God and man and hence also between man and his neighbor, namely, the word, speech.* Speech is the "primal act"[14] of spirit. Thus it is already associated with the first relation affecting man in his natural existence, with creation. Speech "is entire from the beginning: man became when he first spoke."[15] Only in revelation, however, does speech come alive. Speech in the human being is merely the refraction "of the true event because in truth language does not reside in man but man stands in language and speaks out of it – so it is with all words, all spirit."[16] Through its method, grounded in actual relation, the new thinking leads away from the abstraction of idealistic thought, which could know only "yes" and "no." Dialectics returns to its source, to the spoken dialogue. Thinking could merely create a static, lifeless world, a world of objects; only the word creates the real world."The idealistic world is not created through the word, but through thought."[17] This formulation already suggests the idea that speech is "truly analogue – and therefore more than analogue" and hence "that which we hear as a living word in our I and which resounds towards us out of our Thou"[18] must correspond to the word of the Bible. Speech is analogue to God's word in the Bible, and since it is more than analogue it is God's word itself. Here the innermost motif of speech thinking becomes clear. Speech thinking is not merely the representation of the living dialogue between God and man but is also faith thinking in the sense that it is oriented to the Bible, where God spoke when He created and spoke when He revealed Himself. Thus the speech of the Bible becomes the speech of the thinker. He describes the orbit in which he believes with the words in which he trusts.[19]

[14] M. Buber, *op. cit.*, p. 141.
[15] 110.
[16] M- Buber, *op. cit.*, p. 89.
[17] 141.
[18] 198.
[19] Cf. 150–151.

* In German *die Sprache*, which means both language and speech. Rosenzweig generally means the latter. Language is an established pattern of verbal symbols – as such it is independent of time. Speech, on the other hand, requires time and a partner, one who responds. "Speaking," Rosenzweig writes, "means speaking to some one . . . And this some one is always a quite different some one, and he has not merely ears, like 'all the world,' but also a mouth." ("The New Thinking," N. Glatzer, *Franz Rosenzweig: His Life and Thought*, p. 200). Rosenzweig expresses here the root-idea of dialogue, which he shares with Eugen Rosenstock-Huessy and Buber. Cf. *ibid.*, p. 200f (editor's note).

Thus relation as a basic concept of existence makes speech as method intelligible. Further, the notion that this relation occurs through an act, and that reality is therefore not a being but an event, opens a vista to the problem of *time*. Speech thinking itself is bound to time, nourished by time.[20] It must take time seriously.[21] Speech is possible only successively; it can not say everything at once. The temporality of existence is supported by a metaphysical world-time. "Not in time...occurs that which occurs, but rather time itself occurs."[22] "Just as every single event has its present, its past and its future, without which it can not be known or at least known only distortedly, so too reality as a whole. Reality also has its past and its future, specifically, an everlasting past and an eternal future."[23] Past reality is creation, present reality is revelation and future reality is redemption. Indeed, it is only the designation of existence as creation, i.e., its being distinguished by the character of the past, that gives the world its fixed place.[24] World-time becomes guarantor for the objectivity of God, world and man – creation, revelation and redemption become the history of God.

How fundamental an importance the time-motif has for Rosenzweig, becomes clear only in the third part of *The Star*, in the realm of vision. Eternity, not as time of endless duration, but as simultaneousness of the three qualitatively different times, forms the basic concept for being-in-community. Judaism and Christianity join together the times of creation, revelation and redemption as the eternity of life and the eternity of the way, respectively. Their description is directly determined by the systematic interest in "an eternity that is" (*einer seienden Ewigkeit*).* Furthermore, eternity as the convergence of the three times not only unites with the existence of Judaism and Christianity, but is equated with truth. Present, past and future coalesce in God; thus God is truth. The history of God is history only when viewed from the human perspective. From the standpoint of God history coalesces into being. The eternity of life and the eternity of the way can only represent the eternity of God relatively. In fact, it is only because creation, revelation and redemption are coincident from God's perspective that this life and way are possible. Hence, world-time leads to *the climax of the system: "God is truth."* Out of this fixed point the parts of the All become arranged in their final order.

[20] Cf. *Kl. Sch.*, p. 387.
[21] Cf. *Ibid.*
[22] *Ibid.*, p. 384.
[23] *Ibid.*, p. 385.
[24] Cf. 133.

* *Kl. Sch.*, p. 392. In this case also one could not speak of a co-existence of man with other beings. By integrating himself as Jew or Christian with other "eternities that are" man once more attains a level of human existence, namely, existence in community. Cf. note p. 10.

"God is truth," this sentence in which all else culminates, is Rosenzweig's answer to the horror of death that he witnessed in the World War. The fact that Rosenzweig gave this answer attests to his rootedness in Judaism. It demonstrates this more than does the Star of David, the "Star of Redemption," introduced as a symbol summarizing the book, and more even than the biblical language employed in *The Star*. This answer testifies to his natural belonging to a people that throughout its four-thousand year history has been a living witness to God as truth and has drawn its strength and its breath of life from this witness.

This absolute truth, however, belongs to the eternal hypercosmos (*Ueberwelt*); it is grasped in vision. Man in his earthly existence learns only that God loves him. With respect to God's supreme being, human existence in all its modfications and even in its crystallization in the Jewish and Christian communities constitutes a critical factor. All that remains for man is the experience of revelation and with it the certainty that God has created and that man has been commanded to love his neighbor. Judaism and Christianity receive only a portion of the truth, which they have to verify. The notion of verification is the sign of finite human existence even at its final and highest point. With this, human life once more becomes end, just as it had been beginning. The system consummates itself, coming to a close in a circle.

And yet this last correspondence to idealism also illustrates the fundamental difference which parallels the distinction between the conceivable All of idealism, which did not know the individual, and the All of realism which arises through the very gathering together of these individuals. Hegel's system claimed to be absolutely and generally applicable. Rosenzweig, in contrast, is aware that philosophy is a finite undertaking.* "Let everyone try his hand once at philosophizing...But...the book...must itself be accounted for, instead of sustaining itself or being supported by other books of its kind. This vindication occurs in everyday life."[25] Philosophy that seeks to solve the problems of human life and human existence must be justified by the life of the philosopher.

It is beyond the scope of the following study to offer an exhaustive analysis of *The Star of Redemption*, inasmuch as *The Star*, in the framework of its system, raises the salient problems of Western philosophy. The aim of this work is simply to serve as a first orientation and thereby at the same time to stimulate more comprehensive and more thorough research. Moreover, the

---

[25] *Kl. Sch.*, p. 397.

* Cf. M. Heidegger, *Vom Wesen des Grundes*, (Halle: M. Niemeyer, 1929), p. 3, where he also speaks of philosophy as an innermost, finite effort.

theological questions, as dealt with in general in the second part and in particular in the third part of *The Star*, must be reserved for a theological study. The present contribution will:

1) set forth Schelling's positive philosophy, to which the basic idea of *The Star* points as its *historical example;*

2) give *a brief survey of Rosenzweig's work in its entirety;*

3) pursue *several motifs of The Star of Redemption* which were merely sketched above.

In so doing this study places Rosenzweig's life work itself under the aspects of creation, revelation and redemption, which in art, and only in art, lose their character as experienced realities and become categories under which a multiplicity of matters can be classified. Rosenzweig says of these categories:

"A naturalistic foundation as it were always belonged to the category of *creation;*

what was specifically 'aesthetic,' professional, difficult, to be attained with might and main, always belonged to the category of *revelation;*

the actual, the visible, the ultimate result, that for whose sake alone all else had to precede, always belonged to the category of *redemption.*"[26]

---

[26] 248–249.

A. SCHELLING'S POSITIVE PHILOSOPHY

A. SCHELLING'S POSITIVE PHILOSOPHY

Schelling's later thought is one of the most difficult areas of modern philosophy and until recently has remained practically unexplored. In the nineteenth century, apart from the purely expository books of Konstantin Franz[1] and Kuno Fischer,[2] only Eduard von Hartmann investigated in a short essay[3] the relation of Schelling's later thought to the history of philosophy. Schelling's truly imposing work, which claimed to have both conquered and crowned German idealism, scarcely received any notice, and to the extent that it did, was judged unfavorably. The reason for this may very well be, as Kuno Fischer believes,[4] the unfavorable timing of its appearance in print – the years 1856–1858, which marked the end of the epoch of Friedrich Wilhelm IV and immediately preceded the beginning of the militaristic Bismarckian era. Schelling's thought no longer found an echo in a world which had other interests. This neglect, however, can also be explained by reasons internal to his thought. Schelling's later thought grew from the soil of idealism. Step by step it led away from idealism, yet even in its final independence it considered idealism to be its indispensable precondition. Idealism was always recognized by him as negative philosophy which, together with its positive counterpart, constituted the one philosophy. Schelling's positive philosophy in turn was a philosophy of existence nourished by faith in revelation. In Schelling's words, it added the "that" (of factuality) to the "what" of negative philosophy. The positivism of the nineteenth century, which was oriented to the natural sciences, could not be expected to show any understanding for this combination. Thus E. von Hartmann, for instance, while appreciating Schelling's inductive method comments: "The attachment to a pure rational course and the admiration for the illusion of the absolute science must be *forgiven* in a man who has devoted the best part of his life to

[1] Konstantin Frantz, *Schellings positive Philosophie*, Part 1 (Aalen: Scientia Verlag, 1968, Neudruck der Ausgabe Koethen 1879–1880).

[2] Kuno Fischer, *Schellings Leben, Werke und Lehre*, 4th edition (Heidelberg: Winter, 1899).

[3] E. von Hartmann, *Schellings positive Philosophie als Einheit von Hegel und Schopenhauer* (Berlin: O. Loewenstein, 1869).

[4] K. Fischer, *op. cit.*, Preface, p. x.

this science."[5] So, too was it inevitable that Neokantianism, which maintained its leading role until the 1920s, would take offence at Schelling's later thought. The positivists were disturbed by the close attachment to idealism, the Neokantians by the notion of being that was not preceded by thought, and both held in common an aversion to Schelling's affirmation of revelation. To the positivists revelation did not appear to be an empirical fact,[6] while to the Neokantian idealists it appeared as such a fact, but a fact that was to be rendered superfluous by the religion of reason.

Not until the present day has there been a reawakening of interest in Schelling's later thought. The lively discussion over the pros and cons of Heidegger's philosophy of existence, which has opened up a new horizon for the discussion of problems of being, in conjunction with the external inducement provided by the centenary of Schelling's death, once more turned the attention of philosophers and theologians to positive philosophy, which hitherto had been neglected and little appreciated. Among the recent scholars of Schelling special mention should be made of Walter Schulz, who in his comprehensive book perceives Schelling's later thought as the answer to "the question on the possibility of the self-constitution of pure subjectivity."[7] In his lecture given at the Schelling conference of 1954 held in Ragaz, Switzerland, Schulz accordingly calls positive philosophy absolute reason's critical reflection on itself.[8] "Only when it is absolute can reason...limit itself.... Reason has no boundary that is not boundary for reason. And only a boundary set by reason itself can be boundary for reason."[9] This interpretation, which seeks to "retrieve" Schelling for idealism, certainly preserves the unity of Schelling the idealist. This ocuurs, however, at the expense of the freedom of the personal God, His actuation of being that is prior to thought. God's freedom expresses itself in creation and revelation and for its part demands a kind of thinking which confines itself to its own boundaries. So, too the existentialist thinkers Kierkegaard, Nietzsche and Heidegger – whose predecessor the later Schelling was and to whom Schulz devotes a special chapter of his book[10] – advance to a dubious proximity to idealism, though they themselves explicitly resisted idealism, since they felt sure they were standing on quite different ground. Karl Jaspers judges Schelling's positive

    [5] E. von Hartmann, op. cit., p. 21.
    [6] Cf. ibid., p. 35.
    [7] W. Schulz, Die Vollendung des deutschen Idealismus in der Spaetphilosophie Schellings (Stuttgart: Kohlhammer, 1955), p. 5.
    [8] Studia Philosophica, Jahrbuch der Schweizerischen Philosophischen Gesellschaft, Vol. 14 (1954), p. 247.
    [9] Ibid., p. 250.
    [10] Schulz, op. cit., pp. 271–306.

philosophy from the perspective of his own voluntaristic philosophy of existence. He considers Schelling's greatness to be that he related the question of the sovereignty of reason to the realm of transcendence: Why is there an Aught at all, why is there not Nought? However, says Jaspers, instead of "expressing the depth of experience through being answerless,"[11] it is precisely an answer that Schelling wants. Further, Jaspers continues, it is Schelling's misfortune that he characterizes transcendence as freedom, and thereby lapses into objectification. In view of the fact that Schelling made many unfinished starts, he offers numerous possibilities for completion as well as exegesis, all according to the observer's own standpoint. This leads to varying results. Paul Tillich, the existentialist theologian, already presented a detailed analysis of positive philosophy in his dissertation.[12] He has remained faithful to Schelling, and throughout the development of his own thought, as he says,[13] has never forgotten his dependence on Schelling. Tillich points precisely to the existential character of Schelling's philosophy, seeking it even in the latter's philosophy of nature and his system of identity. He rightly finds the distinguishing mark and the final formulation of this character in Schelling's positive philosophy, which already anticipated the basic concepts of modern existentialist thinking. Tillich thus follows a path which makes it possible to relate the later Schelling to the nineteenth century philosophers of life who struggled against idealism as well as to the present-day philosophy of existence.

The present study limits itself to dealing with Schelling's positive philosophy as a basis for understanding the philosophy of Rosenzweig. Accordingly, the stages of Schelling's thinking that moved him away from idealism can only be adumbrated. This will be followed by a brief exposition of positive philosophy and by a consideration of its particular problems in so far as they allow for comparison with Rosenzweig.

---

[11] K. Jaspers, "Schellings Groesse und sein Verhaengnis," lecture at the Schelling conference in Ragaz, *Studia Philosophica*, Vol. 14, p. 21.

[12] P. Tillich, *Die religionsgeschichtliche Konstruktion in Schellings positiver Philosophie* (Breslau: Fleischmann, 1910).

[13] Tillich, "Schelling und die Anfänge des existentialistischen Protestes," lecture in commemoration of Schelling's centenary, *Zeitschrift fuer philosophische Forschung*, Vol. 9 (1955), p. 197.

a) Schelling's Development prior to Positive Philosophy

"The Program for a System of German Idealism" of 1796 which, as Rosen-zweig was able to demonstrate,[14] can be ascribed to Schelling with certainly. contains the first exposition of those trains of thought which achieved pro-minence one by one in the course of Schelling's development.[15] The fact that already at the beginning of his thinking these ideas lay together before Schelling as the building blocks of a future system, even though this system was never fully put into effect, helps make the uniformity of his development clear. Nevertheless, the chronological succession of these thoughts did not completely resemble their systematic juxtaposition, so that Schelling did not merely carry out what he had previously expounded. Rather, he instituted decisive modifications in these thoughts. The element of unrest that re-currently impugned each systematic summation, the leaven that was present in Schelling's thought from the very beginning, is his consciousness of the reality of nature, human life and God, a consciousness which moved him powerfully. Thus the periods of Schelling's thought – philosophy of nature (c. 1797-1799), aesthetic idealism (c. 1800-1801), philosophy of identity (c. 1801-1804), theory of freedom (c. 1804-1813) and positive philosophy (c. 1813-1854) – can be understood as a progression whose advance is determined through the relation of this unrest to each crystallization of the system, and whose beginning and conclusion, in spite of their many similarities, look quite different.

Fichte's theory of science, dating from 1794, had made the acting ego the principle for explaining the world; nature was the means through which the ethical aim was to be realized. Schelling's philosophy of nature was at first to be no more than a further development of this theory. Because the self-containedness of nature fared badly in Fichte's theory,* Schelling wanted to trace the working of reason in nature itself. While Fichte had constructed a series descending from the I, the lowest rank of which was nature, Schelling sought to establish an ascending series that began from nature and ended with the I. This different point of departure, which sprang from studies in the natural sciences, gradually led Schelling to ascribe to nature an autonomy which it could not have in the framework of a strict I-philosophy. The

---

[14] F. Rosenzweig, "Das aelteste Systemprogramm des deutschen Idealismus," *Kl. Sch.*, pp. 230–277.

[15] Cf. *ibid.*, p. 267.

* Cf. F. Rosenzweig, "*Das aelteste Systemprogramm des deutschen Idealismus,*" *Kl. Sch.*, pp. 242–245, for a discussion of Fichte's influence on the philosophy of nature of Schelling.

philosophy of nature, which at first had been conceived of as a part of the theory of science, quickly assumed a place of equality next to it, the series of objects next to the series of subjects. This necessitated a third principle to unite both series. -- In conformity with Kant's *Critique of Judgment*, which had already influenced his philosophy of nature, Schelling found this uniting function in aesthetics. In this way Schelling's romantic philosophy became a consequence of philosophy of nature, which stressed the object. Romantic philosophy itself was only a transitional link to the system of identity, which anchored the equilibrium of subject and object in the identity or the absolute indifference of both.

With this, on the one hand, the step beyond Fichte towards absolute idealism was taken. On the other hand, exactly because it was supposed to give expression to the equivalence of subject and object, the supreme principle was not the absolute subject as with Hegel, but rather a point of indifference between the two poles, a point that of necessity received a quality of being. It is not absolute thinking but absolute being of the I, which intuits itself directly and through this intellectual intuition produces itself. Thinking is associated with the finite I, intuition with the absolute I. Seen from the perspective of Hegel's absolute subject, for whom intuition is merely an element in the thought process that is to be overcome, this positing of intuition as absolute is an aberration from the path of idealism. Kroner says even of Schelling's early writings: "Schelling is not aware...that in the highest principle he unintentionally mixes the colors of objectivity more strongly than those of subjectivity. This is done, certainly, as part of the endeavor...to make as radical a separation as possible between the sphere of absoluteness and the sphere of the finite I...If, in order to arrive at the absoluteness, it is necessary to relinquish together with the finiteness of the I its very I-ness (*Ichhaftigkeit*), then the goods for which this sacrifice was made were acquired at too great a price."[16] Regarding the philosophy of nature as the kernel for the systems of identity Kroner comments: "The dissociation of the philosophy of nature from the context of the I-philosophy...can not possibly be given a transcendental justification."*

Schelling now faces difficulties in deriving the finite from the principle of identity, which remains beyond all contradictions, and in explaining the origin of difference from absolute indifference. By designating the absolute as God, what was at first only a logical problem became a religious problem, and in this way acquired a special acuteness. The problem of thought merged with

[16] R. Kroner, *Von Kant bis Hegel* (Tuebingen: Mohr, 1921–1924), Vol. 1, pp. 550–551.

* R. Kroner, *Von Kant bis Hegel*, Vol. 1, p. 609. On this point Kroner stands in sharp contrast to Schulz, who transcendentally justifies even Schelling's positive philosophy.

the question of theodicy. The point in question was no longer merely a matter of logical derivation, but of the actual origin of finite things, and of evil in the world. With the inclusion of religion into the system the entire distress and severity of human existence gained influence over the formulation of the absolute. If the independence of nature towards the I had diverted Schelling's philosophy from logical idealism, then the greater consideration accorded to human life brought about the gradual estrangement from idealism in general. Hoelderin's tragic end* had blatantly revealed the inadequacy of the romantic synthesis for life. To be sure, romanticism also knew life and its inherent contradiction, but for it "living...(was) not something irrational...but the root or zenith of rationality itself. The universe as totality of the living is therefore never torn apart by primal oppositions or by a flood of arbitrariness impervious to meaning, but rather from its primordial beginning it is sheltered in the monism of the rational,which is perhaps raised to divine absoluteness."[17] Through the basic presupposition of identity, contradiction's sting was removed from the outset. As soon as human life showed this contradiction to be insoluble, this discovery had to be expressed in a different version of the absolute. In his book *Philosophie und Religion* (1804), Schelling for the first time turns his attention to the reality of the finite which is outside thought. He no longer attempts to derive the finite from the absolute, but rather explains its origin as a falling-away (*Abfall*), that is, as a free act of the finite. The weight of this reality is even more prominent in *Philosophische Untersuchungen ueber das Wesen der menschlichen Freiheit* (*Philosophical Inquiries into the Nature of Human Freedom*, 1809), where human freedom is led away from the conflictless sphere of the idealistic concept of freedom and is perceived as a real decision between good and evil. This positive, fulfilled freedom can no longer be reconciled with an absolute existing in harmonious equilibrium. Rather, this freedom demands a God who is Himself disunited and whose nature, lying within Him as dark foundation, is conquered by His freedom and made into past. God has made the decision that man ought to carry out in real life. Here, as well as in *Die Weltalter* (*The Ages of the World*, 1811), the absolute becomes the justification for the fact that the contradiction, in all its harshness, is present in the world.

From here it is merely one step more to Schelling's positive philosophy.

---

[17] Hinrich Knittermeyer, *Schelling und die romantische Schule* (Muenchen: E. Reinhardt, 1929), p. 348.

* Friedrich Hoelderlin (1770–1843), German poet, whose poems on the fragility and isolation of human existence received a tragic coda in the pitiful insanity that marked his last forty years (editor's note).

Until now the reality outside thought had furnished an increasingly more forceful strand in the idealistic construction. In positive philosophy this reality becomes the true absolute, which can be known only through revelation. To be sure, the absolute is also related to the concept, and the identity of thought and being is explicitly retained. "In this unity, however, the priority is not on the side of thought. Being is first, thinking only second or subsequent."[18]

b) Positive Philosophy

Schelling's positive philosophy is contained in the four volumes of the second part of his collected writings[1] and is divided into philosophy of mythology and philosophy of revelation. Philosophy of revelation is, strictly speaking, also called positive philosophy, and within its framework the designation "positive" is to be further limited to the philosophy of Christianity found in the last volume.

These three gradations of positive, and thereby also of negative, are themselves futher graded. In its widest dimension positive philosophy marks itself off against all of Western philosophy, from the Greek up to idealism. Schelling labels Western philosophy as negative or purely rational, while considering his own system of identity to be the climax of idealism. He generally expresses a negative opinion of Hegel, blaming him for what is the basic presupposition of every absolute idealism, that is, for wanting to include existence within the idea. Thus, for instance, he says: "The true improvement that could have been made to my philosophy would have been to limit it to its merely logical significance. Hegel, however, made a much more definite claim than did his predecessors to have also comprhended the positive."[2] If in another place Schelling believes that his system of identity did not even raise the question of existence,[3] this is only to be understood as a result of his changed position, from which he looks back on his own work and sees it in the further development of his own theory, but merely as a one-sided elaboration of the subjective factor in the absolutely mixed identity between subject and absoluteness of the subject in Hegel's system, for which the object is only a factor in the subject's path to itself, rational philosophy reaches its peak and

[18] Schelling, *Werke*, Part II, Vol. 1, p. 587.

[1] *Fr.W.J.V. Schellings Saemtliche Werke*, Part 2, ed. K.Fr.A. Schelling (Stutgart: J.G. Gotta, 1856–1861). In the following citations the Roman numeral will refer to the part and the Arab numeral to the volume.

[2] *Ibid*, II, 3, p. 86.

[3] Cf. *ibid.*, I, 10, pp. 148–149.

by this means the antithesis negative-positive first assumes its full sharpness. It is solely the dialectic method that he values in Hegel. "While the others, to be sure, were nearly only staggering, he [Hegel] at least adhered on the whole to the [dialectic] method. The energy with which he propounded this false system, but a system all the same, could have brought inestimable benefit to science, had it been turned in the proper direction."[4]

Since positive philosophy also develops its principles dialectically before applying them to mythology and revelation, it also has a rational, i.e., negative part, which would be negative philosophy in the stricter sense. This rational part presents the positive principles first in conjunction with mythology, but then in conjunction with revelation itself – and this is the third and strictest sense of negative philosophy. The latter two gradations, however, merge into one another, since the introduction and the first part of the philosophy of revelation lead only to a repetition and a more precise formulation of the positive principles that were already developed in both introductions and the first part of the philosophy of mythology.

If one were briefly to sketch the character of positive philosophy in general, Schelling himself could be cited. He designated the meaning of human existence as the ultimate and most profound problem of all philosophy. Nature and history reach their zenith in the human being, but "man and his actions are far from making the world comprehensible. Man himself is the most incomprehensible of all and inexorably drives me to the opinion that all being is wretched... It is precisely he, the human being, who pushes me to the final, desperate question: Why is there Aught at all? Why is there not Nought?"[5] Positive philosophy is the science that is to answer this question. It is especially needed at times when life's indispensable convictions are undermined and the need emerges to take possession of them in a new way. One would think that Schelling is speaking of our times when he continues: "The more glaringly one depicts the discord, the dissension, the manifestations of our day that threaten disintegration, the surer he who is truly informed can see in all this only omens...of a great and abiding restoration ...which...however...must be preceded by the merciless destruction of all that has become decayed, brittle and defective. There must be an end to this struggle, however, for there can not be endless progress, that is, progress without purpose and meaning. Mankind does not advance *ad infinitum*; mankind has an aim."[6] It is concern of philosophy to draw attention to this aim. This is, to be sure, as Schelling says with obvious reference to Hegel, the

---

[4] *Ibid.*, II, 3, p. 87.
[5] *Ibid.*, II, 3, p. 7.
[6] *Ibid.*, II, 3, p. 10.

task not of a weak philosophy but of a strong philosophy, one that can stand up to life, one that "far from feeling helpless in the face of life and its colossal reality...draws its strength from reality itself and therefore in its turn also produces things that are real and lasting."[7] Philosophy is not to be "a mere tangent" to human life, but rather "it must deeply penetrate into life; it must become the center around which all forces revolve."[8] It wants to satisfy not a formal and momentary thirst for knowledge but a real thirst. It wants to provide a system "that would be strong enough in the future to also stand the test of life, that would not run the risk of gradually fading when faced with the great objects of reality,...but rather would itself acquire strength and vigor with the unfolding experience of life and with a profound, penetrating knowledge of reality."[9] If these powerful sentences of Schelling are contrasted with Hegel's utterance: "When philosophy paints its gray on gray, then an image of life has become old, and with gray on gray it is not possible to rejuvenate the image, but merely to know it; the owl of Minerva begins its flight only with the approach of twilight,"[10] then the blatant difference between positive philosophy, close to life, standing face to face with reality, and rational philosophy, keeping a distance from life through noble resignation, becomes strikingly evident.*

The two crucial questions of life which positive philosophy is to solve are the actions of man and man's relation to God. Freedom and religion thus constitute the subject matter of positive philosophy – freedom not understood in a formal sense and religion not understood as religion of reason. Rather, freedom is a question of real capacity for decision, of act fulfilled by content, and religion is a question of real relation of man to the personal God.** And it appears that man's action and the living God refer to each other. God as an idea suffices for man only if he surrenders himself as acting agent, and consequently rids himself of his selfness and flees into meditative life, into contemplative cognition. But "the renunciation of action can not be carried

[7] *Ibid.*, II, 3, p. 11.

[8] *Ibid.*, II, 3, p. 178.

[9] *Ibid.*, II, 3, p. 177.

[10] Hegel, *Vollstaendige Werke*, herausg. durch einen Verein von Freunden des Verewigten (Berlin: Duncker, 1832 ff.) Vol. 7, pp. 20–21.

* Rosenzweig is of the opinion, however, that in carrying out his ideas, Hegel has not always adhered to this mood. Cf. F. Rosenzweig, *Hegel und der Staat* (Muenchen: R. Oldenbourg, 1920), Vol. 2, p. 82.

** Hermann Cohen believes that also for Kant religion is not identical with the religion of reason. Even with all the autonomy of the moral human being religion remains man's most profound core, the primal source of personality and of moral strength and moral disposition. Ethics certainly is also the innermost core, but nevertheless only a theoretical strength, whereas religion remains a practical primal strength. Cf. H. Cohen, *Kants Begruendung der Ethik* (Berlin: B. Cassirer, 1910), p. 481.

through; action must be taken. As soon, though, as active life again enters the picture, and reality again demands its own rights, the ideal (passive) God also no longer suffices."[11] Thus, in order to perceive the personal God, Volitional thinking is necessary. If the transition from negative to positive philosophy is to be accomplished, there is a need for "a practical stimulus. Thinking, however, contains nothing practical. The concept is merely contemplative and is interested only in the necessary, while here it is a question of that which is outside necessity, that which is willed. The I . . . knows how at the basis of all moral action lies the falling away (*Abfall*) from God . . . making the life of the I problematic, so that it will enjoy neither peace not quiet until this breach is healed. No happiness can help the Self other than That which at the same time redeems it. For this reason the Self craves for God Himself. It is Him, Him that it wants, the God that acts, with whom is providence, the God who can confront the factuality of the falling away as One who is Himself factual, in short He who is the *Lord* of being . . . For person seeks person."[12] Positive philosophy is thus only for the discerning and the free, for those who know that rational philosophy can not satisfy man's true concerns. Freedom is its source and freedom is its aim.

In spite of this close association between freedom and the personal God, an association that at times approaches the identification of the two (cf. the passage, "freedom is our highest thing, our duty, we want it as ultimate cause of all things"[13]), positive philosophy nevertheless is not religion itself. Rather, it merely wants to understand religion, which is a reality of human life. Though "it has the content of religion as its own content,"[14] positive philosophy must reject revelation as a *formal* principle. "For he who wants and is able to believe does not philosophize, and he who philosophizes thereby proclaims that mere belief does not suffice for him."[15] Positive philosophy acknowledges religion, i.e., that yearning for the real God and for redemption, which found its historical outcome in the fact of mythology and revelation, and subsequently applies its general principles to this fact in order to make it comprehensible. There is no philosophy which can prove that God *must have* created the world or which can know *a priori* the divine will for revelation. But once the world and revelation are empirical facts and once they are recognized as an act of God's free decision, philosophy can make the act, the execution, comprehensible. God is above reason; man acts precisely in the highest commandments of ethics above reason, but *a posteriori* the transcen-

---

[11] Schelling, *Werke*, II, 1, p. 560.
[12] *Ibid.*, II, 1, pp. 565–566.
[13] *Ibid.*, II, 3, p. 256.
[14] *Ibid.*, II, 3, p. 134.
[15] *Ibid.*, II, 3, p. 135.

dent is also accessible to human cognition. Since, however, negative philosophy did not have the means to grasp such a boundless matter, it was
destined to distort the contents of revelation. "There is no point in excusing
this obscurity by saying the teaching [on revelation] is a secret. For either it
really is a secret – in which case we would have to refrain from speaking about
it at all and certainly not want to enclose it a firm, rigid definition – or it is an
open secret, i.e., one that for us has ceased to be a secret. In order, then, for the
secret to be something for us, that is, in order for it to be truly revealed, it must
of necessity also be understandable."[16] Positive philosophy, therefore, is
believing science. It takes the existence of a personal God, which can not be
proved by reason – and Kant's critique of the proofs of God remains valid – as
being proved by the fact of creation and revelation, that is, by believing
experience (glaeubige Erfahrung) and then treats this experience philosophically. Faith and knowledge are not to stand next to each other separately so
that man must behave dualistically, now as a creature of reason and now as a
creature of faith, without being able to justify his faith before his reason.
Rather, both are to belong to each other. Reason demands faith at the point
where it reaches its limits, so that faith bestows genuine truth to the per-
ceptions of reason. For "all knowledge that is merely rational is basically only
unknowing knowledge."[17] Reason for its part also is able to comprehend
faith. Faith is the end of negative philosophy and the beginning of positive
philosophy. It is an objectively grounded cognition which itself can become a
principle for science.

How, then is positive philosophy related to experience, i.e., in this case to
the fact of revelation? In what sense is it empiricism? To begin with, sen-
sualism is excluded. "It is wrong to limit empiricism in general to that which
merely is susceptible to the senses as though this were its only object. This is
because a freely willing and acting intelligence, for instance – such as each one
us is – does not manifest itself to the senses as such, as intelligence. Nevertheless it is empirical, and indeed can be perceived only empirically. For no one
knows what is inside a man unless he expresses himself. A man can be
recognized by his intellectual and moral character only a posteriori, that is, by
his utterances and actions. Let us suppose now that the question is one of an
acting and freely willing intelligence that is a presupposition for the world.
Even this will not be recognizable a priori, but only through its actions, which
fall within the field of experience. Thus, even though it is transcendental it will
be known only empirically."[18] "Only decision and action can substantiate a

[16] Ibid., II, 4, p. 31.
[17] Ibid., II, 4, p. 118.
[18] Ibid., II, 3, p. 113.

true experience. If, for instance, experience has no place in geometry, this is precisely because in this field everything can be accomplished by pure thought, because here no event is to be presupposed."[19] Schelling distinguishes between sensate and mystical empiricism. While sensate empiricism does not even share the opposition to rationalism with positive philosophy – for every sensate experience has a necessary relation to the concept – mystical experience is in accordance with the aim of positive philosophy. Both want to know that which is beyond the senses, except that one does this in a mystical manner and the other in a rational manner. The lowest level of mystical empiricism is that which takes divine revelation as an *external* fact for the proof of that which is beyond the senses. Next comes affective philosophy (*Gefuehlsphilosophie*), which becomes convinced of the existence of God through feeling. Theosophy is to be reckoned as belonging to the third level, where man envisions the divine essence and the essence of creation in a state of ecstasy. In the derivation either from revelation or an individual feeling of that which is beyond the sense there is something mystical.

It may seem as though Schelling's philosophy corresponds to the first kind of mystical empiricism. The difference is one between blind faith and comprehended, i.e., philosophical faith. Positive philosophy considers the existence of God as an absolute premise which can not be proved but which can only be experienced through revelation, hence through believing experience. In so far as positive philosophy comprehends this experience, however, that is, explains it according to general principles, it thereby proves the divinity of its premise. For "God is not . . . the transcendent. He is the transcendent that has been made immanent (i.e., that has become the content of reason)."[20] Here lies the key for understanding the fact that the same principles explain revelation as well as nature and history and at the same time form the concept of God: nature and history are a continuous revelation of God and the proof of His existence. "We shall therefore say: The premise whose concept is this and this (that which is above being) might have *such* a consequence (we shall not say: it will necessarily have such a consequence, for then we would be reverting to necessary movement, i.e., to movement determined by a mere concept; we shall only say: it can have such a consequence, if it wishes . . .). But now this consequence actually exists (this sentence is a sentence based on experience; the existence of such a consequence is a fact, a *datum* of experience). Therefore this fact, the existence of such a consequence, shows us that the premise itself also exists in the way in which we had comprehended it,

---

[19] *Ibid.*, II, 3, p. 114.
[20] *Ibid.*, II, 3, p. 170.

that is to say, it shows us that *God exists.*"[21] The existence of the absolute premise is thus proved by revelation, while its essence is proved by revelation *illuminated by speculation.* In other words, the existence of the consequence proves the existence of the premise, while the existence of *such* a consequence proves the existence of this premise as God.

The difference between negative and positive philosophy with regard to empiricism is briefly expressed by Schelling as follows: "Negative philosophy is *a prioric* empiricism; it is the apriority of the empirical, but precisely on account of this is not itself empiricism. Positive philosophy, on the contrary, is empirical apriority or the empiricism of the *a priori* in so far as it proves the premise by what comes after as being God."[22] Negative philosophy prescribed the law of the intellect to the empirical and thereby participated creatively in existence. Positive philosophy recognizes existence as lying outside of thought and comprehends it *ex post facto.* The identity of thought and being remains the basic presupposition. Without it *no* philosophy, including positive philosophy, would be possible, and faith would be all that remained. But while negative philosophy had placed thought in front of being in this identity, so that being became dependent on thought, positive philosophy – convinced that reality can not be exhausted by thought – stressed the priority of being, which thought serves as explanation. "If reason is all being (and hence conversely all being is reason), there will be no small difficulty in furnishing the non-rational (*die Unvernunft*) which is nevertheless needed to explain the actual world."[23] Only both taken together, being and thought, constitute the complete philosophy.

The concept of uniform philosophy, containing the negative and the positive as parts having *equal* rights, takes up the idea of the system of identity once more at a higher level. Schelling leaves philosophical religion, to which positive philosophy is supposed to lead, completely undetermined, so that the dialectic triad [of thesis, antithesis and synthesis], which is nowadays carried out everywhere in the theory of principles, fails to materialize in the structure of the system. Rather, both components, the negative and the positive, challenge and support each other. "Only a properly understood negative philosophy brings about positive philosophy and, conversely, positive philosophy is possible only against the background of a properly understood negative philosophy. Negative philosophy, when it withdraws into its limits, makes positive philosophy recognizable for the first time and thereupon

---

[21] *Ibid.*, II, 3, p. 129.
[22] *Ibid.*, II, 3, p. 130.
[23] *Ibid.*, II, 4, p. 23.

makes it not only possible, but also necessary."[24] To be sure, Schelling does not develop this systematically conceived basic thesis into a well-rounded system, but from this point of departure he embarks on a theoretical confrontation with negative philosophy. The further development of both aspects of uniform philosophy by means of positive philosophy is no longer simply because of revelation, but is now required *in principle*.

These expositions submit the history of the whole of Western philosophy to a thorough inspection. They dwell especially lovingly on Aristotle and Kant, the two great empiricists, and revolve around the Aristotelian pair of concepts "what" and "that"* or "potential" and "act" (*Actus*). "Negative philosophy is designated as such because it is concerned only with the possibility (the what), because it perceives everything as it is in pure thought independent of all existence. To be sure, existing things are deduced within it (otherwise it would not be a science of reason, i.e., an *a prioric* science, for the *a priori* is not *a priori* without an *a posteriori*), but this does not mean that within this philosophy it is deduced that the things exist. It is negative also because it has the ultimate, which in itself is act (and therefore as opposed to existing things is above existence), only as a *concept*. The other philosophy, in contrast, is positive because it proceeds from existence, that is, from the actuation of being (*Actus-Sein*) which is found in primary science as necessarily existing in the concept (as naturally being act). This actuation of being is at first only pure "that," whence it proceeds to the "what" (to that which is being)** in order to lead that which is existing in such a manner to the point at which it shows itself as real (existent) Lord of being (of the world), as personal, real God. By this means all other being is at the same time explained in its existence as deduced from this first "that" and thus a positive system, i.e., a system that explains reality, is constituted."[25] "In so far as the question is concerned with the "what"...this question...is addressed...to reason, whereas only experience can teach...*that* something whatsoever exists."[26] Aristotle and Kant, both of whom proceeded from experience, arrived by the path of induction to the border of negative philosophy. Aristotle ascends from the empirical to the logical. "From the bosom of the indefiniteness and

---

[24] *Ibid.*, II, 3, p. 80.

[25] *Ibid.*, II, 1, pp. 563–564.

[26] *Ibid.*, II, 3, p. 58.

* On this point cf. Hans Ehrenberg, *Fichte* (Muenchen: Drei Masken Verlag, 1923), p. 126 ff. and pp. 191–213, where it is shown that for Fichte too there was a third period, in which the basic concepts of his philosophy are "what" and "that," though for him revelation ultimately means for all that only philosophy itself.

** Elsewhere Schelling calls this step inverse transcendence, which Kant did not forbid. Schelling, *op. cit.*, II, 3, pp. 169–170.

infinity of the potential, of that which is possible, nature raises itself by degrees towards the end... In proportion to the advance toward the end, being rules over non-being, act over potential...The ultimate is...the potential established entirely as act."[27] Since Aristotle began with experience, he deems, to be sure, this ultimate as actually existing – unlike negative philosophy which considers it merely as idea. Inasmuch, however, for Aristotle also it was the essence of things and not their existence that mattered, he does not make use of God as that which is actually existing. For him God is merely end and not principle of a new science. This ultimate as pure act in *concept* is the highest point negative philosophy can reach. – Kant also perceived God as an ultimate, necessary concept of reason. His ideal of pure reason is not something general, not idea, but rather something particular, individual, that is to say impenetrable, something containing the material of all possible and actual being. Yet this also is not the actual God, but the God *conceived* as actual,whose existence remains transcendent. Kant calls the being that precedes all thought a true abyss for human reason. His God says: "I am from eternity to eternity; there is nothing besides me, except that which is something by my will alone, but then, whence am I?" In Schelling's opinion, these words do not contain a rejection of the notion of a bieng that precedes thought, but merely the expression of the notion's incomprehensibility. Accordingly, he sees in the Kantian ideal of pure reason the bridge which can lead from negative to positive philosophy. If Hegel said that what is rational is real, Schelling is satisfied with saying that what is rational is *possible*. Rational being and reason itself can not be taken as absolute, for from the standpoint of the absolute it is possible that there would be no reason. "It is not reason that is the cause of the perfect spirit, but rather it is only because this spirit *is* that there is reason. The foundation of all philosophical rationalism, i.e., of every system that raises reason to a *principle*, is thereby destroyed."[28] And if rationalism justifies itself by saying that without it there would be no science this does not help. "For why does there even have to be science?"[29] Reason is the infinite *potential*, the ability of cognition, and its content is the infinite *potential* of being. It knows that things, *if* they exist, must be constituted in such and such a way. With regard to essence real existence is accidental and accessible only to experience. "Thought extends in every respect to coincidence with that which is present in experience."[30]

[27] *Ibid.*, II, 3, pp. 103–104.
[28] *Ibid.*, II, 3, p. 248.
[29] *Ibid.*, II, 1, p. 586.
[30] *Ibid.*, II, 3, p. 102.

Thought abandons that which has passed into the realm of being in order to leave it to experience, while itself moving forward to the next higher level.

Inasmuch as positive philosophy starts from absolute, transcendent existence, its negative part, that is, the exposition of its principles, will be philosophy of being, i.e., ontology. These principles are not formal concepts, but modalities of being or potentials. Schelling thereby takes up once more the problems of being of ancient philosophy. From Schelling the threads lead into the present to Martin Heidegger, whose theory of existentials[31] has its historical counterpart in Schelling's theory of potentials and whose notion of the transcendence of existence and its links with freedom[32] finds its counterpart in Schelling's positive philosophy.

c) Individual Problems

1. The Theory of Potentials[1]

Potentials are the factors of being on its dialectic path towards absolute actuation of being (actu Sein). As they themselves are principles, these factors can not contain this absolute transcendent being. Rather they merely lead up to it and thereby explain existence on the level of thought. One might call this dialectic movement positive dialectics, i.e., dialectic that though it is negative as a movement of thought, nevertheless it rests on the presupposition of a being transcendent to thought and is an implementation of the principle of the identity of thought and being, with priority given to the latter. This presupposition, which is fundamentally different as opposed to Hegel, also substantiates the difference between the two thinkers in the manner of realization.

Hegel's dialectics, which incorporates the highest principle of his system into the movement of thought, is consequently the *self*-movement of the idea, which unfolds itself in its particular factors and in this otherness is on the way to itself. The absolute spirit is point of departure as well as aim. It lives in the various categories as their driving power toward the principle and in turn needs the otherness of the categories in order to posit itself as principle. The movement is circular, for thinking is subject and object of this dialectic.

With Schelling it is otherwise. In his preface to Cousin's book he characterizes the self-movement of the idea as a fatal fundamental error, "the most

---

[31] Cf. M. Heidegger, *Sein und Zeit*, pp. 54–129.

[32] M. Heidegger, *Vom Wesen des Grundes*.

[1] For the development of the theory of potentials prior to positive philosophy cf. P. Tillich, *Die religionsgeschichtliche Konstruktion in Schellings positiver Philosophie*, pp. 5–14.

peculiar fiction or hypostatization."[2] As a result of its transcendence, Schelling's highest principle, the actuation of being, which remains outside thought, can not itself be active within the movement of thought. Together with all categories in which the idea no longer operates, it thus becomes the *object* of dialectics. Already in connection with the philosophy of nature Kroner speaks of an ontic, not logical dialectics of Schelling, because the dialectics becomes absolute without a subject that fulfils it and on whose terms of cognition it is to be based.[3] From the point of view of Hegel's dialectics this critique is justified and it is also found in Rosenzwig's book on Hegel, in which Rosenzwig calls Schelling's potentials an "external joining together" because they are not supported by the concept of consciousness.[4] This critique would have to take even greater offence at the ontic dialectics of positive philosophy, where it is no longer intellectual intuition that posits *a posteriori* idea and being as identical and without contradiction, but rather where absolute being is non-rational and accessible only to a free, volitional thinking. This free thinking as subject of dialectics faces the transcendent being as object, which it seeks as aim. In order to attain this aim it takes possession of categories that are equally objective. In spite of the fact that the moving force is now the volition of the free spirit – and philosophy "after all is itself and in name a volition, a science that freely determines for itself its subject"[5] – and in spite of the fact that the aim also remains non-rational, the dialectics nevertheless does not become something arbitrary and accidental. This volition remains subjugated to the form of dialectics and this aim is attained only by means of the totality of categories that are overcome dialectics nevertheless does not become something arbitrary and accidental. straight line. Thought *wills* the actuation of being. Therefore it *must* think it first as pure potential, then as pure act, then as spirit and personality, until at this highest point of the dialectics only the absolute actuation of being remains.

Schelling characterizes this kind of dialectics, with reference to Plato,[6] as thinking experience (*Denkerfahrung*).* "In order to know what being

---

[2] Schelling, *Werke*, I, 10, p. 212.

[3] Cf. R. Kroner, *Von Kant bis Hegel*, Vol. 2, pp. 29–42.

[4] F. Rosenzweig, *Hegel und der Staat*, pp. 131, 183.

[5] Schelling, *Werke*, II, 3, p. 93.

[6] Cf. *ibid.*, II, 1, p. 321 ff.

* Paul Tillich identifies this pure thinking experience with intellectual intuition. (Cf. P. Tillich, *Die religionsgeschichtliche Konstruktion in Schellings positiver Philosophie*, p. 15.) If, however, this experience was able to master the opposition between real and ideal, now that the opposition is between non-rational and rational, it will hardly be able to do so. Emphasis should therefore be given to the volitional character of Schelling's dialectics, which is oriented more to Platonic remembering (*Wiedererinnerung*) than it is to intellectual intuition. On this point cf. Schelling, *op. cit.*, II, 3, p. 287.

is,...one must...really try to think it, so that one will come to experience (*erfahren*) what it is. *Tentandum et experiendum est.* (It is to be tried and experienced.)"[7] Accordingly, thinking proceeds hypothetically and teleologically. Its aim, absolute reality, is already presupposed from the beginning. All possibilities are tried successively in order to be then gradually eliminated, with each level signifying the reality of what on the previous level had been possibility. This inductive path from possibility to reality produces non-rational being. The method of elimination, which alone is capable of positing a principle outside thought, has, like every inquiry, a critical nature. Thought confines itself within its limits and makes visible the aim which is outside it. In this self-limitation there is a certain similarity to the idealistic-critical dialectics such as S. Marck has founded in this century,[8] which on the basis of R. Hoenigswald's psychology of thought posits Hegel's absolute dialectics as a boundary concept. Compared with this, however, Schelling's theory of potentials is not a dialectics of finite intellect, which positively excludes reason, but a dialectics of finite reason, which sets absolute freedom as its limit. It is no longer a dialectics of the creative reason of idealism – even the finite cognition of critical dialectics remains creative – but rather a dialectics of the merely reflective reason of realism, i.e., of the philosophy of freedom.

The difference from Hegel's dialectics indeed lies above all in the dissociation of the movement of thought from the principle and therefore in the objectivization of the principle as well as the categories – the latter are the necessary means for the attainment of the former. But the categories nevertheless display a substantial affinity to the principle, as is the case with Hegel. This principle is not absolute knowledge, but absolute transcendent being. Correspondingly, the potentials are not purely logical, but rather are on the border between the rational and the non-rational, in accordance with their nature as negative means to positive philosophy. The non-rational aspect of the categories together with the one-dimensionality of the movement turns Schelling's theory of potentials into a kind of *Realdialektik*, a dialectic of historical life; for history also is only possible if being is not entirely soluble in thinking. The potentials belong on the one hand to thought. Reason itself is potential, ability, possibility; the potentials are "abilities of being (*Seinkoennende*) of various classes."[9] On the other hand, the potentials are "real, acting and to that extent actual forces. They stand in the middle between that which is concrete and that which is merely abstract concept, inasmuch as they are true universals, no less than the concepts, only

---

[7] *Ibid.*, II, 1, p. 330.

[8] Cf. S. Marck, *Die Dialektik in der Philosophie der Gegenwart*, Vol. 2, p. 88.

[9] Schelling, *Werke*, II, 2, p. 114.

in a higher sense, universals which are yet at the same time realities and not unrealities as are the abstract concepts."[10] "Being, to be sure, is content of pure thought only as potential. That which is potential, however, is by its very nature, as it were, on the point of being."[11] The potential owes this unmediated relationship to reality to the volitional factor that is contained within it; for "wherever will intervenes it is a matter of reality."* And the unmediated ability of being "in order to attain being, needs nothing but mere will. This concept of volition can certainly be justified, since every ability is really only will at rest, just as every will is only ability that has been made active."[12]**

Furthermore, since for thought the potentials are impenetrable and hence personal, they are individually determined. Schelling says for instance in the philosophy of mythology, where he refers to Persephone as potential: "Certainly, one will not be tempted to represent the merely abstract concepts of ordinary philosophy as persons. The philosophy we are propounding, however, deals not with mere concepts, but with true realities, actual essences. That primal possibility is not a category, but a real, intelligible essence – even if it can be perceived only by the intellect. It is not something general (not possibility as a whole) but the particular possibility which is unique and exists only once."[13] Accordingly, "we should have *names* for it, instead of saying: being-in-itself, being-outside-itself. This is a drawback which has given rise to the invention of special word-saving signs ($-A$, $+A$, $\pm A$), in order to know each potential by a name, as it were. At the same time these signs should serve to designate each potential as an essence of its own, indeed a unique essence."[14]

With this the discussion of the form and the essence of the potential leads to the exposition of its content. The modes of being, the differentations of the infinite potential of being that are designated by $-A$, $+A$, $\pm A$ are that which is able to be, that which must be and that which ought to be . The

---

[10] *Ibid.*, II, 2, p. 115.
[11] *Ibid.*, II, 3, p. 102.
[12] *Ibid.*, II, 3, p. 205.
[13] *Ibid.*, II, 2, p. 156.
[14] *Ibid.*, II, 1, p. 336.

* Schelling, *op. cit.*, II, 1, p. 579. In that will and freedom are made the criteria of reality, Schelling's positive philosophy is at the same time differentiated from every form of materialism.

** This relation to the will is already inherent in the character of the potential on the whole, as the prevailing application of conative categories to all three potentials shows. If in his interpretation of Schelling E. von Hartmann locates the will only in the first potential and the idea only in the second potential and is thus obliged to ignore many passages or to pronounce them as inconsistent, this must be understood from his own philosophical position. For him will and idea are attributes of a substance which comprehends them as identical and seeks to prove them as elements in all empirical being. Cf. E. von Hartmann, *op. cit.*, pp. 40 ff, 60.

beginning of conceived being is that which is able to be. It is the potential as potential, that is, in its pure possibility. The second instance of being is pure being, or the potential conceived as act. The distinction between potential and actual, i.e., between reason and existence, is thus repeated in reason itself. In order for the first potential not to pass directly into being – which is possible for it as will at rest – it must be detained by pure being, by conceived act. "The infinite lack of being of the first potential can only be satisfied by the infinite profusion of being of the second and by just this means the former can be maintained as ability."[15] Both potentials are posited simultaneously, but one can not stop at this duality. In the first, being is mere potential; in the second, the ability of being is potential, that is, the one is always latent in the other. These definitions, however, directly exclude each other. They can coincide only in the third mode, where the other two possibilities are barred, as it were. Only here are potential and act (always taken conceptually) one. "For that which is in possession of itself and which remains without itself, that which in act remains potential and in being remains force, language has no other word than spirit."[16] In keeping with their conative character the three potentials can also be expressed in categories of will. That which is able to be is like a will at rest, i.e., a will not willing. "Being as pure being in contrast . . . is like a clear willing without will, as it were."[17] "The third can be defined only as that which is really free to be or not to be."[18]

Schelling expresses the qualitative difference of the potentials in yet another way by saying that every potential is the attribute of that which comes next, and that which comes next is the substance of that which came before. The first potential is "not for itself but rather is subjugated and subordinated to a higher potential, to that which is pure being."[19] "They [the first and the second potentials] are not themselves substance, but merely specifications of the supra-real one."[20] This also holds for all three potentials together as against the absolute act. As soon as being is, the potentials become its attributes. "These elements, that were able to appear as principles, are lowered to mere attributes of the one that in them completely and totally takes possession of itself."[21] Where these attributes are two in number, that is to say on the level of spirit, which is the substance of the first two potentials, one might think of Spinoza's notion of the substance. The point of divergence

[15] *Ibid.*, II, 2, p. 49.
[16] *Ibid.*, II, 2, p. 57.
[17] *Ibid.*, II, 2, p. 49.
[18] *Ibid.*, II, 3, p. 235.
[19] *Ibid.*, II, 1, p. 389.
[20] *Ibid.*, II, 3, p. 218.
[21] *Ibid.*, II, 1, p. 317.

lies only in the fact that with Schelling the attributes are graded among themselves in the same way as the attributes taken together are graded vis-à-vis the substance. This difference from Spinoza is even more evident in the concept of God.

2. The Concept of God

Schelling had already distinguished between nature and freedom in God in his theory of freedom.[22] This was done on the one hand to derive the existence of the finite from God and on the other hand to give God Himself a basis for His existence. For something that exists must be conceived as individual, as spiritual personality and since this is not possible without complete freedom it needs an opposition – Schelling later says "A will... demands a cause."[23] By the positing and overcoming of this opposition the personality gives living proof of its freedom, or one might also say that personality is possible only as unity of two inner contradictions. This concept of God is thoroughly anthropomorphic. Schelling justifies this in a letter to Eschenmayer in 1812 as follows: if one were to affirm a personal God, then one would also have to conceive Him as personality, that is to say, with human manifestations of life. "Either no anthropomorphism whatsoever, and then there will also be no representation of a personal God acting consciously and intentionally (which already makes Him quite human) or an unlimited anthropomorphism, a thorough and total humanization of God (excepting the one matter of necessary being)."[24] The distinction between nature and freedom in God as a condition for His personality parallels the distinction between pantheism and theism which Schelling sets forth in a polemic[25] written in reaction to Jacobi's critique of the theory of freedom. Pantheism does not contradict theism but is its necessary preliminary stage. For just as there is no living, personal God without the self-development of God from His nature – "all consciousness is concentration, gathering, con-solidation of Himself. This negating power of an essence, a power going back to Himself, is the true power of personality within God, the power of selfhood, of ego-ness"[26] – so is there no genuine theism that does not contain naturalism as an element that is to be overcome. "As long as the God of modern theism remains a simple essence that is supposed to be purely essential – but in fact lacks essence – as He is in all the recent systems, as long as a true duality is not recognized in God and a restrictive, negative force is

[22] *Ibid.*, I, 5, pp. 331–416.
[23] *Ibid.*, II, 1, p. 246.
[24] *Ibid.*, I, 8, p. 167.
[25] *Ibid.*, I, 5, pp. 19–136.
[26] *Ibid.*, I, 8, p. 74.

not placed opposite the affirmative, expansive force, the denial of a personal God will be scientific sincerity and the assertion af such a God will be lack of sincerity."[27] In the theory of freedom the development of God into personality still takes place in the world process. In *Die Weltalter*[28] God subsequently becomes independent with regard to the world and thereby acquires the freedom for creation, a freedom, though, which approaches realization only in positive philosophy. Becoming conscious now occurs in God Himself as an eternal becoming. God posits His nature as eternal past. He also recognizes Himself in His nature as He who *is*, as the eternally present, and finally in addition as "He who will be since He sees Himself as eternal freedom as opposed to His nature and thereby sees this nature as possible background for a future willing."[29] Thus He is the Eternal, "He who was, He who is, and He who shall be."[30] Eternity here is not an empty, abstract concept of time, but is arranged according to modes of time, and is a succession of qualitative times.

On the basis of these earlier formulations of the concept of God its version in Schelling's positive philosophy can easily be made clear. God, in so far as He can be conceptualized, is the summation of the potentials. He is the third potential that contains the first two potentials after gradually overcoming them; He is the absolute spirit that has potential and act or nature and freedom as attributes and as such is the highest and ultimate concept of reason.

The relation of the three potentials in God is also similar to the relation between pantheism, theism and monotheism. Pantheism, which makes God's nature His essence, is the precondition of theism which turns God's freedom, His separateness from all else, into His essence. Both are overcome by monotheism with its personal concept of God, where God as person must be the spiritual unity of these two elements.

If being in the first potential – i.e., as being that is able – is not arrested by the second potential but passes over into being, it loses its freedom; for in being it ceases to be the source of being and becomes blind, involuntary substance, "a true non-God as with Spinoza."[31] Pantheism itself loses all freedom with respect to this blind being, whose source it can not know. Spinoza can not account to himself how this blind and infinite being could have modifications. The principle of pantheism, however, belongs to the concept of God in so far as it is spirit; it must not be ignored but overcome.

---

[27] *Ibid.*, I, 8, p. 73.
[28] *Ibid.*, I, 8, pp. 195–344.
[29] *Ibid.*, I, 8, p. 264.
[30] *Ibid.*, I, 8, p. 263.
[31] Cf. *Ibid.*, II, 2, p. 38.

For pantheism owes its spell over minds to the religious basic-idea that being is only with God and thus all being is only the being of God. "This basic-idea is the sinew of all religious consciousness, which can not be touched without being shaken in its depths."[32]

Theism, on the contrary, which knows God only in the second potential, that is, as essential freedom, as moral essence, and which denies that He is the ability that directly passes into being, divests "Him exactly by these means of every possibility of movement and turns Him, albeit in a way different than Spinoza, into an absolutely impotent essence no less immovable than pantheism's concept of God. Hence theism is also forced to acknowledge that every true creation, for instance, is something quite incomprehensible to reason."[33]

It is only monotheism that makes the basic idea of pantheism, namely, that all being is with God, truly fertile by penetrating to the concept of the living God. All being is with the living God as well, but in a threefold differentiation, as a threefold element of a spiritual personality. If the first potential corresponded to Spinozism as it is, then the potential of monotheism can indeed be compared to Spinoza's notion of the substance, but what was rigid and constrained has here been brought into movement and has become living.

Just as it is certain, however, that monotheism not only *thinks* of the personal God but acknowledges revelation, so, too, is it certain that the actual God is more than its concept. God unites the three potentials with the absolute premise of transcendent existence. His conceived being is only the negative condition for His real being. He makes His essential eternity the basis for His actual eternity and thus turns Himself into eternal beginning of Himself. God is the transcendent "that" of the immanent "what" and it is only on that account that He is truly free as opposed to being. He can be or not be; He is the *Lord* of being. "For Him this being-as-spirit is also again only a type or manner of being. This not being tied even to Himself gives Him that absolute, that transcendent, abundant freedom, the notion of which . . . exploits all the vessels of our thinking and cognition in such a way that we feel that now we have attained the highest level . . . than which nothing higher can be conceived."[34] This absolute transcendence rests in freedom, a freedom that our concepts can not reach and which can only be experienced by revelation. We make this transcendence immanent by conceiving it as God, something which is possible only because that absolute premise is related to the concept. God *is* being, He is the absolute reality that has all possibilities

---

[32] *Ibid.*, II, 2, p. 69.
[33] *Ibid.*, II, 2, p. 41.
[34] *Ibid.*, II, 3, p. 256.

behind Him. But God is also *being* and for this reason is comprehensible. By Himself He would have only a name.

The freedom of creation and revelation is based on the transcendent existence of God that can no longer be conceived. He created because He willed and He revealed Himself because He willed. For Schelling revelation means not the personal experience of the believing man, but the historical fact, specifically the fact of Christian revelation alone. Schelling views this revelation not as an aggregate of doctrines but as the fact of the life and deeds of Jesus, which at the same time also signifies for him redemption. Meanwhile he places the revelation at Mt. Sinai and the existence of the Jewish people who believed in revelation before Jesus at the side of paganism and thereby evaluates it in the spirit of the New Testament as a preparation for Christianity.

3. Creation, Rational Philosophy and Paganism

God found the possibility to fulfil His will for creation in His essence, that is to say, in the ambiguity of the first potential. That which previously on the level of concept was the potential within the potential is now, inasmuch as potential character becomes actual in the absolute premise, the potential in actuation, namely, that which as the *ability to be* really *is*. This possibility, which has a share in God's reality, is now elevated by God to a real being *different* from Himself. God initiates the process of creation, in which the potentials become real causes and come into tension with one another. Through this elevation of the potential to the actual God makes Himself potential and hides, so to speak, behind His creation. The process of creation is at first the process of nature, at the end of which human consciousness arises. Afterwards the process repeats itself in human consciousness as a theogonic process, i.e., as a process that produces God.

In this derivation of the fact of world and of man from God's will alone, one might see a cancellation of these two, especially where the world is concerned. For nature "in a certain sense is an error; no one will be inclined to attribute to it the same reality he attributes to God and to his own spirit."[35] On the other hand the creature also receives a certain right of its own, even if it is only because Schelling is searching for a motive for creation. God created because in this real separation He differentiates Himself in His forms. The true aim of creation, however, is "the creature...whom God perceives as future, as possible,"[36] is the particular man, who is the ultimate purpose of creation.

[35] *Ibid.*, II, 2, p. 645.
[36] *Ibid.*, II, 2, p. 109.

In the human being the gaining of autonomy vis-à-vis God appears in another way. Man has freedom, spirit, and his spirit opposes the divine. In the world process – where God lets the potentials operate as real causes, so that these potentials themselves are detached from God (Schelling expresses this detachment of the potentials from God by designating as B what was earlier called A)[37] – a fourth comprehensive principle is needed. This principle is the soul, which *is* those three causes exactly in the same way that God *is* being (Schelling therefore calls it a_0). God is the "that" of undivided being, while the soul is the "that" of divided being. The soul is act, in order not to be God Himself, but to be something different. "The soul...is only *what* God is, but not *like* God."[38]

In addition to this relationship to the potentials acting in the world process, the soul has a special relationship to God. Contrasted with the potentials the soul is act, but contrased with God it is potential, for "it is *what* God is" means "it is God in potential."[39] Thus the soul touches God and can secure entry into divine being for all else. At the same time, however, the potential being as opposed to God holds the possibility to be the act as opposed to God, to stand out from the world process, to isolate itself and hence to be *like* God. This falling away takes place through willing and is an act of spirit, of reason. "Spirit originally is only the willing of the soul, which longs for the wide open spaces and for freedom."[40] The soul is "its own act, the cause of itself in a totally different sense than what Spinoza said about his absolute substance. It is that pure positing of itself, with which Fichte was able to do more than he himself realized."[41] With his alienation from God on the paths of pure reason man himself pretends to be creator. Originally, however, he was destined not to elevate himself but to mediate between nature and the creator with his mere will, a will standing motionless within. Through the elevation of his spirit man steps forth from this relationship with nature, which on account of its quiet willing which acts without external movement can be characterized as magic, and thereby loses the majesty of God. The falling away of the spirit is at the same time original sin. The spirit's punishment is that man, who flees from God, falls under the rule of moral laws (accodingly the state is also derived from original sin) under which he can not be happy. For the law is concerned only with the society as a whole; to the individual it offers nothing. Here, however, "where the purpose of the law, the negation of the I, has all

---

[37] *Ibid.*, II, 1, p. 391.
[38] *Ibid.*, II, 1, p. 418.
[39] *Ibid.*, II, 1, p. 418.
[40] *Ibid.*, II, 1, p. 461.
[41] *Ibid.*, II, 1, p. 420.

but been attained, a turning point occurs."[42] Spirit withdraws into itself and again leaves room for the soul. Man at first seeks escape in the meditative, contemplative life, where he again finds God as idea. Since, however, he can not be satisfied with the life of art and science and hence with a hypothetical God, and since reality demands action, man presses forward to the personal God of revelation.

This path of rational philosophy, which leads to revelation, is parallel to the historical path of paganism to Christianity. Paganism is perceived as a theogonic process in which the potentials act as real forces set in tension, as in the process of creation – and the theogonic process is nothing but a repetition of the process of creation in human consciousness. After a gradual overcoming of the division the potentials produce God. Human consciousness is the aim and end of the process of nature. Its place is there, where the potentials are again in their unity, where they are God, that is to say, where they are again A. Human consciousness, and "primeval man is essentially only consciousness,"[43] is according to its substance, i.e., by its very nature, God-positing. Primeval man has neither a communicated nor a self-produced cognition of God, but rather the basis that precedes all thought and cognition, his essence, binds him to God. Consciousness, however, posits God only in so far as it does not move, but it can also remove itself from its place. For it is A that is based upon B, the beginning of creation, A that has within it B as potential. The process through which human essence became God-positing in this way once more finds a beginning in human consciousness, only that now it proceeds in representations. The process contains the factors of God individually and separately; at its end God's unity is restored. The individual factors, i.e., God in His division, are the gods of paganism, the polytheism that was a real though false religion and which has found its outcome in mythology. God in His unity is the personal God of monotheism who becomes manifest in revelation.

The theogonic movement, which is based on the potentiality of the consciousness that by its nature posits God, can not be mistaken for that act of freedom through which man has placed himself beyond all potential and has aspired to be a creator like God. In the theogonic process man remains in the potential. He is creature and the entire movement, exactly like the process of nature, is a real event, which takes its course independently of human freedom and human thinking. Thus the movement is objective, even though it occurs in human consciousness. It is history, history of religion, namely history of God Himself who in the development of nature and of the religions is on the way to

[42] *Ibid.*, II, 1, p. 556.
[43] *Ibid.*, II, 1, p. 118.

Himself. Nature and history are the succession of objective principles. Although in relation to these objective principles the lawfulness of rational philosophy can now be considered subjective – it is after all not a historical, real movement but a movement of thought – from the standpoint of God's transcendent freedom, i.e., from revelation, both the theogonic process and rationalism nevertheless appear as necessities of varying degree. Here that first distinction between positive and negative philosophy in the narrower and broader senses recurs: both the necessity in the process of nature and history, which is objective because it is based on potentials and the subjective necessity of the I-philosophy remain fixed in the essence. Only at their end does the real God arise. One time He restores Himself out of the division of the potentials that are His essence, that is, in an objective way, and another time the I recognizes Him as highest and ultimate, thereby reestablishing Him subjectively. In polytheism the real God is a God searching for *Himself*, thence the prophetic bent in paganism. In rationalism God is He who *is* sought. Both are preparatory stages and presuppositions for revelation.

4. History and Time

The concept of theogony as well as the process of nature, both of which signify a real growth of God, justify the designation of Schelling's philosophy as a historical philosophy. Certainly not because the theogonic process is a real-dialectic movement and Schelling thereby offers a construction of the history of religion – this would be the task of the philosophy *of* history – but rather because freedom and act are its highest principles and because the movement of the potentials is the result of God's free act, the act of creation. To be sure, Schelling's philosophy also conceives empirical history according to general principles. In addition to the process of nature and the history of paganism, it also constructs a history of the Christian Church according to three periods: Petrine, i.e., Catholic, Pauline, i.e., Protestant, and Johannine, i.e., a church that is to be brought about in the future.[44] This conception of empirical history, however, is possible only on the basis of the conception of a supra-empirical, nonrational history which expresses itself in deeds, exactly as human history is consummated in a definite time – this is the notion of the patristic construction of history – and is merely one factor in absolute history. The motif of God's eternal becoming in *Die Weltalter*, where God evolves from nature and freedom to personality, combines with the earlier idea of the theory of freedom, in which this evolution was equated with the world process. The connection lies in the new foundation that positive philosophy adds to Schelling's earlier philosophy, in the freedom of God which is outside of the

[44] *Ibid.*, II, 4, p. 302 ff.

concept of Him, the freedom which expresses itself in creation and revelation. By means of the actuation that is in His act of creation God posits Himself as becoming. The world is no longer the becoming of God in totality; neither does it fall entirely outside this becoming. Rather, it is a factor of this becoming. The life of God, which prior to creation is a flow rotating around itself, is separated by God's actuation and turned into a linear movement, whereby it achieves true beginning, middle and end. God is prior to this world, in this world and after this world.

The qualitative concept of time that in *Die Weltalter* was demanded by divine becoming* now receives a more rigorous formulation from the standpoint of the philosophy of the absolute act. Every action makes a real incision into time. Present, past and future, which as stages of becoming could merge into one another, here, where God's development occurs through his free action, are sharply demarcated against each other. Only creation establishes time in general. Prior to creation there was only absolute eternity, which is above time and which precedes in thought the first moment, which is *of* eternity – and all that comes about through positing is not eternal, but only of eternity. Now, creation *posits* this first moment by creating time as prehistoric eternity, that is, as past. "There is no time as long as there is no past. The single possible way to posit for itself a beginning of time... is precisely for something that previously was non-time to be posited as time, cosequently as past."[45] With creation a new era, the present, begins and after this time of creation future eternity follows. This world, however, can not reach future eternity, which surpasses the world just as past eternity preceded it. Thus, through the creation of the world a positive eternity is founded in contrast with the first, timeless, merely conceptual history, a positive eternity which is an organism of eternal times that are really discernible and that can be called historical. For historical time is time that is limited and that limits, time which no longer "lacks the best, namely the beginning."[46] In this segmented eternity, which has an eternal beginning and an eternal conclusion, divine history runs its course, while world time, i.e., the eternal present, is only a member of the system of times. The eternal present is prevented from reaching the future and is thus repressed time, which can only posit itself over and over again, and whose scheme is $A + A + A + A \ldots$ In it there is "neither true past nor true future."[47] Due to its uniformity, however, which is based on the fact that it is

[45] *Ibid.*, II, 4, p. 109.
[46] *Ibid.*, II, 1, p. 232.
[47] *Ibid.*, II, 4, p. 109.

* On Schelling's conception of time in the philosophy of *Die Weltalter* see the detailed investigation of Wolfgang Wieland, *Schellings Lehre von der Zeit* (Heidelberg: C. Winter, 1956).

only one member in the system of absolute times, it can also be said of the eternal present that it represents a positing of human spirit, the form of the sensate quality of the I which generates its own world for itself in origin sin, just as in general with Schelling the line between creation and original sin is not always made clear.

All the problems of positive philosophy pointed out here return in Rosenzweig's *Star of Redemption*. Rosenzweig, that penetrating investigator of the works of Schelling and Hegel, lived, like Schelling, in idealism and following Schelling's path went beyond it, in the course of which, however, he far exceeds the solutions of his gifted predecessor.

B. THE WORK OF FRANZ ROSENZWEIG BEFORE AND AFTER *THE STAR OF REDEMPTION*

B. THE WORK OF FRANZ ROSENZWEIG
BEFORE AND AFTER
THE STAR OF REDEMPTION

Six years after Franz Rosenzweig's death a selection from his correspondence appeared which contains, according to the editors, approximately one-tenth of the letters written by him from 1904 until 1929.* They begin at the time when the 18 year old high school graduate left his parental home in Kassel and entered university, and span his student years 1905–1914, the war years 1914–1918 – in the last months of which, on the Macedonian front, *The Star of Redemption* was produced – the period of Jewish activity in Kassel and Frankfurt/Main 1919–1921, and the long years of the fatal illness – which lasted longer than he himself had expected – from the beginning of 1922 to the end of 1929. Rosenzweig died at the age of 43. Through the diversity of the subjects and situations treated in the letters as well as through the diversity of their recipients, the correspondence affords us insight into the personality of Rosenzweig and into his brief life that was full of turning points. The discussion between Judaism and Christianity which was so important for Rosenzweig's spiritual development, and which found its final formulation in the third part of *The Star of Redemption*, occupies a prominent place among the themes of the letters. This theme is dealt with in the numerous letters to Hans and Rudolf Ehrenberg and above all in the correspondence with Eugen Rosenstock that is included as an appendix.** There are few letters from the brief period in which Rosenzweig concentrated on the composition of *The Star*, which was penned in one stroke "on the front, in flight, and in a field hospital."[1] The later letters, on the other hand, faithfully accompany and reflect his work, in particular the translation of the Bible and the Jewish writings. Nowhere in the letters are his thoughts

---

[1] *Briefe*, p. 470.

* Franz Rosenzweig, *Briefe*, Unter Mitwirkung von Ernst Simon ausgewaehlt und herausgegeben von Edith Rosenzweig (Berlin: Schocken, 1935). Hereafter referred to as *Briefe*.

** Cf. Alexander Altmann, "Franz Rosenzweig and Eugen Rosenstock-Huessy, an Introduction to their Letters on Judaism and Christianity," *The Journal of Religion*, XXIV, No. 4 (1944) and Eugen Rosenstock-Huessy, ed., *Judaism Despite Christianity* (Alabama: University of Alabama Press, 1968).

presented with the objectivity and coherence of the published work which confronts its author, demands examination and verification and then is presented standing on its own to the reading public. Rather, his thoughts appear in inchoate form as personal and sometimes contradictory expressions of a *tête-à-tête* with the respective correspondents, an exchange dependent on the moment, on moods, on friendship or aversion with respect to other individuals, whether they be those to whom the letters are addressed or those who are discussed. Thus the letters are not relevant for an understanding of Rosenzweig's systematic thought. They can merely give us some idea of the formation or modification of this or that thought in the thinker's soul, which was always turned and open to experience. The letters make Rosenzweig the person attractive and endear him to us.

Nahum N. Glatzer, who was bound to Rosenzweig during his Frankfurt period in friendship and study in common, has published another personal document in English, a biography of Rosenzweig with fragments from his philosophical writings.[2] This is a book that can offer a first acquaintance with Rosenzweig to a large circle of readers. In the introduction Glatzer, drawing from his close association with the thinker, vividly depicts the stations of Rosenzweig's life and the main subjects of his thought. Since he saw Rosenzweig after the completion of *The Star of Redemption* and during the years of his Jewish activity in Frankfurt, he calls special attention to Rosenzweig's breakthrough to faith that occurred in 1913 and to the return to Judaism under the impact of the Jewish Day of Atonement. In Glatzer's view, a skeptical conception of history alienated Rosenzweig from Christianity, which propagates itself among the peoples of history, and led him to a history-less Judaism. The biography is composed of letters, some of which were previously unpublished, and of jottings from the thinker's diary published for the first time. It also contains doctors' reports from Rosenzweig's period of illness, as well as oral accounts by his mother and some friends. Glatzer joins all this together with simple connecting remarks. A selection of Rosenzweig's writings, including parts of *The Star* as well as of *Kleinere Schriften*, are added in a separate section.

Aside from the aforementioned, friends of Rosenzweig have offered a picture of him in individual essays differing in form and content in two commemorative books published shortly after his death.[3] These essays also

    [2] N. Glatzer, *Franz Rosenzweig, His Life and Thought* (New York: Schocken, 1953).
    [3] *Franz Rosenzweig, Eine Gedenkschrift*, im Auftrag des Vorstands der Israelitischen Gemeinde Frankfurt a. M., herausg. von Dr. Eugen Mayer (Frankfurt: M. Braun, 1930) and *Franz Rosenzweig, ein Buch des Gedenkens*, Elfte Publikation der Soncino-Gesellschaft der Freunde des juedischen Buches zu Berlin, herausg. von Hermann Meyer (Berlin: Soncino, 1930).

give us an idea of the man standing behind the work, precisely because they are written from very different points of view and thus reveal ever new aspects of Rosenzweig's personality.

It would therefore be tempting to use the available material and connect Rosenzweig's work with his personal life. The character of this philosophy, which grew *out* of his life and which has as its subject matter problems of existence and undertakes to solve them *for* life, plainly calls for this kind of approach. The statement which Rosenzweig made about Hegel applies to no one more than to himself: "The formation of the new outlook took place for the most part not as a dry, conceptual occurrence in thought, but was deeply embedded in the stream of personal life. In order to understand this development, therefore, one should not seek to remove it from the stream to dry land."[4] Nevertheless, the onlooker whose grateful admiration is based merely on knowledge of the printed word and not on knowledge of the thinker's personality, does not have adequate and legitimate means for this kind of biographical method. Personality rounds itself out and appears complete to another person only "face to face,"[5] or when sufficient *distance in time* has drawn all the contours of a person, contours that no contemporary can any longer alter or supplement. Rosenzweig understood the thought of Hermann Cohen as well as of Hegel through their lives. To Hegel he had that distance in time and to Cohen that personal proximity which alone are able to remove the feeling of diffidence one has before the innermost region of a thinker. He describes his impression of Cohen as follows: "There I saw him...and at once I knew: this is ...a philosopher. For the first time the name philosopher forced itself upon me. Here was the personal base, the heart, the love, the hate – in short a man about whom it was worth to philosophize."[6]

The biographical mode of exposition must be the privilege of friends. For the person who was granted neither personal proximity nor distance in time, the only way left is to proceed solely along the "dry land." The following survey of Rosenzweig's collected works is to show the essential relationship of *The Star of Redemption* to the earlier and later writings and thereby to elucidate the central position this book occupies within the context of his entire production.

---

[4] Rosenzweig, *Hegel und der Staat*, Vol. 1, p. 3.
[5] *Briefe*, p. 197. The reference is to Cohen.
[6] *Ibid.*, p. 229.

a) The Earlier Writings

During his university years 1905-1912, Franz Rosenzweig applied himself first to the study of *medicine*, then to *history* and *philosophy*. In 1913-1914, after leaving the university, he turned to *theological* interests. Thus the threefold factuality of world, man and God in *The Star of Redemption* might at least have been prepared by his occupation with the three positive, empirical sciences that presuppose these factualities.

Literary testimony is lacking for the first period, which focused on the natural sciences. Nonetheless, the concept of the world that was constructed later, which perceives the world not mathematically and statically, but biologically and dynamically as a coalescence of individuum and species, suggests a connection with Rosenzweig's initial medical studies.

The connection between the study of history and philosophy and his later train of thought is demonstrable through the two volume work *Hegel und der Staat*. Rosenzweig began the work in 1909 and in 1912 submitted one chapter of it as a doctoral thesis. It was not completed, however, until 1914, as indicated by the numerous references[7] to his essay *"Das aelteste Systemprogramm des deutschen Idealismus"* written in 1914 and as Rosenzweig also states in the preface of the book.[8] It was published in 1920 with minor additions at a time when his attitude had already changed. The book's content, method and direction take their point of departure in the historic factuality of man and overcome it philosphically.

The book gives the substance of Hegel's discussion of the historical power of the state, and traces his political philosophy in its various stages. Hegel at first sees the state as dependent on the spirit of the people, which he understands to be not enlightened and rational but rather romantic and natural. – He then shapes his conception of the state against the background of a classical philosophy of history that combines the ancient state and Christianity into a historical construction and that raises above the present the ideal of a renewal of antiquity in which the unity of civil and religious life, disrupted in the Christian era, is to be restored. Therefore in the present the state can only have the duty of protecting the rights of the individual. – Both these conceptions are governed by the notion of the free individual, in contrast to whom the state is indeed powerful, but does not signify mere power. The withdrawal from this concept of man together with the higher estimation of the Christian world era brings about a further transformation of

---

[7] Cf. *Hegel und der Staat*, Vol. 1, p. 46 and Vol. 2, p. 83.
[8] *Ibid.*, Vol. 1, Preface, p. ii.

the ideal of the state. Hegel sees the fulfilment of time already in the present
and gradually comes to justify the present-day state. At first he perceives the
state as fate confronting the individual and commanding subjugation, whereas later, after his interest in the state had temporarily receded in the period
of Napoleonic rule, the state is to him the autonomous power totally uncon-
cerned with the individual. This latter view is that of Hegel's finished system
of 1820, in which the state, as reality, participates in the equation of reason
and reality as it is carried out in the philosophy of spirit.

From the book's abundance of themes only two main notions that were to
become important for Rosenzweig's philosophy are to be sketched here: the
construction of history and the manner in which the state is arranged in the
system. – The historical construction which results in the ideal of the state of
Hegel's second period is closely related to, and codetermined by, a specific
conception of the history of *religion*. Hegel saw the forerunner of Christianity
not in Judaism but in Hellenism, and not specifically in Greek philosophy and
religion but in the Greek plastic arts, in the "imagination of this religion, its
fine arts."[9] He divides the history of religion into three stages, "the first of
which is first Catholic and then Protestant. Catholicism is dominated by the
a 'beautiful mythology.'"[10] – The second epoch of religion is Christianity,
which is first Catholic and then Protstant. Catholicism is dominated by the
notion of the reconciliation of God and nature, while Protestantism is
governed by the notion of their incompatibility, so that the medieval view of
the Sabbath of the world returns here to the weekday. – The synthesis of these
contradictory forces at work in the history of Christianity is to bring the third
stage, the religion of the future. This "absolute religion" is a cult born out of
national life. It can come about only when the ideal of the state, the renewal of
the *politeia* of antiquity, will have been realized.

The appreciation of antiquity and its association with Christianity in a
construction of world history belongs to the German classical-idealist tradition. It is found in Hegel as well as in Schelling, even if the latter does not deal
with the state. The influence of Schiller and Wilhelm von Humboldt on Hegel is explicitly mentioned in *Hegel und der Staat*.[11] If later in *The Star of
Redemption* Rosenzweig sees paganism as the forerunner of revelation, ap-
parently only following Schelling's mature philosophy, he does nevertheless
move beyond Schelling. Following in the footsteps of the young Hegel, whose
Greek ideal comprises religion, state and art, Rosenzweig includes not only

---

[9] *Ibid.*, Vol. 1, p. 220.
[10] *Ibid.*, Vol. 1, p. 201.
[11] Cf. *ibid.*, Vol. 1, p. 44.

the mythical God, but also the plastic cosmos and the tragic hero in the pagan preliminary stage of revelation. On the other hand, Rosenzweig does not see the Christian era as supreme, as did the later Schelling – who did so with some hesitation – and the mature Hegel. Rather, by juxtaposing Judaism to Christianity and uniting them both in the messianic future, he takes up in this primal Jewish notion the classicists' dream of an ideal third world era.

Another idea of Hegel's political philosophy became equally significant for Rosenzweig. Within the system that ascends from logic by way of philosophy of nature to the philosophy of spirit – in which spirit arranges itself into subjective, objective and absolute – the state, as the unity of law and morality, occupies the stage of objective spirit. The state presupposes man, as he arises at the end of subjective spirit as free will, while the state itself is the presupposition for political community. This last point, that the state is among states and hence is an individuum, bestows upon the state the reality it needs in order to enter a relationship with man, who is equally real in that he is an individual. The state is the unconditional relationship between individual and community.

The positing of relation as absolute and the regarding of individuality as a sign of reality – the latter as in Schelling's positive philosophy – occurs, to be sure, in the framework of Hegel's philosophy of *state*, which does not occupy the highest stage on the system of the absolute spirit. Hegel's political philosophy receives its ultimate justification only by means of the reality of the absolute spirit itself – Rosenzweig calls it a realistic metaphysics of state.[12] Nevertheless, this entirely non-idealistic notion which Rosenzweig derives from the Hegelian system, does not signify an anticipation of his own later fundamental views.

It is possible to show other parallels between Hegel and Rosenzweig with regard to the content of their thought. There is, for instance, the concept of life in the dialectics of the young Hegel, in which life is the movement from guilt to fate, combining both in a supreme unity, an idea that was also to have an influence on the materialistic dialectics of Karl Marx.[13] Then there is Hegel's interpretation of the Christian church, whose essential character is "the transition of feeling to existence, the apotheosizing removal of that which originally had been directly human and present in love."[14] The threads, leading to *The Star of Redemption*, however, can be shown in a much clearer fashion by the method than by the contents.

Richard Kroner calls *Hegel und der Staat* together with Wilhelm Dilthey's

---

[12] *Ibid.*, Vol. 2, p. 173.

[13] Cf. Herbert Marcuse, *Zum Problem der Dialektik. Gesellschaft* (Berlin: 1931), p. 541.

[14] *Hegel und der Staat*, Vol. 1, p. 196.

work on Hegel and other thinkers a true *biography*, i.e., a tracing of the spiritual experience that has as its proper subject matter the genesis and formation of the ideas, a history of the inner growth of the thinking personality, its struggles, wanderings, discoveries, the resolution of the work in the subjectivityand inwardness of the soul.[15] In his book on Hegel Rosenzweig says, in connection with Hegel's essay of 1802-1803, "*Ueber die wissenschaftlichen Behandlungsarten des Naturrechts*" ("On the Methods for Scientific Treatment of Natural Law"), that only in the spiritual history of the great individual man is the alliance of forces between socio-economic freedom and strict political consolidation scientifically comprehensible. It would be difficult to explain this alliance in a general-conceptual fashion.[16] *Hegel und der Staat* is not the only place where Rosenzweig employs this kind of exposition, which brings the work and the thinking personality into congruence. Later, in his essay "*Das aelteste Systemprogramm des deutschen Idealismus*," this method is carried out in all those passages which deal with "the inner arrangement of the development of Schelling's thoughts"[17] and which relate this development to the personal life of the philosopher. Rosenzweig again uses this biographical method after the writing of *The Star of Redemption* in the "*Einleitung in die Akademieausgabe der juedischen Schriften Hermann Cohens*." Here he tries "to make visible the shape of his [Cohen's] personal demiurge behind his literary cosmos"[18] not only on the basis of material that was handed down but on the basis of his personal contact with the thinker. It is his intention to show by means of Cohen's mode of expression that "over the depths lie surfaces, and under the surfaces rest depths; they are joined in the unity of man."[19]

The biographical method presupposes the empirical reality of man and his inner development. It examines the intellectual expressions and then seeks to order, classify and thereby understand them. Thus it is at the same time empiricism – the establishment of spiritual facts through experience – and philosophy, somewhat in Dilthey's sense. Dilthey's thoughts on the essential historical significance of man, who does not *have* history but *is* history, and on the role of philosophy as the understanding of life originate in the same ontological approach that is here the basis for Rosenzweig. Thus, if Rosenzweig says of Dilthey that he has "the most sensitive feeling for pure psychic

---

[15] Cf. R. Kroner, *Von Kant bis Hegel*, Vol. 1, p. 18. For this kind of biography also see the works of Eugen Kuehnemann: *Schiller* (Muenchen: C.H. Beck, 1905); *Herder* (Muenchen: C.H. Beck, 1912); *Kant* (Muenchen: C.H. Beck, 1923); *Goethe* (Leipzig: Insel-Verlag, 1930).

[16] Cf. *Hegel und der Staat*, Vol. 1, p. 159.

[17] *Kl. Sch.*, p. 264.

[18] *Ibid.*, p. 299.

[19] *Ibid.*, p. 300.

reality as such, a feeling coming from positivist training,"[20] this is more than mere assertion. It is the recognition of kinship. The image of the "flowing stream" that Rosenzweig repeatedly employs for thinking in his writings may also be related to this notion of the inner history of the human soul, a history which expresses itself in thought.[21]

Thus to begin with Rosenzweig wants to give a "*narration* of the development"[22] of Hegel's conception of the state in accordance with the empirical givenness of the thoughts in the thinker's soul. "That which is ultimately inexplicable in personal life evades analytical treatment. It simply wants to be taken up."[23] On the other hand, he also speaks of his "exposition that classifies"[24] and of "disclosing in order to distinguish."[25] The method, taking as its point of departure Hegel's personal life and fate, thus demonstrates how this conditioned the transformation of his ideal of the state and shows how his political philosophy was given its final form by expanding finally into a consciousness of time. In keeping with this starting point, the method also returns again to historical factuality. It does this – in conformity with Friedrich Meinecke's school of intellectual history* – by describing the philosophy of Hegel in its history-creating strength and by demonstrating that Bismarck's actions were grounded in Hegel's conception of the state.

This connection between empiricism and philosophy, which turns mere stringing together of facts into a scientific method, finally establishes itself also in the tendency of the book. Rosenzweig once more places the political thinking of Hegel in its historical context and presents the equation of reason and reality as the unification of the diverging streams of 18th century political thought and as the foundation for the 19th century's conception of the state. In this way he not only attempts to interpret the history of ideas, but also seeks to actively influence his time through his book and thereby render a service to German life. "Hegel's limited and rigid idea of the state . . . was to decompose itself, as it were, in front of the eyes of the reader in its develop-

---

[20] *Hegel und der Staat*, Vol. 1, Preface, p. xii.

[21] Some of the numerous places (where this image appears): *Hegel und der Staat*, Vol. 1, p. 221; "Die Bauleute," *Kl. Sch.*, p. 118; "Ein Gedenkblatt," *Kl. Sch.*, p. 292.

[22] *Hegel und der Staat*, Vol. 1, pp. 11, 175.

[23] *Ibid.*, Vol. 1, p. 73.

[24] *Ibid.*, Vol. 1, p. 25.

[25] Cf. *ibid.*, Vol. 1, pp. 82–83.

* For a discussion of Rosenzweig's relation to Meinecke, as well as his general view of history as expressed in his journals, see Paul Mendes-Flohr and Jehuda Reinharz, "From Relativism to Religious Faith. The Testimony of Franz Rosenzweig's Unpublished Diaries," *Leo Baeck Institute Year Book* XXII (1977) (editor's note).

ment through the life of its thinker so that it could offer the prospect of a German future more spacious inwardly as well as outwardly."[26]

Now even if in *Hegel und der Staat* we encounter human historical factuality in threefold form – as history which Hegel confronts, as history of the individual soul that expresses itself in thoughts and thereby once more produces history, and as history which Rosenzweig himself faces as interpreter and as actor – it nevertheless should be pointed out that all this finds its place within idealism. For not only are the content and method of the book related to Hegel's philosophy, but also a wonderfully vivid description such as that of the *Phenomenology of Spirit*,[27] lets one sense Rosenzweig's own sympathetic participation in the thought that he is depicting.

Rosenzweig's next work, "*Das aelteste Systemprogramm des deutschen Idealismus*,"[28] written in 1914, investigates the authorship of a program for a system of idealism written in Hegel's hand and eventually attributes it to the young Schelling. Later, shortly before working on *The Star of Redemption*, Rosenzweig in a memorial pamphlet for Cohen published in 1918, indeed speaks of a basic distrust of all academic philosophy,[29] which he claims to have already held from the beginning of his stay in Berlin. In relation to Cohen this distrust of his could only mean a distrust of all idealism. Nevertheless this essay on German idealism, which was written soon after Rosenzweig's arrival in Berlin, does not yet show any deviation from the "magic circle"[30] of idealism. Here he still sees Schelling's philosophy *after* 1804 entirely through the eyes of idealism and labels it as "late-romantic and reactionary philosophy of history and faith."[31] We must therefore look for the relatio of idealism to *The Star of Redemption* not in realistic beginnings, but rather precisely in that which Rosenzweig's philosophy owes to idealism, that is the concept of the system.

After having demonstrated Schelling's authorship of the program, Rosenzweig proceeds to demonstrate that the system as a whole is a disclosure of German idealism. All the splendor thereby falls upon Hegel. With Schelling, Rosenzweig finds that the proper systematization is lacking. He considers this first draft to be the only rounded-out system that Schelling had produced. "He [Schelling] never attained that inner certainty of the ultimate standpoint

---

[26] *Ibid.*, Vol. 1, Preface, p. xii.

[27] *Ibid.*, Vol. 1, pp. 209–210.

[28] Kl. Sch., pp. 230–277.

[29] Cf. *ibid.*, p. 291.

[30] With reference to Fichte this designation of idealism is found in "Das aelteste Systemprogramm," *Ibid.*, p. 275 and with reference to idealism in general in "Einleitung in die Akademieausgabe der juedischen Schriften Hermann Cohens," *ibid.*, p. 335.

[31] *Ibid.*, p. 264.

that would have enabled him to take full possession of the inheritance he claimed."[32] Antiquity also did not know the system in the sense of *Weltanschauung* just as little as did scholasticism, which was dependent on antiquity, and which for that reason could not carry out the notion of a uniform spiritual penetration of the whole world as demanded in reality by Christianity. In spite of Spinoza, only idealism brought the idea of the system to maturity. Hegel, the consummator of idealism, is the first to offer the complete system. That this religious idea of penetration thereby plays a role in Hegel's thought was already stated by Rosenzweig in *Hegel und der Staat*: "With its urge to realize reason Christianity became for him [Hegel] the primeval phenomenon of the harmony of reality and rationality."[33] Hegel's system undertook for the first time "the philosophical conquest of the real world."[34] And if Rosenzweig says "the task of all philosophy has ever since remained not merely to declare the unity of total being but to define it somehow by linking it to that which is,"[35] then in *The Star of Redemption* he has undertaken his own solution to this task that has been placed on all philosophy.

The short essay "*Atheistische Theologie*"[36] also derives from the same year, 1914. Through comparison with theological currents in Protestantism, it turns against a Jewish theology divorced from revelation. "The thinker...will...not be able to eliminate God to whom the historicity of history is subjected through His historical act...His theology may be as scientific as it wants to and can be: it can not avoid the idea of revelation."[37] In the brief note "*Ueger das juedische Volkstum*"[38] written in 1915 as the introduction to a critical essay on Hermann Cohen's "*Deutschtum und Judentum*" Rosenzweig outlines the idea, which appears later in full form, that the Jewish people is a unique, eternal people, bound neither to the land nor to the moment. "Even he among us who sees temporal salvation in the sinking of roots in a land...even he knows,...that there is still a difference between this temporal salvation which he desires and for which he aspires and that redemption for which he hopes...For us alone the surroundings may never entirely replace the world and the moment may never entirely replace the future."[39]

As a soldier on the Macedonian front in 1916 Rosenzweig, to whom

---

[32] *Ibid.*, p. 269.
[33] *Hegel und der Staat*, Vol. 2, p. 182.
[34] *Kl. Sch.*, p. 271.
[35] *Ibid.*, pp. 273–274.
[36] *Ibid.*, pp. 278–290.
[37] *Ibid.*, p. 290.
[38] *Ibid.*, pp. 26–28.
[39] *Ibid.*, p. 27.

questions of learning and teaching were always near and dear, drew up a school curriculum, "*Volksschule und Reichsschule.*"[40] The curriculum seeks to set the German school system on a new and unified basis of education. Rosenzweig calls this curriculum "an answer to the demands of the day."[41] The school should "seek the connection with the actual life of the spirit of the era with the demands that the world-historical moment makes on the people."[42] It should offer not utilitarian training but spiritual cultivation. It should never accumulate material but rather provide the ability to understand it. The last year of school is to be devoted entirely to philosophy, but to a philosophy that is not joined externally to the other subjects as a new subject. It must grow organically from that which had been learned previously in the study of languages, natural sciences and history. It does not set itself "on the totality as a common hat";[43] it is not "queen" but truly "crown" of the various positive sciences. The sparks of later thoughts already flash everywhere in this audacious curriculum. Thus Rosenzweig rejects the type of the pure dialectician, "whose mind grinds itself down like two millstones between which no grain has been thrown," though he concedes "that a certain tendency of this kind is precisely that which makes the great philosopher."[45] Education is for Rosenzweig "always personal, always the man himself, never something merely had by him."[46] In the study of language he is more interested in the structure of language than in understanding the actual language and literature.[47] Opposite the dialectics of idealist thought he places the "I-You-He" of the personal pronoun,"[48] just as he already speaks of the "religion of the vital present, in which things past and things future are known only in their flaming up in things present."[49]

In an appeal addressed to Cohen, "*Zeit ist's,*"[50] written in 1917, also in Macedonia, Rosenzweig expresses his opinion about the same questions as they appertain to Jewish education.* Here he makes positive proposals for the

[40] *Ibid.*, pp. 420–466.
[41] *Ibid.*, p. 424.
[42] *Ibid.*, p. 463.
[43] *Ibid.*, p. 453.
[44] *Ibid.*, p. 459.
[45] *Ibid.*, p. 456.
[46] *Ibid.*, p. 433.
[47] Cf. *ibid.*, p. 435.
[48] *Ibid.*, p. 454.
[49] *Ibid.*, p. 455.
[50] *Ibid.*, pp. 56–78.

* Cf. Ernst Simon, "Franz Rosenzweig's Place in Jewish Education" (Hebrew) in *On Franz Rosenzweig* (Jerusalem: Beit Hillel – Magnes Press, 1956).

remodelling of the Jewish educational system. He urges Cohen to work for
the establishment of an academy for the science of Judaism whose members
were to be at the same time both scholars and teachers, so that Jewish
theological work would be combined with the creation of a class of teachers
trained in theology.This demand for a close relation between theory and
practice, between science and life, is already thoroughly in keeping with sense.
of *The Star of Redemption*. It is also possible to point to a correspondence of
contents with *The Star* in the curriculum which Rosenzweig outlines in all its
details. "To us Judaism is more than a force of the past or a curiosity of the
present; to us it is the aim of the future. But in so far as it is future it is a world
of its own...and on that account is rooted in everyone's soul by its own
language."[51] The autonomy of the Jewish world is expressed "most con-
spicuously" for Rosenzweig in the Jewish calendar, in its own "liturgical
year."[52] The Jewish week, the Jewish festival year and the annual cycle of
Sabbaths serve as the guidelines for the selection and arrangement of the
Jewish material to be taught.

In addition, several brief political essays were written at the front in 1917:
"*Realpolitik*,"[53] "*Nordwest und Suedost*,"[54] "*Die neue Levante*,"[55] "*Vox
Dei*"[56] and "*Die Sachverstaendigen*."[57] These essays belong to the range of
ideas expressed in his book on Hegel in that through interpreting historical
connections they seek to influence the contemporary political situation. "*Die
Sachverstaendigen*" discusses the composition of parliament which, Rosenzweig maintains, should be composed not of specialists but of average men
blind to the concerns of the specialist. Just as Rosenzweig rejects philosophers
as kings, so he raises sound common sense to the throne.

From the year 1917 there is also a letter to Rudolf Ehrenberg, which
Rosenzweig called the "germ cell"[58] of *The Star of Redemption*. It is not a
program for a system, not a draft of a comprehsive, well-rounded disqui-
sition. It is truly a cell that offers the first point of departure and the
conceptual basis from which the system was able to grow, leaving some things
behind and adding much. Idealism is shaken. After philosophizing reason
"has absorbed everything into itself and has proclaimed its sole existence,
man suddenly discovers that he, who for the longest time was digested

---

[51] *Ibid.*, p. 58.
[52] *Ibid.*, p. 59.
[53] *Ibid.*, pp. 409–414.
[54] *Archiv fuer exakte Wirtschaftsforschung*, Vol. 8 (1917).
[55] *Das neue Deutschland*, June 15, 1917.
[56] *Kl. Sch.*, pp. 400–408.
[57] *Ibid.*, pp. 415–419.
[58] *Ibid.*, pp. 357–372.

philosophically...still is...That is to say...I, the wholly private person, I, with a first and last name, I, dust and ashes, still *am*."[59] "Thinking must establish itself if it is to be able to establish being...The suspicion remains, however,...that apart from this relation to being the self-establishment of thinking is a mere logical game."[60] Rosenzweig finds in revelation the "philosophical Archimedean point"[61] which for him, in the words of Eugen Rosenstock, is "orientation." "After revelation there is a real above and below in nature, an above and below that are no longer relative...and a real, permanent before and after in time."[62] God, world and man are already represented in their conceptual formulas $A = A$, $A = B$, $B = B$ as are, to some extent, their relations in reality.

In the sequence of Rosenzweig's writings we are herewith standing immediately before his main work, *The Star of Redemption*, which was written in the years 1918-1919.[63] In connection with Rosenzweig's theological studies in the years 1913-1914, however, it is necessary to also examine the influence of Hermann Cohen on the evolution of *The Star of Redemption*. Therefore reference shall already be made at this point to a later, important work, "*Einleitung in die Akademieausgabe der juedischen Schriften Hermann Cohens*,"[64] written in 1923 and previously mentioned because of its biographical method. As supplement to this, reference shall also be made to a brief letter from 1921, "*Hermann Cohens Nachlasswerk*,"[65] and an even briefer "*Gedenkblatt*,"[66] written in 1918 after Cohen's death. All of these are important evidence of Cohen's influence. Rosenzweig explicitly speaks of a lecture by Cohen in the winter of 1913-1914, which his "happy ears heard,"[67] and of a "magnificant, unannounced tutorial"[68] on the Psalms. With regard to content, the lecture coincides with the book Cohen published in 1915, *Der Begriff der Religion im System der Philosophie*. This book, in turn, is a preliminary systematic study for Cohen's late work, *Religion of Reason from the Sources of Judaism*,[69] part of which Rosenzweig read at the front in the beginning of

---

[59] *Ibid.*, p. 359.

[60] *Ibid.*, pp. 359–360.

[61] *Ibid.*, p. 357.

[62] *Ibid.*, p. 308. Cf. also *Briefe*, p. 211.

[63] Rosenzweig even supplies the exact dates in his letters: from August 22, 1918 to February 16, 1919. *Briefe*, pp. 370, 568.

[64] *Kl. Sch.*, pp. 299–350.

[65] *Ibid.*, pp. 294–298.

[66] *Ibid.*, pp. 291–293.

[67] *Ibid.*, p. 337.

[68] *Ibid.*, p. 343.

[69] On this point cf. *ibid.*, p. 331.

1918,[70] and of which he said that it would still be read "when the language in which Cohen wrote it would be understood only by scholars."[71]

The aspect of Cohen's thought to which Rosenzweig attributes such impotance is, when briefly summarized, that Cohen "affirmed the unique God as opposed to the spell of pantheism, even in its most spiritualized form, the God who can not be compared to any creature and who is the origin of nature *and* reason. Against all the claims of culture Cohen asserted the inalienable right of the soul."[72] Closely related to this is the discovery of correlation as the basic concept of religion. Man and nature are not merged in God's being, but stand face to face with God and are close to Him. This nearness of God furnishes all the components of the correlation with autonomy and hence reality. "For two things which are in reciprocal relation to one another are not in danger of disputing each other's reality, unlike the idealist concept of producer which almost necessarily must dispute its production."[73] God is no longer identified with reason. Rather, He is the ultimate ground of all idealism and "since idealism only articulates the unspoken secret of all previous philosophy, God is the ultimate ground of all philosophy."[74] Reason itself is God's creation; it is "created reason."[75] For Cohen monotheism signifies a mystery. The faith and existence of the Jewish people of faith (*Glaubensvolkes*) is a miracle – with faith not something that contradicts existence but rather something that derives its impetus "from its harmony with the thinking spirit and with silent existence."[76] All this is accomplished through consideration of the individual. "The individual, who in his sin and repentance has no understanding for the totality of mankind, but must consider himself exactly as unique as God"[77] finds his place in religion, where he seeks the forgiving and redeeming God.

Rosenzweig considers religious feeling to be codetermining even in Cohen's philosophical *system*. He speaks of the " systematic omnipresence"[78] of religion and points to the fact that already in the *Ethik des reinen Willens* redemption, i.e., the realization of the ideal in the present, appears in place of the "barren" notion of progress. With Cohen eternity does not mean "the sum of all time; . . . that which constitutes time is the future and eternity is the most distant future, that which is related to the moment and which is carried

---

[70] Cf. *Briefe*, pp. 281, 393.
[71] *Kl. Sch.*, p. 350.
[72] *Ibid.*, p. 306.
[73] *Ibid.*, p. 335.
[74] *Ibid.*, p. 336.
[75] Cf. *ibid.*, p. 336.
[76] *Ibid.*, p. 341.
[77] *Ibid.*, p. 332.
[78] *Ibid.*, p. 334.

out in the moment's 'nutshell.'"[79] "His [Cohen's] 'messianism' was...not an excuse for idleness,...rather he always hoped for salvation to come 'soon in our days.' Cohen, the logician and the moral philosopher, drew his concepts of time and eternity from this hope." Moreover, "he...believed...he would yet live to see the commencement of the messianic union of religions."[80]

If one takes into consideration the great importance these thoughts had already come to have for Rosenzweig at the point of time at which he offered this interpretation, that is, four years after the completion of *The Star of Redemption*, one will understand that though he mentions Cohen's principal reservations, he does not enlarge upon them in great detail. As a result they fall into the background. These reservations of Cohen include, for instance, the restriction of human individuality to the *completion* of the I of ethics,[81] which in the approach to the infinite task (*Aufgabe*) always has merely the reality of a *moment*.[82] Another reservation is the strict rejection of all anthropomorphism with regard to God.[83] The late composition of Rosenzweig's introduction must further be taken into account due to the noticeable change in its position towards systems. In 1918 Rosenzweig still praised Cohen for offering a system, since he "did not push aside with pseudo-scientific superiority the eternal fundamental questions of humanity, questions revolving around life and death. Neither did he envelop them in feeble emotional and intellectual frills. Rather, he took hold of them with greatness and purity."[84] In light of this it certainly signifies a shift of emphasis to speech thinking if now, in 1923, Rosenzweig says that *Religion of Reason* towers above Cohen's philosophical system to such an extent that it "will still live even when this system will have gone the way of all systems."[85] — And from Rosenzweig's own final standpoint correlation, the I-Thou relation, which heretofore with Cohen had had its place only in aesthetics and then became the basis for religion, now appears to him as the unconscious and future-filled discovery of a new logic. When Rosenzweig first became acquainted with the thought of Cohen he undoubtedly did not come to these conclusions. Indeed, he himself says that though he was well aware of these ideas at the time of the composition of *The Star of Redemption*, the decisive influence came not from them but from Eugen Rosenstock's *Angewandte Seelenkunde*.[86]

---

[79] *Ibid.*, p. 321.
[80] *Ibid.*, p. 322.
[81] Cf. H. Cohen, *Religion of Reason out of the Sources of Judaism*, pp. 11–15.
[82] *Ibid.*, p. 204.
[83] *Ibid.*, pp. 159–160.
[84] *Kl. Sch.*, p. 292.
[85] *Ibid.*, p. 306.
[86] Cf. *ibid.*, p. 388.

It may not be said, then that Rosenzweig's philosophy was called forth or brought to light by any of the conceptual agreements and parallels that have been mentioned. Though realistic elements were already present alongside of idealism, the relation between Rosenzweig's earlier and later views nevertheless is not one of cause and effect. Rather, those three factualities – world, man and God – were prepared merely as possiblities. In the development of Rosenzweig's thought these factualities stand, just as they are found in *The Star of Redemption*, under the dominion of "perhaps." In order for them to be turned into building blocks for a structure there was a need for that inner conversion of the thinker which occurred under the impression of death during the war. The significance of this conversion can not be overestimated, even though there is no evidence of it in Rosenzweig's first years in the war, "for perhaps the great events in a man's life always begin undetected by human eyes."[87] It was this reversal alone that led Rosenzweig to join Hegel's systematics to Schelling's positive philosophy and to add what appeared to him the truly revolutionary innovation, that is, the philosophical method which was no longer based on the isolated I but on I-Thou, on speech thinking. Thus from the aspect of the completed work it is indeed not the contents of the earlier writings which we should see as the important stimuli of Rosenzweig's philosophy but rather the three thinkers with whom he dealt, Hegel, Schelling and Cohen and specifically all three in their most mature form. By creatively utilizing the output of their lives the work arose which Rosenzweig considered to be his unique and essential work, and after which, according to his friends,* he did not want to write any other book.

The Star of Redemption is the peak towering above all of Rosenzweig's work. Before this book his earlier writings recede as old thinking in which the new thinking was only latently present, just as the later writings receive their meaning from this book and appear as its consequences. If in the *earlier* work mostly realistic tendencies can be ascertained which are concerned with the foundations of *The Star* and its first section, then the *later* writings are tied to its second and third sections.

---

[87] ·*Ibid.*, p. 325.

* Cf. for example Martin Buber, Soncino *Gedenkbuch*, p. 29; Ernst Simon, *ibid.*, p. 35; Richard Koch, *Gedenkschrift der Frankfurter Gemeinde*, p. 28. Cf. also *Briefe*, pp. 406–407, where Rosenzweig writes that he must be grateful to fate to have allowed him at the age of 32 to know that he has behind him a "work," a truly eternal work (according to what is humanly called "eternal"). His life from here on is no more than a great present, something which Goethe could only say on his 82nd birthday after the completion of *Faust*.

b) The Later Writings

Among the works written later there are three that directly comment on *The Star of Redemption*. In 1921, in response to the request of the Frommann publishing house for a popular account of his philosophy, Rosenzweig wrote the *Buechlein vom gesunden und kranken Menschenverstand*.* He depicts in a satirical manner "sick" idealist thinking and lets it be cured by treatment in a sanatorium where the patient learns to absorb world, man and God by the simple seeing of experience. A concluding chapter on death, the "brother of life," leads toward the opening of *The Star of Redemption*. The satirical form, however, does not suit its subject. It does not facilitate the understanding of the new thinking for the naive reader, while it leaves the thinking reader on the surface of matters. Rosenzweig himself was dissatisfied with the booklet. In all the letters where he mentions it he speaks disparagingly of it** and withdrew it from print. In contrast he calls the *"Anmerkungen zu Jehuda Halevi"* of 1923 "instructive examples of the practical application of the new thinking"[1] and labels the the comprehensive essay *"Das neue Denken,"* written in 1925, a commentary on *The Star* in the form of "some supplementary remarks."[2]

The philosophy of *The Star of Redemption* is fruitful for the other later writings – for speech thinking, for his views on Judaism and for this philosophy's practical application to, and confirmation in life. These writings can thus be divided into *three groups*. The first of these groups comprises the *translations and works on speech theory*, the second includes the *Jewish writings of general content*, and the third group contains the many *small works* which were written on specific *occasions* about specific personalities and as reviews and criticisms of various books. The borderline between the individual groups, however, is often fluid.

---

[1] *Kl. Sch.*, p. 388.
[2] *Ibid.*, p. 373.

* Nahum N. Glatzer has published an English translation of the book: *Understanding the Sick and the Healthy*, edited with an introduction by Nahum N. Glatzer (New York: Noonday Press, 1954).
** See *Briefe*, pp. 406–407; expressions can be found such as "dirty half-baked article" (*ibid.*, p. 409); *"Vestigia terrent"* (*ibid.*, p. 436); "a description that remained unprinted because it is bad" (*Ibid.*, p. 475).

The first translation is "*Sechzig Hymnen und Gedichte des Jehuda Halevi,*"[3] dating from 1922–1923. It is followed, apart from some minor translations, by the important undertaking of the translation of the Bible into German together with Martin Buber,* an undertaking revolutionary for the method of its execution. The close bond between both these translations and speech theory is clearly demonstrated in the theoretical accounts that accompany them, the "*Nachwort zu den Hymnen und Gedichten des Jehuda Halevi*"[4] from 1922 and "*Die Schrift und Luther*"[5] from 1926. In the "*Nachwort*" Rosenzweig designates as the task of the translator not the Germanization of the foreign language, but rather the preservation of the foreign language's characteristics of style and allusions of content in German. In order to solve this task it becomes necessary, therefore, to reshape the German language in foreign molds and in this way to bring about linguistic creativity. The presupposition for this renewal of one language by way of another is the "essential unity of all languages."[6] Such a presupposition not only makes translation possible but also determines the goal of translation, which has to serve "universal human understanding,"[7] the "coming of that day [when the name of the Lord shall be one]."[8] Just as translation proceeds from the unity of language, it also strives toward this unity, that is to say, it is based on the same principles as speech thinking. Translating is, as it were, *practical* speech thinking, not the expression of revelation and redemption themselves, but revealing of one language in another for the purpose of redemption.

In addition to being the basis for the practical work of translation, the principles of speech thinking also provide the motivation for the demand of being read orally, for being spoken and heard, a demand that Rosenzweig makes for all poetry. Thus, for instance, in his translation of the Hebrew grace after meals[9] he adapts the rhythm of the German exactly to the traditional Hebrew melody. "Poems are...originally not intended for being read, but

---

[3] F. Rosenzweig, *Sechzig Hymnen und Gedichte des Jehuda Halevi* (Konstanz: 1924).

[4] Published as an independent essay in *Kl. Sch.*, pp. 200–219.

[5] *Ibid.*, pp. 141–166.

[6] *Ibid.*, p. 203.

[7] *Ibid.*, p. 203.

[8] *Ibid.*, p. 205.

[9] F. Rosenzweig, *Der Tischdank* (Berlin: Juedische Buecherei, 1920).

* Martin Buber gives the time of the Bible translation's beginning as Spring, 1925 in his essay "*Aus den Anfaengen unserer Schriftuebertragung,*" which appeared in the periodical *Der Orden Bne Briss* (Berlin), March, 1930. Cf. als *Briefe*, p. 533. In the essay in question in which he describes the method of their joint effort, Buber offers an explanation for the note added to the translation: "translation into German *undertaken* by Martin Buber together with Franz Rosenzweig." Rosenzweig was motivated to use this phrase by his illness, which daily threatened him with death. Isaiah is the last book in which Rosenzweig collaborated.

...for being recited and heard."[10] And if he speaks of Goethe's "powerless wish": "Never read, only sing!"[11] this should be an indication to us of the profound relation that exists between speech thinking and Rosenzweig's own love of music, that musicality and talent for listening which, as with Herder, enabled him to listen into the voice and speech of men and hence to hear them in their innermost core.

The significance of speech thinking is even more conspicuous in connection with the translation of the Bible. If earlier we characterized translation as applied speech thinking, then here the application truly returns to its prototype. The language of the Bible is the language of creation and revelation. In it that occurrence which speech thinking wants to reproduce is already represented; in it one may seek a decisive impulse for the new thinking. So it is that precisely with regard to the translation of the Bible Rosenzweig can declare in "*Die Schrift und Luther*" that "all speech is really dialogue to begin with and hence translating."[12] His esteem of the Bible is characterized elsewhere in a well-formulated passage: "The Bible is the most important book. This can be proved, and even the most fanatical hater of the Bible must acknowledge this, at least as far as the past is concerned, and by his fanatical hatred he is also acknowledging this even in the present. For the Bible does not raise a question of personal taste or psychic talent or spiritual inclination, but rather a question of world history that has occurred until now."[13] Accordingly, translations of the Bible come under a world-historical perspective. The great works such as the Septuagint, the Vulgate and Luther's Bible, are accompaniment and preparation for world-historical events. Again and again God's question to man "Where are you" resounds from this book. Each time when men give a new answer to it they thereby introduce a new era of history, so Paul with the foundation of Christianity, so Augustine with the establishment of the city of God, so Luther with the Reformation.[14] "In every instance a new phase in this conversation is preceded by a translation, the translation into the language of tragedy, the translation into the language of *Corpus Juris*, the translation into the *Phenomenology of the Spirit*. When this conversation will come to an end, no one knows, but then, no one knew when it began. Thus it can not be terminated by

---

[10] *Kl. Sch.*, p. 216.

[11] *Ibid.*, p. 216. Cf. on this what is said in another place concerning prose text: "One must be able to read Cohen with one's ears."*Ibid.*, p. 320.

[12] *Ibid.*, p. 141.

[13] *Ibid.*, p. 179, in the essay "Das Formgeheimnis der biblischen Erzaehlungen."

[14] Cf. also "Nachwort zu Jehudah Halevi," *ibid.*, p. 205.

the unwillingness, knowing better or complacent cleverness of any man, but only by the will, the knowledge and the wisdom of Him who began it."[15]

In the Bible translation speech thinking is important not only by virtue of its principles, but above all by virtue of its ability to depict the reality of faith. Whereas previously we had examined the stylistic considerations behind Rosenzweig's demand for the reshaping of the German language into foreign forms and for the preservation of the oral character of the text, we shall now review the theological reasons prompting this demand. As we shall see, the conception of faith of *The Star of Redemption* determines the aim and method of this translation.

In addition to the "doubly grounded national uniqueness of Luther's Bible"[16] – unique as founder of the written language and unique through the point in time at which the spirit of the German language had matured towards Hebrew – there is its ecclesiastical uniqueness, i.e., its significance as representative of the Protestant Church. In spite of this unrepeatability of Luther's work, Buber and Rosenzweig undertook the translation, because it is permitted and even imperative "to again pose translation's question of faith to the book,"[17] because the voice of this book "if it anywhere has become familiar, habitual, possession, . . . must ever again appear anew as an alien, unfamiliar sound from outside to disturb the satisfied saturation of the presumed owner."* This faith is not rigid dogma but the readiness to experience the faith and skepticism that *occur* to men. It is also the readiness, when the voice of God calls to men, not to run away but to obey. Thus it is faith as experience which nevertheless can not be called subjective, precisely on account of its experienced objective content. With respect to this faith the psychology of religion, "the favorite science of the modern learned fools of Gotham, which . . . dismantles the telescope while hoping to find therein the stars"[18] has lost its significance. When applied to Scripture this means faith is the readiness to hear the word of God everywhere "in such a way that it is suddenly inscribed in the very center of this man's heart, so that for the duration of a

---

[15]   *Ibid.*, p. 166.

[16]   *Ibid.*, p. 149.

[17]   *Ibid.*, p. 145.

[18]   *Ibid.*, p. 153.

* *Kl. Sch.*, p. 151. The extent to which the conception of faith which lies at the foundation of this view deviates from idealism becomes clear when this sentence is placed opposite Schleiermacher's remark: "Not every person has religion who believes in a sacred writing, but only the man who has a lively and immediate understanding of it, and who, therefore, so far as he himself is concerned, could most easily do without it." F. Schleiermacher, *On Religion. Speeches to its Cultured Despisers*, translated by John Oman (New York: Harper and Row, 1958), p. 91.

heartbeat the divine in the humanly written will be just as clear and as certain as a voice his heart could hear calling at that same moment."[19]

The nature of the translation is determined by such faith, just as Luther also derived the criteria for his translation of the Bible from his faith, which in his case was Christian dogma. Accordingly, in every place where Luther saw in the Old Testament no more than a simple narration, he translated it into familiar, simple, colloquial German. In those places, however, where it provided him with a living teaching and living solace, that is, where he perceived it as pointing to Christ, he preserved the form of the language and reproduced the peculiarity of the Hebrew in German. "And if one believes that not only where a transcribed dogma points the way, but that on principle everywhere in the Bible the possibility is concealed that one day, at its time, at my time, the divine word will reveal itself through the human word, then it will become necessary for the translator, as far as his language allows it, to follow, be it through imitation or through allusion, the characteristic expressions of that human speech which is pregnant with revelation."[20]

One way to "transplant the living growth of Hebrew speech into a Western language"[21] is, significantly, the restoration of the oral character of the language through the introduction of "breathing phrases," i.e., the natural intervals which in reading aloud are caused by the breathing of the person who is reciting. These intervals are to return to the translation "the free, oral soul of the word which was stifled in the writtenness of Scripture."[22] Rosenzweig discusses this matter in detail in a separate essay, "*Die Schrift und das Wort*,"[23] written in 1925.

The other means of expressing the holiness of Scripture is the literal translation. To that end the root-stratum of the Hebrew words has to be excavated to that point at which there is something in common between the roots of the Hebrew and the German words – the unity of language being after all the presupposition for the translation. Moreover, even the meaning and the sensate quality of the root, which lie beyond the science of language, provide the guiding principle for the choice of the German expression.

This "reverential faithfulness to the word of Scripture,"[24] which indeed gives the Bible a high degree of that "strange, unfamiliar tone from outside" and thus occasioned rejection and misunderstanding, is the subject of two

[19] *Ibid.*, p. 154.
[20] *Ibid.*, p. 160.
[21] *Ibid.*, p. 162.
[22] *Ibid.*, p. 162.
[23] *Ibid.*, pp. 134–140.
[24] *Ibid.*, p. 165.

brief articles written together with Buber, "*Die Bibel auf Deutsch*"[25] and "*Zu einer Uebersetzung und einer Rezension*,"[26] both dating from 1926. With passionate fervor the latter turns against the opinion, which admittedly had been suggested by the translation of Jehuda Halevi's poems, that the exact rendering of the textual peculiarities had been made on aesthetic grounds. In reality, "the living variety of style...has arisen piece by piece from the endeavor to give a precise rendering of what was written. That is, it has arisen from the Scripture itself from its speech, from the tone, origin and meaning of its words, from the cadence, structure and content of its syntax."[27] – In a letter to Jacob Rosenheim published in 1927 under the title "*Die Einheit der Bibel*,"[28] Rosenzweig gives expression to the fact that the "literal character of the terminology," while conforming to the orthodox view in its result, nevertheless derives from a different basis of faith. The Bible forms a unity that can not be shaken by any objection of critical science not because the text that has been transmitted is word for word what was handed to Moses on Mt. Sinai, but because God's teachings are believed to be present in every word. The concept of creation which the Bible seeks to teach consists precisely of the harmonization of Chapters 1 and 2 of Genesis, "that is, the 'cosmological' creation of the first chapter, which leads toward man, and the 'anthropological' creation of the second chapter, which commences with man,"[29] while revelation is the combination of God's appearance and God's command. This belief, which stands behind the faithfulness of the translation, behind "its method and its degree,"[30] is "not a dogmatic self-binding, but a being-bound that embraces the entire human being,"[31] an attitude which also includes science. No dualism of science and faith is allowed to establish itself here, whether on the basis of science as introduced by Kant, or on the basis of faith as Barth and Gogarten have advocated in our day. "If science and religion do not want to have any knowledge of each other, yet nevertheless know each other, neither science nor religion are worth anything. There is only one truth. No honest person can pray to a God whom as a scientist he denies. And he who prays can not deny God... God is not the subject of science; its subject is the world. But God has created the world, and hence, the subject of science. Thus God is indeed...transcendent to science, but also transcendental. Science does not hold God, but without Him it would not be; God is not in

---

[25] *Frankfurter Zeitung*, May 18, 1926.
[26] *Der Morgen*, Year 2, Vol. 1 (1926–1927), pp. 111–113.
[27] *Ibid.*, p. 112.
[28] *Kl. Sch.*, pp. 128–133.
[29] *Ibid.*, p. 129.
[30] *Ibid.*, p. 131.
[31] *Ibid.*, p. 133.

science, but science is under Him."[32] Rosenzweig had already once articulated this thought, which forms one of the main points of his philosophy, in the "*Einleitung in die Akademieausgabe der juedischen Schriften Hermann Cohens*": "A healthy man needs both, faith and thinking. Where faith supposes it can hold its ground without having to depend on thinking, then in the long run either faith must solidify or thinking must atrophy. Thus for the sake of man's wholeness faith and thinking may not remain strangers to each other."[33]

The principle decisive for the manner of the translation, according to which the Bible is to be taken in its entirety as the bearer of the dialogue between God and man, now leads to the disclosure of dialogic elements also in the Bible's narrative parts. In the essay "*Das Formgeheimnis der biblischen Erzaehlungen*"[34] from the year 1928, Rosenzweig tells of a discovery made by Buber. In the repetition of certain words in the narrative texts of the Bible Buber detected a coherence of content that usually is unnoticeable, whereby the narration becomes more than a message, namely teaching. A secret dialogue thus runs throughout the biblical narrative in the form of the interlocking of similar words. These stories are revelatory message" which turns towards man and at the same time answers his question with a "teaching that commands."[35] In the psalms, the prophets and the laws the dialogue is evident even without this form, for they awaken entirely of their own accord the human partner, who is reciting them in prayer, believing in them, and fulfilling them. "The subterranean didactics of the secret dialogue assume full importance only where the open dialogue can no longer arise from the book and proceed outward, that is, in the epic texts."[36] Here the dialogue turns "a distant audience into the partners of a conversation... This conversation, which is question and answer, assertion and contradiction, statement and supplement, gives to those who have awoken to deed, hope and love the one thing they still lack. It gives them this in such a modest way that it does not dogmatically paralyze deed, hope and love, but rather lends wings to spirit; it gives them: knowledge, teaching, revelation."[37] – Rosenzweig again formulates his conviction in the dialogic character of the biblical narratives in a letter to Joseph Carlebach from 1929: "We are convinced that the Bible seeks to teach in every place, also in its 'narrative' and 'poetic' parts, sometimes explicitly, but

---

[32] *Ibid.*, p. 132.
[33] *Ibid.*, p. 312.
[34] *Ibid.*, pp. 167–181.
[35] *Ibid.*, p. 172.
[36] *Ibid.*, p. 180.
[37] *Ibid.*, p. 181.

usually only through the strong yet unobtrusive means of linguistic allusions."[38] Shortly prior to this, in answer to the objections of Carlebach,
who had warned against the exaggerated literalness of the translation, Rosenzweig makes a remark that is significnat with regard to his part in the
translation. He commented that he was "the one" who, out of "theological
madness" ("*rabies theologica*") penetrated into the meaning of the words,
while Buber, on the contrary, took "the part of the poor reader." – The
literalness of the translation is again treated in a brief review of a French
translation of the Bible in 1929,[39] a translation which lacks this struggle with
the spirit of the foreign language. In this review Rosenzweig adopts the words
of Goethe, who characterizes such a translation as the product of an age of
parody, an age that endeavors "to appropiate for itself the foreign meaning
and to present it again with its own meaning."

The specific problem of translating the name of God is discussed in one of
the last essays, from 1929: "*Der Ewige – Mendelssohn und der Gottesname.*"[40]
Rosenzweig sees the great merit of Mendelssohn's translation of the Bible as
lying in the fact that he bound the rendering of God's name to the revelation
of the name. He nevertheless rejects the translation of this revealed name as
"The Eternal One," for the revealed name is to express not the necessary, all-
time existence, which for Mendelssohn was associated with the concept of
eternity more even than was the solicitous and providential presence. Rather,
it is to express only that which is wholly presence. (And if in this context
Rosenzweig remarks: "We today would, if at all, rather make the opposite
'inference' – from the solicitous God to the existing God,"[41] then one
could see in this "if at all" a subsequent reservation regarding the central idea
of *The Star of Redemption*. For it is precisely on this point, that the presence of
revelation guarantees the existence of God, that the entire philosophy of
Rosenzweig stands or falls. Denying this idea would mean taking away the
philosophical character of *The Star of Redemption* and making it merely a
book for edification.) If the translation is to render the sense of presence that
lies in the name–and "the transparence of the name, its being illuminated
with meaning"[42] distinguishes this name from a mere idol's name–it must
comprehend this presence "in the three dimensions of the personal pronoun:
the speaker, the spoken to, and the spoken about. The meaning of the One
who in any given time is present in one of the three modes, in each instance

---

[38] *Briefe*, p. 626.
[39] *Der Morgen*, Year 5, Vol. 1 (1929–1930), p. 95. Review of *La Bible Traduite*.
[40] *Kl. Sch.*, pp. 182–198. See also *Briefe*, pp. 554, 599 ff.
[41] *Kl. Sch.*, p. 187.
[42] *Ibid.*, p. 189.

according to the intended kind of presence, condenses itself into one word only in the personal pronoun";[43] that is to say, in a pronoun that through being stressed with special type makes visible the tension with its context and that "for the blink of an eye, as it were, glances upwards toward heaven from the midst of the sentence."[44] Thus it is to be translated: "that which is present to them, existing with them, that is–HE; that which is present to an I, existing with me, that is–THOU; that which is present to a thou, existing with you, that is–I."* Only through this continuing linkage of the name with revelation does the Bible become a unity "under the principle of monotheism";[45] for monotheism is not the cognition of God as the One, but rather the un-mediated identification of the One with the revealed. "And it is this very identification that forges the entire Bible into one unit through the ardor of its call of *Here am I* which bursts forth from the burning bush into the name of God, in that it everywhere carries out the equation of the God of creation with the God who is present to me, to you and to each and every one."[46]

The essay "*Neuhebraeisch*"[47] of 1925 marks the transition to the second group of Rosenzweig's writings, the Jewish writings, in that it contains speech theory and also deals with the special role of the Hebrew language in Judaism. As in *The Star of Redemption*, the Hebrew language is viewed as the holy language of the holy people, a language which serves as sign and guarantee for the people's eternity and which is acquired at the price of the immediacy of life and the surrender to the moment. The theory of Jacob Klatzkin, who wants to translate Spinoza's *Ethics* into Hebrew as if this were an ordinary colloquial language, contradicts itself through its application in that the holiness of the language unties the "fetters of normality." To be sure, "it is not the task of a translation of Spinoza to turn this great tempter's apparent profundity into genuine insights;... the peculiarity of the holy language can

---

[43] *Ibid.*, p. 188.
[44] *Ibid.*, p. 190.
[45] *Ibid.*, p. 191.
[46] *Ibid.*, p. 192.
[47] *Ibid.*, pp. 220–227.

* *Kl. Sch.*, p. 189. It might be pointed out that the translation of the Hebrew *Ohel Moed* (tent of congregation) which is translated by Luther as "tabernacle of foundation" ("*Huette des Stifts*") and by Buber and Rosenzweig as "tent of presence" ("*Zelt der Gegenwart*") is also determined by this approach to revelation as presence and meeting. (Cf. M. Buber, *Ueber die Wortwahl in einer Verdeutschung der Schrift* (Hellerau: Hegner, 1930), pp. 11–13, and Rosen-zweig, "*Die Schrift und Luther*," *Kl. Sch.*, p. 164. The same is true of the rendering of the various forms of sacrifice as *Darnahung* (drawing near), *Darhoehung* (raising high), and *Hinleite* (leading hither), in which a relation is to be expressed. (Cf. Buber, *loc. cit.*, pp. 7–8).

only make its own way incidentally."[48] If, however, the translator renders the *quod erat demonstrandum* of Spinoza with the Talmudic term *sh'ma miney* ("hear it from this"), even though Hebrew has at its disposal a word for "proof" stemming from the realm of seeing, one is "an immediate witness as to how in the middle of the camp of the enemy, at the very heart of the 'geometric' method, the essence of revelation, which is hostile to the image and to the form, manages to break through. 'You saw no form, only a voice.' (Deut. 4:12)."[49]

The lecture of 1919, "*Geist und Epochen der juedischen Geschichte*,"[50] is to be counted among the second group of writings. It reflects the views of *The Star of Redemption* concerning the Jewish people, a people "free of that power to which other peoples are usually subjected – the power of time; alone among the peoples...it is eternal."[51] Its land is to it the land of the divine promise. Its language is not like the language of other peoples, but rather is the language of prayer, holy language. Custom and law do not change for it; they are divine revelation. In this way the eras of Jewish history lose their significance, for the eternality of the people prevails over them. Even Zionism which strives to turn the Jews into a normal people, pays tribute to this eternal character by making the demand for a state of social justice, an ideal state.

Also belonging to this group of Jewish writings are the three longer essays of 1923, above all "*Apologetisches Denken*"[52] and "*Ein Rabbinerbuch*."[53] Though both these essays relate to specific books, they nevertheless go substantially beyond their framework and have a general Jewish content. The first essay treats the meaning and value of apologetics, while the second essay, in a sharply critical manner, deals with the tasks and limitations of the sermon. In the third of these essays, "*Die Bauleute*,"[54] the question of Jewish law is posed from the viewpoint of the new conception of faith and is answered in such a way that the fulfilment of the law comes to be placed in the middle between "must" and can," that is, between objective norm and subjective ability.

---

[48] *Ibid.*, p. 226.
[49] *Ibid.*, p. 227.
[50] *Ibid.*, pp. 12–25.
[51] *Ibid.*, p. 19.
[52] *Ibid.*, pp. 31–42.
[53] *Ibid.*, pp. 43–49.
[54] *Ibid.*, pp. 106–121.

The essay from 1920, "*Bildung und kein Ende*,"[55]* stands on the border between the second and the third groups. Its subject matter is the relation of Jewish education to the Jewish man, but at the same time it had a specific task, that is, to serve as a programmatic work for the *Freie juedische Lehrhaus* that Rosenzweig founded in Frankfurt/Main.[56] The views of *The Star of Redemption* are again decisive here. Rosenzweig demands first of all not Jewish education and teaching per se, but a man whose humanity is expressed in his Judaism and who in his boundlessness can be delimited only by an equally boundless Christianity and paganism. Past and future, science and teaching draw their strength only from this man's life in the present. In order to create this Judaism that is grounded in the existence of man, in order to educate Jewish men, it is necessary to provide forms in which man alone can penetrate to his innermost core, that is, time for speech and space for speech. Readiness and trust are the beginning of all educational work. The path to Jewish contents leads through the soul of Jewish men, it rests "on their strength to desire, their urge to question, their courage to doubt."[57] Rosenzweig's position here is doubly significant, in that he is not concerned with something coming to him from outside, but rather is setting up guidelines for his own teaching activity and thereby seeking to lead himself from the world of books to the praxis of life. Shortly afterward his illness began, a paralysis which deprived him of movement and speech and which no longer permitted practical activity. During the eight years of hopeless infirmity that followed, he nevertheless preserved the courage to live and work. With the help of his wife, who translated his meagre hints into speech and writing, he still composed a variety of works, in which the sharpness and the profundity of his thinking remained unbroken. If his contemporaries and posterity have admired this victory of a strong will over a failing body, then they must in any case see behind Rosenzweig the man, the philosopher from whose great intellectual work such personal courage sprang.

In actuality, all the works written during the years of illness, the translations as well as the Jewish treatises, belong to the sphere of this trial, to this faithfulness to the task even under desperate conditions. Moreover, the many *short works written for particular occasions* testify to the thinker's alert eye which was directed toward contemporary life and to his constant partici-

---

[55] *Ibid.*, pp. 79–93.

[56] In addition see "Entwurf der Rede zur Eroeffnung des Freien Juedischen Lehrhauses," *ibid.*, pp. 100–102.

[57] *Ibid.*, p. 93.

* This essay, under the title "Towards a Renaissance of Jewish Learning," appears along with "The Builders" ("*Die Bauleute*") and "It Is Time" ("*Zeit ist's*") in F. Rosenzweig, *On Jewish Learning*, with an introduction by N. Glatzer (New York: Schocken, 1965) (translator's note).

pation in life's questions and duties. There are articles on great personalities, both of the present, such as Cohen, Rabbi Nobel, Buber, and Stefan George, as well as of the past, such as Lessing and Mendelssohn, whose names were revived by the commemorative celebrations of 1929. These articles take a position regarding Zionism, discuss practical plans and demands born of the moment, and weigh and evaluate artistic and literary phenomena, such as the series of articles written in 1928-1929 with ample knowledge and the most sensitive feeling for music, "*Der Konzertsaal auf der Schallplatte*,"[58] which dwell with special fondness on recordings of cultic music, or the review of books on Hegel from the years 1921-1922 and the review of volumes of the *Encyclopedia Judaica* from the years 1928-1929. Some of these brief pieces are related to *The Star of Redemption* not only by their character as written for a certain occasion but also by their content.

The 1922 review of Dilthey's book on Hegel[59] throws important light on Rosenzweig's relation to Dilthey as well as to Hegel after the completion of *The Star of Redemption*. Hegel is to him the "dispossessed potentate" who "perhaps was the last one to have the courage to seek to solve without reservations of conditions the ancient riddle of cognition," while Dilthey was the one who was just about to cause that dispossession and was unable to do so only because the time was not yet ripe for giving a new constitution to the spiritual realm where Hegel had once reigned. "Probably never before had anyone faced the Hegelian system with so much considered suspicion and at the same time full of deep-seated reverence. Nevertheless he [Dilthey] remained face to face with the system. He did not have a comprehensive view, not from the outside, certainly not from above. For this even he was still standing too close to Hegel." And later on: "The world has changed. It is after all more than chance that this biography of Hegel has remained a fragment." If one takes into consideration the kinship of Dilthey's work with Rosenzweig's *Hegel und der Staat* and the claim of speech thinking to be the new constitution of the spiritual realm, then the view is justified that Rosenzweig's book on Hegel was already a first step toward the new thinking of *The Star of Redemption*.

Also of importance is the "*Anmerkung ueber Anthropomorphismus*"[60] of 1928, which can be juxtaposed to Schelling's letter to Eschenmayer.[61] In both, anthropomorphism is affirmed and substantiated, in both cases through the rejection of the argument based on the faultiness of human cognition.

---

[58] *Ibid.*, pp. 478–502.

[59] *Ibid.*, pp. 511–512.

[60] *Ibid.*, pp. 525–533.

[61] Cf. above, p. 51, where it was mentioned in connection with Schelling's positive philosophy.

Schelling had expressed this by saying that one must conceive of a personal God as soon as one asserts Him. Rosenzweig says that *our* language, *our* thinking, our experience are the only means of cognition we have at our disposal. The difference between the two lies in the fact that Schelling justifies anthropomorphism for thinking, i.e., for the first part of *The Star of Redemption*, while Rosenzweig establishes it for faith experience, i.e., for the second part. This experience is not experience of an object, but experience of an encounter. Therefore it allows neither the dogmatic assertion that God *is* a person and thus man was also created a person – which would mean that man is in the image of God, that is, the theomorphism of man – nor the skeptical statement that man is person and consequently God also *is* person – which would mean anthropomorphism, God in the image of man. In faith experience God may be seen as person only to the extent that He shows Himself as person in the living relation. "Where there is something to be seen, God has an eye for it; where man calls, God lends an ear;...where man extends his hands in supplication, God's hand can clasp it."[62] No attribute or being is herewith expressed about God. Rather, lying within all this is "an unlimited trust in His unlimited powers to encounter the corporeality and the spirituality of ourselves and of all creation always and at all times, to encounter bodily and spiritually, in body and soul."[63] Without this "courage to trust that the actually experienced experiences of God originate actually and directly in God"[64] monotheism is impugned, for alongside of a non-living God who is merely essence religious consciousness demands – and here history offers the proof – "half- and quarter gods" that are closer to man. Rosenzweig again finds the example for the new thinking in biblical thinking. There too, the characteristics of God are never joined together into a picture, but rather always relate to a creaturely presence standing opposite. Thus the language of the Bible, which for spirituality says "spirit" (according to the Hebrew word *ruach* which refers to spirit and wind) and for personality says "face," in renunciation of a rigid statement, provides "guidance to a thinking faithful to experience." It is not personality that is common to God and man, but rather language. "God speaks all languages."[65]

In the essay "*Die Bibel und die Weltkultur*,"[66] written in 1929, the views of *The Star of Redemption* on the relation of Judaism to Christianity and thus

---

[62] *Kl. Sch.*, p. 529.
[63] *Ibid.*, p. 530.
[64] *Ibid.*, p. 531.
[65] *Ibid.*, p. 530.
[66] *Enzyklopaedia Judaica*, Vol. 4, column 748ff; appears under the title "Weltgeschichtliche Bedeutung der Bibel" in *Kl. Sch.*, pp. 124–127.

also the relation between the Old and New Testaments are taken up in such a way that the former represents the solid foundation that guarantees for the latter the connection with the created world. One of the last small treatises, "*Vertauschte Fronten*,"[67] written in May of 1929, the last year of his life, should also be mentioned. On the occasion of the appearance of the second edition of Hermann Cohen's *Religion of Reason out of the Sources of Judaism* it once again emphasizes the difference between the Cohen of the Marburg school and the later Cohen, the one who was the discoverer of correlation as basic concept. Beyond that, however, it expresses Rosenzweig's great satisfaction that his own philosophical achievement, speech thinking, had meantime found a worthy representative in Martin Heidegger. He who before the thoughts of *The Star* had crystallized into written form had said of himself "only posthumously shall I speak out entirely,"[68] can now confirm that "that which only five years ago, when I stated it in the introduction to Cohen's Jewish writings, might have seemed a personal opinion about contemporary philosophical trends, has meanwhile become common knowledge. Recently at Davos that conversation took place before a European forum between Cassirer, Cohen's most prominent student, and Heidegger, the present occupant of Cohen's chair at Marburg...Here Heidegger, the student of Husserl, the Aristotelian scholastic, whose occupancy of Cohen's chair must appear to every "old Marburgian" only as an irony of the history of ideas, has advocated in opposition to Cassirer a philosophical position, the position of our, of the new thinking, which is entirely in keeping with the line proceeding from the 'last Cohen.'" If Heidegger, as opposed to Cassirer, gives to philosophy the task to reveal to man, to that "specific, finite creature" his own "nothingness, with all its freedom" and "to call him back from the lazy aspect of man which makes use merely of the works of the spirit, into the severity of his fate," and if he says that "what he designates as 'existence' (*Dasein*) can not be expressed by any one of Cassirer's terms," then Rosenzweig sees therein a sign of the times, a sign that the fronts have changed. "The school with its pedants dies; the master lives."

---

[67] *Ibid.*, pp. 354–356.
[68] *Briefe*, p. 200.

C. *THE STAR OF REDEMPTION*

C. *THE STAR OF REDEMPTION*

I. THINKING OR THE THESIS

a) *The priority of Being to Thinking*

The thesis of Schelling's positive philosophy which states that thinking can not contain being and that the latter therefore can only be experienced in faith, is the central pillar of Franz Rosenzweig's philosophy. This thesis determines the relation of the first part of Rosenzweig's system to the second part and beyond that leads to the synthesis of thinking and faith, to believing science. Within the first part of the system, that is within thinking, it also determines the construction of the elements.

This synthesis of thinking and faith, however, which rests on the priority of being to thinking, takes place in the case of Rosenzweig in a manner differing from that of Schelling. Schelling bases his system – although it never reached its full realization but rather remained at the stage of a "program for a system," as at the beginning of his philosophizing – on the juxtaposition of thinking and faith. In this dichotomy he renews his concept of identity. Just as Schelling applies the theory of potentials to the concept of God and to mythology, he also applies it to revelation. Schelling calls this elucidation of revelation by means of general philosophical principles believing science. Negative philosphy – here already taken in the stricter sense as the negative part of positive philosophy – is the thinking that leads toward absolute act (*actus*). Negative philosophy so conceived and the philosophy of revelation, which in turn rationalizes the absolute act through the potentials, counterbalance each other. Since both have the theory of potentials in common – negative philosophy as preparation for the non-rational principle and positive philosophy, believing science, as subsequent comprehension of this non-rational actuated being – they are assimilated to each other to a great extent. Both hang, like the arms of a scale, on their point of suspension – absolute actuated being.

Rosenzweig, in contrast, erects his system in three stages. Thinking – as in

Schelling's system the negative part of positive philosophy, and as theory of elements corresponding exactly to the theory of potentials in its position as preparation for faith – is supplemented and strengthened by faith. Both thinking and faith come together in believing thinking. Thinking, faith and believing thinking are related to each other as thesis, antithesis and synthesis. For Rosenzweig, then, the synthesis of thinking and faith is effected by a dialectic overcoming of thinking through faith. He thus gives preference to Hegel's systematic structure rather than to Schelling's. The reason for this lies, strangely enough, in his non-rationalism, which exceeds that of Schelling's. This difference is expressed by contrasting conceptions of revelation. For Schelling revelation from the beginning signified the historical fact of Christian revelation, which is recorded in documents and verified by the Church, and which, because of this, was already more accessible to the employment of rational principles. Rosenzweig, however, sees in revelation not the historical fact, but rather the believing experience of the individual soul that resists the reification of revelation into concepts. The non-rational element is so strong in revelation that the second part of the system can no longer be compared to the first. The absolute act, in which with regard to Schelling mythology and revelation were anchored in a like manner while it itself remained independent of them, here in Rosenzweig has a much greater and more emphasized significance. In all of its non-rationality it, the absolute act, enters the second part of Rosenzweig's system. This is explained by the fact that the method by which it is made comprehensible, speech thinking, is not rational. Thus a subsequent stage, the third part of Rosenzweig's system, becomes necessary in which this flowing life and activity, which can be perceived only successively, is again combined into a synthesis with the thinking of the part.

With Schelling as well as with Rosenzweig the principle of the priority and transcendence of being thus leads, in spite of different paths, to the same result, to the synthesis of thinking and faith. In both cases this principle does not lead to the negation of thinking, something which also is possible. This can be explained by the philosophers' identical point of departure, by the rooting of their philosophy in a question whose origin is not religious but rather universal-human. Both arrive at the principle of the priority of being to thinking and thereby at the synthesis of thinking and faith for the sake of man, whose innermost desires can not be satisfied by thinking alone, but whose thinking also is not to be negated.

Schelling joined positive to negative philosophy in order to solve the problems of human existence and human action in reality. He demanded a personal, acting God, the God of faith, on behalf of the individual, yet in doing so he sought to obviate a bifurcation of the individual into a rational and believing essence. Thereby Schelling expressed his concern to maintain the inner unity of thinking and faith. And if Rosenzweig allows the era in which the philosopher philosophizes as an individual human being possessing his own proper name, to begin with Schopenhauer and to continue with Nietzsche,[1] then he is overlooking the fact that Schelling's later philosophy, which was formed at the same time as and later to Schopenhauer's work, derives from the same attitude. Here again the differences between Schelling and Rosenzweig lie only in the manner of fulfilment. In the case of Schelling the point of departure, the human problem, diminishes in importance with the further pursuance of his views. To be sure, he ultimately philosophizes on behalf of man, but solely *from God*; man and world have only a very limited independence. The freedom of man is counter-divine (*gegengoettlich*), indeed is the essence of sin. Further, God participates in the world reluctantly. It is precisely because of this neglect of the existential situation of man that Kierkegaard and German dialectic theology reject Schelling's synthesis of thinking and faith, while affirming his understanding of faith.

Rosenzweig also philosophizes for the sake of man. Nothing explains the inner ground of his realism, his shattering of the All, better than that passage in the concluding section of *The Star*:"And this itself – how gladly one would like to regard it as All, and oneself as the gloriously irresponsible 'speck of dust in the All,' rather than as its reponsible center about which everything rotates or as the pillar on whose stability the world rests."[2] For him, too this question on the meaning of human existence is at the same time the question on the compatibility of man's believing attitude and thinking attitude. Unlike Schelling, however, Rosenzweig thinks for the sake of man *towards God*. He takes man and world for the foundation of the system as factualities classified equally with the factuality of God. Only through the advance of the system itself, especially in the translation by means of the antithesis of faith, does he arrive at the conception of God as the One above all. Generally speaking, a system, even should it culimate in God, contains the danger that the human question will be "deprived of its poisonous fangs,"[3] for "system of course already implies in itself independent universal applicability."[4] Rosenzweig meets this danger by relativizing by means of his understanding of revelation the system's self-sufficiency expressed in the Hegelian epigram "God is truth." For Rosenzweig, God is beyond the conceptual purview of a philo-

[1] Cf. 8.
[2] 414.
[3] 8.
[4] 8.

sophical system. With the characterization of truth as a fact that requires the trust of the entire man, of whom reason is only one dimension, Rosenzweig arrives at the concept of verification. Here his conception of the system, which with regard to its content is already fulfilled in believing science, is once more explicitly united with faith by human existence. Accordingly, the human viewpoint guarantees the synthesis of faith and thinking even beyond the system.

The principle of the priority of being to thinking was thus occasioned by the problematics of human existence for both Schelling as well as Rosenzweig. Both also made use of this principle in such a way that faith and thinking remained related to one another. Nevertheless, in the case of Rosenzweig this principle from the very beginning received a different form precisely because of the fuller attention given to man. The system begins, as mentioned previously, with three factualities and thus the priority of being to thinking is *threefold*. It is not only a question of God's absolute being, as in Schelling's philosophy, but the being of man and of the world as well as of God.

Rosenzweig's point of departure is the fact of death, which idealism wanted to ignore and obscure. Death, which in war he experienced as "a something from which there is no appeal, which is not to be done away with,"[5] makes him conscious of the factuality of human existence that precedes thought. Man is thus outside the context of the conceptual All; the presumed self-sufficiency of this All is shattered. Along with the All the unity of thinking is also destroyed, so that the world, deprived of this unity, in like manner becomes something individual, and finds its place beside God. The experience of death thus signifies at the same time the experience of the threefold factuality of man, world and God. Herein the priority of being to thinking is given expression, that is, the presuppositions of idealism are reversed. "Metaethical man is the leaven which causes the logico-physical unity of the cosmos to fall apart into the metalogical world and the metaphysical God."[6] The prefix "meta" serves to indicate that these three factualities are transcendent to ethics, logic and physics, that they are prior to all thinking and that only they make thinking possible. "We know with the immediate knowledge of experience what God, man and the world, each one taken separately, 'is.' If we did not know, how could we talk about them, and above all, how could we 'reduce' any two of these three [factualities] to the other, or deny the possibility of any of the other two reductions?"[7] "For

---

[5] 4.
[6] 16.
[7] *Kl. Sch.*, p. 380.

we 'believe' in the world, as firmly at least as we believe in God or in our self."[8] "It [knowledge] can not escape these coordinates between which every step that it takes, every move it makes is silhouetted...Thus the Nought of evidential knowledge is here never more than a Nought of knowledge or, more exactly, a Nought of evidencing opposite which the fact which helps to lay the basis of the space wherein knowledge itself lives, works and exists, remains unmovèd in its entire and utter factuality."[9] What Rosenzweig expresses here in words which are at times confusing[10] is nothing but a formulation of the basic principle of the priority of being. This principle entails the conviction that thinking presupposes being, namely, being in its particular threefoldness. As a result, thinking and science no longer reign over being but rather are subservient to it.

This immediate knowledge of the experience that is prior to thinking, this "faith" (which Rosenzweig himself places in quotation marks) is not to be identified without further elaboration as the believing experience of the second part of his system. To be sure, a sentence like the following one: "experience thus does not experience the things which become visible as ultimate factualities in connection with thinking about experience,"[11] could tempt one to take the experience of faith which experiences in relations as being identical with the experience that precedes thought, i.e., the experience of the threefold factuality. Here another sentence of Rosenzweig helps us further: "What was put into *The Star of Redemption* was, first of all, the experience of factuality that precedes all facts of real experience..."[12] The proof for this difference between the two experiences lies, above all, in the fact that in believing experience, the experience of the three factualities that is created *a posteriori* by thinking is maintained as basis and presupposition. Accordingly they stand in the relationship of *general* to *specific* experience which is the relationship of the first part of the system to the second part. Julius Guttmann criticizes the elements on account of this experience of factuality which lies at the basis of their construction. He is of the opinion that the basis of the experience is not clearly expressed and is concealed by the construction, so that it sometimes appears that the elements are introduced by Rosenzweig dogmatically and are not taken from experience. This is especially the case with respect to God, of whom there can be knowledge only by means of the encounter with Him in revelation. The experience of the

[8] 42.
[9] 63.
[10] See, for instance, 60, where he speaks of "that courage for clarity of *vision* to which alone the configuration of things is revealed."
[11] *Kl. Sch.*, p. 382.
[12] *Ibid.*, p. 395.

factuality of God must consequently be identical with the believing experience in the second part of Rosenzweig's system.[13] For Rosenzweig, however, the experience of God's factuality is *prior to the construction of the elements*. This experience was "put in" from the very beginning, and is thus to be understood as a conviction shared even by the unbeliever. This conviction attests that, to speak in Rosenzweig's symbolic language, there is an A or something absolutely universal and infinite, a representation of God that suffices for deriving a conception of Him.

In order to be able to judge the significance of the experience that precedes thought for the construction of the elements, it is important to deal in greater detail with its content. The experience prior to thinking is indeed experience only in threefold being. But in spite of the fact that it is based on the personal experience of death it has merely a general content and does not yet experience the specific "this" and "here" of reality. Nonetheless, this pre-conceptual experience enjoys a certain specificity in so far as it already designates experienced factuality as God, man and world. So it is that, according to its content, general experience contains something absolutely universal and infinite, something absolutely particular and finite, and an interlocking of the universal and the particular. That is to say, the experience of the threefold factuality signifies an experience that in each case is determined with respect to its contents as totally A, as totally B, and as a union of A and B. Were this content not determined by the experience that precedes thought, then applying the same scheme of construction three times could not have produced different forms. Above all, it could not have generated interlocking such as the particularly universal, i.e., the freedom of God, and the universally particular, i.e., the character of man. The construction is concerned only with the "how"; the "what" is already established beforehand. We thus have to take notice of the fact that the finished elements have two layers: the non-rational content which is due to experience and which is expressed in the letters A and B, and the rational form which sets up the construction. Exactly like the potentials of Schelling which, as a result of their voluntaristic character had a non-rational admixture, the elements are partly non-rational, partly rational. The construction is merely to answer the question:"How must God, world and man be constituted in order that they can be perceived as three factualities that are separate from one another and indissoluble by thinking?" The aim of the construction is the "non-rational object"[14] in so far as it is indeed conceived. The thinking construction does not generate this object, however, but only determines the *form* in which it

[13] Julius Guttmann, *Philosophies of Judaism* (New York: Schocken, 1973), p. 427f.
[14] 19.

alone can be a content prior to thinking. This form, then, is that which in the case of Schelling we designated as personality, as individuality. Without exception Rosenzweig employs these terms for the moral personality, that is, personality as part of a whole. We may thus understand this form of the non-rational object as an inner, living embrace of the All along with external determination. "In order that each be something very definite and particular, one God, one man, one world and yet at the same time All: God, man and world" the factualities "must contain opposite poles within themselves."[15] The factuality that anticipates experience thereby gives the construction a quite specific and limited task. It, the construction, can only "follow...the fact,"[16] As Rosenzweig says elsewhere of Plato, whose recollection, the theory of cognition as re-cognition, is characterized by him as the non-idealistic prototype of idealistic dialectics, the construction achieves "a re-creation in thought of the uncreated* being."[17]

b) The Construction of the Elements

The priority of being to thinking having thus limited the scope and meaning of the construction, this presupposition, which is fundamentally different from idealism, also assumes importance within the system, namely at the system's *point of departure*. The subordinate position of thinking in relation to being already makes it clear that the construction can not be a question of any idealistic generation. Rosenzweig himself says that Cohen, whose logic of origin he takes as a model, would be "far from admitting"[1] such an application of his thought. Not the object, but only its form is to be generated, only "the *timbre* of the three-part bass of our world symphony."[2] Even this form stands before our eyes through being demaded by the requirements of the content, so that the construction is from the beginning characterized as teleological. At the same time, however, the construction, exactly like Schelling's theory of potentials, also proceeds hypothetically. This shows itself now when at its onset the realistic presupposition again becomes effective.

In his Critiques Kant had explained God, world and man as objects of the rational sciences, as absolute Nought. To be sure, Rosenzweig thinks that

[15] 306.
[16] 63.
[17] 229.
[1] 21.
[2] 125–126.
* Uncreated by thinking.

Kant himself, by the threefold formulation of this Nought, endowed it with the possibilities of being determined and defined. Thereby he groped for a factuality of which the Nought could appear as a mere expression. "At the very least, two discrete Noughts of knowledge are designated by the thing-in-itself, the *Ding an sich* and the '*intelligible character*,' the metalogical and the metaethical in our terminology. And the dark terms in which he [Kant] occasionally speaks of the mysterious 'root' of both are presumably attempts to grope for a fixed point for the metaphysical Nought of knowledge too."[3] And even if the construction therefore leads Rosenzweig to approach these realistic "intuitions"[4] of Kant, he nevertheless adapt not these but rather precisely the conclusion of Kant the idealist. Kant's critique of rational, metaphysical proofs is fully endorsed by Rosenzweig. "Man is no more capable of proof than are the world and God. If knowledge nonetheless tries to prove one of these three, then it necessarily loses itself in the Nought."[5] The idea, the Nought of idealism, is really an empty, formal Nought.

According to Rosenzweig's other presupposition, however, idea exists only because factuality precedes it, so the endorsement of Kant at once leads to his being surpassed. The idea of Kant is restricted by means of the presupposed reality, just as in Kant's critique the idea itself had restricted intellect; the idea is reduced to something that is self-derived. In this way it enters into an attributive relationship with the factuality that is experienced beforehand, that is, from an empty, formal Nought it becomes the Nought of God, world and man, respectively. Thus the Nought of idealism becomes a differentiating Nought. "The Nought can not imply for us . . . unveiling of the essence of pure being. Rather it is necessary to presuppose a Nought, its Nought, wherever an existing element of the All rests in itself, indissoluble and everlasting."[6]

This is to say that the Nought of the differential, the Nought based on a presupposed factuality, is a hypothetical Nought. Doubt changes from doubt *de omnibus* (of everything) into doubt of that which is established as fact and so becomes a means for refuting itself. "Accordingly, the Nought of these three entities can be only a hypothetical Nought for us, only a Nought of knowledge from which we attain that Aught of knowledge which circumscribes the content of the belief.* That we hold this belief is a fact from which we can free ourselves only hypothetically, by constructing it from the ground up, until we finally reach the point where we realize how the hy-

[3] 21.
[4] 67.
[5] 63.
[6] 20.

* Belief here always means only the belief in the universal factuality of God, world and man.

pothetical must convert into the a-hypothetical, the absolute, the unconditional character of that belief. This alone is what science can and must
achieve for us."[7] This Nought of the differential is a particular Nought that
bursts "fruitfully into reality."[8]

This Nought is completely different, for example, from the Nought of which
Martin Heidegger speaks in his essay *Was ist Metaphysik?*[9] Heidegger's
Nought also is not a formal one; it signifies an absolute, real Nought, a *nihil
absolutum*, that one could also perceive as death. The state of being contained
within this Nought is called existence. "The negation of the Nought occurs
within the being of that which is."[10] In this its significance for being* this
conception of the Nought can only be compared to Rosenzweig's initial
experience of death, that experience which reversed the presupposition of
idealism and established the threefold being prior to thinking.

In the case of Rosenzweig, however, the Nought with which the construction begins comes into action only when the consciousness of being is
already well established. It is placed before this being that precedes thought
merely hypothetically in order to make possible the conceptual, constructive
re-creation of the experienced threefold being. Thus it provides, as it were, a
"methodical auxiliary concept."[11] If the Nought of Heidegger is an extra-
conceptual, non-rational Nought, then the Nought of Rosenzweig is a conceived Nought that is not purely formal only because of the devaluation of
thinking itself. Since thinking is subordinate to the factuality that is prior to
thinking, the Nought becomes differential, i.e., it becomes a Nought that is
conceived on the basis of something experienced. – Only later, when faith
negates thinking as a whole, does the Nought of Rosenzweig also assume the
features of a real Nought, a "dark depth,"[12] by which it then moves nearer to
the Nought of Heidegger.

The adjustment of the construction to a specific goal – "our *goal* is . . . a
highly positive one. We *seek* God"[13] – and the departure from the differential
of Nought and Aught, both of which are consequences of the realistic basic
principle, now offers the possibility for the form of the presupposed factuality
to arise as unity of two opposites. The "particular Nought" corresponds

[7] 42.
[8] 21.
[9] M. Heidegger. *Was its Metaphysik?* (Bonn: F. Cohen, 1929).
[10] *Ibid.*, p. 20.
[11] *Kl. Sch.*, p. 377.
[12] 90.
[13] 23.

  * The difference in the structure of being with regard to Heidegger and Rosenzweig owing to
the negation of the Nought and the experience of death, respectively, will not be entered into here.

exactly to the differential of mathematics. Mathematics also produces neither the "pure" nor "the real itself,"but only the universal. Mathematics is "a continuous derivation of an Aught – and never more than some one Aught, any Aught – from the Nought, and never from the empty, universal Nought, but always from the Nought that belongs peculiarly to precisely this Aught."[14] The purely logical Nought is merely a component of the infinitesimal, of the Nought of magnitude. Here this Nought also is merely the form of a presupposed Aught. As the demarcation between positive and negative, the differential, in so far as an Aught is to be produced from it,* contains two possibilities. "The differental combines in itself the characteristics of the Nought and the Aught. It is a Nought which points to an Aught, its Aught; at the same time it is an Aught which still slumbers in the lap of the Nought...Thus it draws its power to establish reality on the one hand from the forcible negation with which it breaks the lap of the Nought, and on the other hand equally from the calm affirmation of whatever borders on the Nought, to which, as itself infinitesimal, it still and remains attracted. Thus it opens two paths from the Nought to the Aught – the path of the affirmation of what is not Nought, and the path of the negation of the Nought."[15]

The construction which takes up these two paths thereby determines the form of the factual as affirmation of the not-negative, i.e., as infinite and as negation of the negative, i.e., as finite. It was already established as goal of the inquiry that a polar duality must be constituted. That this duality would arise as infinite and finite, however, is something the construction as differential achieves entirely on its own. It is therefore not merely the reconstruction of something that previously had been analytically conceived – as such it would be a mere tautology** and thus in reality superfluous. Rather it truly contributes something new: it determines the opposition as being that of infinite and finite.

"Yea is the beginning."[16] That the course of affirmation is taken up first is based on the fact that the construction is located between the differential and a positive goal. "Nay connot be the beginning, for it could only be a Nay of

---

[14] 20.

[15] 20–21.

[16] 26.

* I.e., an Aught which is always only according to its form.

** If Rosenzweig says elsewhere that there are only tautological answers to the question of essence, then this refers not to what the construction accomplished for the inner formation of God, world and man, but to the external relation of the three to each other, in which one is not a predicate of the other. *Kl. Sch.*, pp. 379–380.

the Nought.* This, however, would presuppose a negatable Nought, a Nay, therefore, that had already decided on a Yea."[17] In each case, then, Yea is what comes first. And this Yea, by affirming the non-Nought, posits the infinite. – The Nay of the Nought is only the second possibility. It posits something absolutely positive, that is something finitely positive, a "finiteness . . . demanded by the immediate propulsion from the negated Nought; for all negation posits something determined, finite, as far as it is not simply the infinite affirmation which occurs in the form of negation."[18] Rosenzweig emphasizes that both Yea and Nay are to be equally original; both presuppose only the Nought. One is not perchance the presupposition of the other. This Nought itself, however, is the Nought of an Aught and therefore the affirmation is logically prior. The Yea precedes the Nay not "in reality" but only "in conceptual sequence (as a possibility af affirmation)."[19]

Rosenzweig also presents this way of construction by means of Yea and Nay as a kind of self-construction of the differential. "The Yea of non-Nought . . . *wells forth* out of the Nought."[20] "Thus the Nay finds its opponent directly in front of itself here. But the metaphor of a pair of wrestlers is misleading. There is no pair. This is a wrestling match not of two partners but of one: the Nought negates itself. It is only in self-negation that the 'other,' the 'opponent,' bursts forth out of it."[21] Therein lies, on the one hand, a transference of real-dialectic thought-processes to the construction. Just as in Schelling's case the potentials owed their suitability as factors of a real-dialectic movement to the volition latent within them, here, too the combination of the construction with the non-rational content suggests a real movement within the elements. To be sure, the construction alone, inasmuch as it is purely rational, would not justify real movement. Only through its application to the experienced content can one speak of a becoming, of a self-movement. Thus we may view the self-construction as an intimation of the history of God that appears in the second part of the system, where Yea and Nay as creation and revelation signify a becoming of God that occurs through a free act. Indeed later, from the standpoint of the second part, the construction is designated self-creation, self-revelation and self-redemption. "Already there [in the first part], so to speak proto- or hypocosmically, there occurred an inner self-creation, self-revelation, self-redemption of each in-

---

[17] 26.
[18] 66.
[19] 32.
[20] 42.
[21] 29.

* On account of the positive goal.

dividual element, God, world, man within itself. We could not have said that
then, even if we had wanted to. Just as little do we still need to state it explicitly
now."[22] Although this change of perspective is also discernible at the conclusion of the first part, where Rosenzweig speaks of "secret generative
forces," of "occult powers that are at work inside God, world and man,"[23]
there is no need to deal with it at this point. We have not yet reached the
antithesis, the believing experience. Rather, we are at the thesis, the thinking,
and accordingly the construction is to be taken seriously, for in order that it
can be negated the construction itself must first be fully implemented.

As for the union by means of the And, this And actually is no longer
directly concerned with the construction out of the differential. Rather, this
union is effected by that which has arisen from both the Yea and the Nay, and
in particular from the Nay. Rosenzweig speaks of "the Yea of creation, the
Nay of generation and the And of configuration."[24] That is to say, the Yea
stands in relation to its result, to the infinite, as begetter, while the Nay in its
begetting of the finite at the same time lays the basis for creative activity of this
finite itself. The And merely grasps *a posteriori* the result of this activity of the
finite. The union of the infinite and the finite thus is already a self-con-
figuration as well, irrespective of the subsequent fluctuations conditioned by
the advance of the system. The finite, on account of its issue from the
differential through direct negation of the Nought, is conceived as active, and
the infinite, which arose out of the indirect affirmation of the Nought, i.e., as
affirmation of its opposite, is conceived as passive. This being the case, the
finite can apprehend the infinite independently and unite with it into a
configuration. The And can not create the configuration;* it is not primordial. "No Aught originates in it [the And]; it is not, like Yea and Nay,
immediate to the Nought; rather it is the sign of the process which permits the
growth of the finished form between what originated in Yea and Nay."[25]

Rosenzweig expresses the result of the construction "finite-and-infinite"
with the symbol $y = x$. He himself calls this a *logical*-mathematical symbol
truth of the sentence, from the qualities that the subject, predicate and copula
have in the sentence. For him, the formulas accordingly are "primeval state-
ments"[26] about God, world and man. Second, he thereby at the same time
lays a basis for the method of the second part of the system, for *speech
thinking*.

[22] 242.
[23] 88.
[24] 63.
[25] 229.
[26] 43.

* It goes without saying that all this always refers only to the form.

In the equation y = x the affirmation, which originally is the sign of determination (*Bestimmung*), is placed on the right side as predicate, while the
negation, as primeval supposition (*Setzung*), is placed on the left side as
subject. "Now ordinarily the affirmative protasis (*Setzung*) designates the
subject, and the negating apodosis (*Bestimmung*) the predicate; here, however, where we are dealing with origins, it is just the other way around."[27]
Only by means of the individualization of the general would the Nay as
predicate and the Yea as subject come to pass. "The apodosis, according to its
original concept [viz. a concluding clause], is precisely positive, the pure
Then,"[28] and "...original supposition, lying before everything individual
[viz. an introductory clause],...is negation, negation, that is, of the
Nought."[29]

In that the Nay, the finite, stands at the left side as subject and the Yea, the
infinite, stands at the right side as predicate, the activity of the finite and the
passivity of the infinite are underlined. They are thereby related to each other
as the logically particular to the logically general. The movement of the Nay
toward the Aught is clarified and at the same time justified as movement of the
subject toward the predicate, Nay and Yea appear as act and essence. Since the
Nay occupies the left side of the equation it moves toward the Yea and thus it
is possible to speak of the "original subject" that "reaches beyond itself with
unlimited power."[30]

The And as sign of the connection between Yea and Nay is symbolized in
the *is*, the copula. Since it joins subject and predicate the copula in itself has a
synthetic character within the sentence. Accordingly, in the equation y = x the
equal sign grants this synthesis its symbolic "form."[31] Inasmuch as the
symbol in its entirety signifies the form of factuality the equal sign is thus the
form within the form. It expresses the direction and once, when it is associated
with human volition, Rosenzweig even designates it as consciousness.[32] This
direction goes together with the subject, i.e., with activity, with respect to God
and man, where the = sign appears on the left side of the equation. In the
formula of the world the direction separates itself and passes over to the
predicate, to passivity, to the right side of the equation. The infinite of the
world has a passive attraction, while the finite is active but directionless.

And just as the symbol y = x helped the result of the construction "finite-
and-infinite" to express particularity and universality, activity and passivity,

[27] 27.
[28] 27.
[29] 27.
[30] 30.
[31] 67.
[32] 67.

act and essence by presenting the Yea and Nay of begetting as predicate and subject and the And as copula in the sentence, so are Yea and Nay in turn the "root words" that establish the living speech, the organon of faith, in the second part of the system. The Yea "posits"[33] each word by itself and thereby not only establishes its "meaning in general"[34] but also secures for each individual word the "identity of its significance,"[35] its "universal applicability"[36] and thirdly "its distinctive meaning."[37] All this, however, applies only to the individual word taken in itself. – The Nay, in contrast, determines the position of the word in the sentence while the And determines the context of the sentence that was prepared in the Nay. "As 'Thus' the Yea confirms the individual word, that is, it assures it of an enduring 'firm' value, independent of the relation which it assumes in regard to the other words within the sentence; the Nay, on the other hand, concerns itself precisely with this relation of the word to the sentence. As 'not-otherwise' it 'locates' this 'locus' of the individual word, a locus which firmly fixes the peculiarity of each word over against the 'others' – not its 'firm' peculiarity but one dependent on the sentence."[38] "The And is the secret companion not of the individual word, but of the verbal context."[39] This explanation, which itself utilizes the reason inherent in speech by relying on literal meaning, offers "the substructure over which the edifice of the Logos, of linguistic reason, is erected."[40]

c) The Concepts God, World and Man

The form "finite-and-infinite," expressed in the equation $y = x$, is now endowed with empirical content. By this procedure the concept of construction is introduced into Rosenzweig's analysis. Hence the factual – i.e., that which according to its content is universal, yet particular and simultaneously a union of the two – becomes comprehensible as the existential realities of God, man and world. Positive concepts, non-rational objects and mixtures of non-rational content and rational form are thereby produced. The content of the construction, its non-rational stratum which is designated by the letters A and

[33] 27.
[34] 65.
[35] 65.
[36] 44, 65.
[37] 65.
[38] 32.
[39] 33.
[40] 33.

B, is joined to the rational, formal stratum of the construction. The contours of the latter are delineated by the position of the particular and universal components of the equation $y = x$ that is posited by the construction. The components of the construction, we may recall, are the subject, predicate and copula. A and B are that which according to their content are infinite and finite, while their respective positions on the left or right side of the equation signify that which is infinite and finite according to its emergence.

With respect to God the Yea affirms something infinite, His essence, and the Nay negates something finite, His freedom. The And joins freedom and essence together into living unity. Strictly speaking, this union results not from the two extremes, but rather from two points that already have been modified by each other. Freedom is characterized by means of the essence lying before it as freedom of practice, i.e., as power, and essence is formed by means of its encounter with divine power as obligation and fate. Thus Yea and Nay, when they appear together, are no longer entirely original. As obligation and power they have already undergone reciprocal influence. "Both infinite power in the free outpour of *Pathos* and infinite constraint in the compulsion of *Moira* – both together form the vitality of God."*

This designation of freedom and essence as power and obligation, respectively, makes use of experienced factuality in addition to the construction. Rosenzweig answers, as it were, the question: How can $y = x$, i.e., how can finite-and-infinite as subject and predicate, act and essence, be expressed when they are applied to God? The answer is that only as the Nay and Yea of *God* are they called freedom and essence. Only because God is that which according to its content is purely universal are these expressions also applicable in His case in their most universal significance. The world and man will have to be designated differently, according to the difference in content. Consequently, the definitive symbol of God, $A = A$, in which the living movement from freedom to essence is once more gathered, stands in the middle between rational form and experienced, i.e., non-rational content. This symbol, on the one hand, reproduces the form $y = x$ that was generated from the construction. On the other hand it expresses that this form is intended for a specific content existing independently of it, intended precisely for an experienced universal A, i.e., for God. The Yea, since it is infinite and *predicate*, *universal, essence*, appears on the *right side*. Because it is the Yea of *God*, that is, universal and infinite according to its *content*, it can be called essence and

---

* *Star*, p. 31. Freedom and essence, whose joining together confers the form of personal life upon each of the three elements, are obviously meant only as regards their inner activity and not as manifestations of the elements.

designated A. The Nay in turn, because it is finite and *subject, particularity, act* appears on the *left side*. Since, however, it is the Nay of *God, that is, universal and infinite according to its content*, it can be called freedom and inserted in the formula as A. Only in the case of God does the direction accompany activity, i.e., join the left side. Only because it is the Nay of God does it direct itself toward essence, and so fulfil the union essentially carried out by activity. If we make it clear to ourselves that the union encompasses activity and direction, then once again the role of the And will be elucidated. It only half participates in the synthesis in that it is not creative but rather leaves activity to the Nay.

Rosenzweig refers to Spinoza[1] and Schelling[2] for his concept of God. He has much in common with both although he nevertheless separates himself from them once more. Only the equation $y = x$ and not $A = A$ can be compared to Spinoza. For Rosenzweig world and man are also substances in Spinoza's sense. Each one, then, fulfils "in its particular way,"[3] i.e., out of a difference in content, the definition of substance as that which is comprehended in and by itself. Thus only the constructed rational form can coincide with the substance of Spinoza.

Above all, it is the mathematical method that is held in common. The *mos geometricus* and the generation from the differential lie on the same plane, even if Spinoza extended the validity of mathematics over a much greater range. For Spinoza mathematics means validity as such, while for Rosenzweig it has a limited task with respect to the concept of God. It erects merely the rational part of this "positive concept," not to mention that even this concept is not the ultimate one and that it does not remain at the "neopagan-Spinozan concealment."[4] – Moreover, even though the equation $y = x$ designates the correlation of two attributes into one substance, this unity is no longer indebted to mathematics – strictly speaking only the attributes are constructed. Rather, this unity arises from a living process among these attributes themselves. In this way it achieves what Spinoza's *mos geometricus* could not attain and what is of the utmost importance for Rosenzweig: the vitality of the unity and hence the form of personal life.

With regard to Schelling's concept of God, we may compare it with the formula $A = A$. Not only it, but the theory of potentials in general, whose special case the concept of God was, can be compared with all three formulas, including $B = A$ and $B = B$, whose emergence we have not yet traced. The

[1] *Kl. Sch.*, p. 379.
[2] 17–18.
[3] *Kl. Sch.*, p. 379.
[4] 200.

formula $y = x$ generates the positive concepts only through its application to the non-rational content. Only by this means can it be juxtaposed to Schelling's potentials, each one of which by itself, as well as in their synthetic consolidation in the third potential, is a positive concept. The definitive formulae of Rosenzweig, which in their separate components as well as in the form of the completed equation are a combination of rational form and non-rational content, correspond to Schelling's concept of God, which makes full use of the theory of potentials. The designation by the individual letters A and B is also shared with Schelling. As in Schelling's case, the letters are a substitute for names. They point to the fact that the objects, in spite of their universality, are nevertheless that primordial universality and that primordial particularity that are given only once. The difference between Rosenzweig and Schelling thus lies not in the result but in the path. It is the difference between *construction and dialectics.*

In accordance with his dialectic path, Schelling allows the second potential to proceed from the first and the third potential from the second. Through this derivation of the potentials one from the other he attains within the potentials an even more vital movement than Rosenzweig attains through the construction. To be sure, Rosenzweig also has a synthesis and vitality, even if his synthesis is of a special kind on account of the peculiar interweaving with the construction: his third stage presupposes the two others. He has no antithesis, however. That is to say, his second stage does not presuppose the first, but rather is equally primary. Here the previously mentioned proximity to Spinoza at the same time signifies his divergence from Schelling. Thus it happens that the two first stages are indeed antithetical according to their meaning as Yea and Nay, but not according to their relationship. The Nay is not the Nay of Yea and is not grounded on the Yea. Rather, it is something that is present independently of the Nay and only then enters into relation with it, even though with the designation of the Nay as logically "younger"[5] Rosenzweig once more approaches dialectics, and even speaks of this anticipation of the Yea as "presupposition."[6] The reciprocal modification of the Yea and Nay also points to a dialectic feature. In any case, Rosenzweig consciously rejects the antithesis for the Nay. It may be because of this rejection of the antithesis that where the concept of the God is concerned he refers to Nietzsche and not to Schelling for the freedom of God. The freedom of Schelling is one that proceeds from essence. Nietzsche, in his hatred of God, knows that freedom

[5] 29.
[6] 136.

of God which is entirely primordial, which directly faces man's defiance and "which drives him to denial because he has to regard it as licence."[7]

With regard to the world, the combination of constructive form and non-rational, experienced content repeats itself. The Yea affirms something infinite which here in the case of the world may be called logos, world-spirit. The Nay negates something finite, which is designated as plenitude of phenomena. In that the infinite again signifies predicate, universal, essence and the finite signifies subject, particularity, act the world plenitude pours into the logos of the world. The And is arranged this time as copula on the side of the Yea and Rosenzweig thereby makes use of the significance of Yea as archetypal word. Here the Yea no longer procures mere universality, as in the essence of God, but rather universal *validity* and universal applicability and hence the intimation that "application really...occurs to it."[8] The Yea as archetypal word thereby supports the concretization of the construction. Thus the direction joins the logos, that is, the logos becomes passively attracting and the image of the world is completed through it.

Here, where it is to designate worldly phenomenon and worldly logos, the formula $y = x$ becomes $B = A$. The Yea, since it signifies that which according to *form* is infinite and universal, appears on the *right side* of the equation. Because it is the Yea of the *world*, that is, something universal according to its *content* it is called logos and designated by A. The Nay, since it is that which is particular according to *form* and emergence, appears on the *left side*. As Nay of the world, that is, something finite and particular according to *content*, it is called plenitude of phenomena and designated by B. A complete correspondence of the two strata is thus in evidence here. The finite and infinite of emergence correspond with a finite and infinite of the content that is experienced from the beginning. It is not accidental that this coincidence of form and content on both sides of the equation exists precisely in the formula of the world alone.

This relationship between something unequivocally finite and particular and something unequivocally infinite and universal, is characteristic of the logic inherent in the objective world. It illumines the influence of the priority of being to thought on the theory of cognition. The logos, as understood by Rosenzweig, is neither creative nor active. This fact also explains why Rosenzweig wants to avoid the "Hegelian connotation"[9] of the world-spirit. Rather, it is precisely the particular, the thing-in-itself, that is active. The

[7] 18.
[8] 44.
[9] 44.

particular undertakes the actual creative act of synthesis, while logos merely completes the synthesis *a posteriori* by means of its need for application. This procedure from primordial duality and the division of the synthesis into factors, which here in the case of the world do not coincide but rather are arranged with one of the two primordialities, contain a kind of correlation. This correlation, however, is clearly marked as realistic on account of the activity of the alogical, in contrast, for example, to the heterothetic principle of Rickert. Kant tried to solve the problems presented to idealism by the inclusion of the alogical within the logical through schematism, while Hegel sought to solve these problems through the creative synthesis of the logos, for which the alogical means its antithesis, in the course of which he was forced to make the alogical logical.* Rosenzweig, in turn, solves these problems in a realistic fashion. To be sure, he does not have the logos proceed from the thing-in-itself – this would be the complete opposite of Hegel. Rather, he grants it independence and only shifts the emphasis of its union with the alogical in general to this alogical in particular. Thus the "intracosmic plenitude of distinctiveness,"[10] which idealism could at best know as a rigid given, here becomes life which breaks into the "vessels and implements...of its infinitely receptive logos."[11] The metalogical view of the world gives "life its vitality"; it "can restore life to its rights."[12]

This movement that has proceeded from the distinctive presents itself again in the world as process between two extremes that have already been influenced by one another. "The structure of the world perfects itself in the individual and the species, more specifically in the movement which carries the individual into the open arms of the species,"[13] Here, however, the world is much more than that which is usually called organic nature. To be sure, the world has "its framework,"[14] but everything that stands in a relationship of particular to its universal, i.e., as individuality, belongs to the world, "stone and plant, state and art...all creation,"[15] and above all the moral personality as part of humanity. On the side of the universal, the species, the law of ethics also explicitly finds its place next to the law of nature.[16] In this

[10] 45.
[11] 46.
[12] 47.
[13] 49.
[14] 219.
[15] 45.
[16] 14–15.

* Cf. on this point S. Marck, *Kant und Hegel* (Tuebingen: Mohr, 1917), p. 85: "From the beginning he [Hegel] knows the non-rational only in the form of an inferior, incomplete rationality...That which is natural and substantial to him never really stands outside thinking but is at once a positing of this thinking itself."

assimilation of ethics to the natural sciences the influence of the Marburg
school on Rosenzweig can be felt. The logos is logos of the so-called "natural" world as well as of the so-called "spiritual"[17] world. "The real 'and' of
the world is . . . the 'and' . . . of the thing and its concept, the individual and his
genus, of man and his community."[18]

It is clear that this world-formula $B = A$, which asserts "the passivity of the
form [and] the activity of content,"[19] must open up a deep chasm between
pure and applied thinking. Applied thinking, which has been taken possession
of the particular, does not point beyond itself. It renounces "the capacity to
demonstrate the unity of its origin"[20] and thereby turns the world into
something finite, self-contained. Kant also had emphasized the special position of applied thinking by his differentiation between formal and transcendental logic. He also could have made the following statement of Rosenzweig: "A merely presupposed reasoning may need to be reasoned about, but
does not reason itself; only a real reasoning reasons, one that is valid for the
world, applied to the world, at home in the world."[21] Similarly, in
Heidegger's opinion, Kant arrived at a finite concept of the world, although
he gave this finiteness an idealistic grounding. The world is finite because
human cognition is finite and is limited by the thing-in-itself. "It certainly also
holds for Kant's concept of the world that the totality it represents refers to
finite existing things. But this relationship to finiteness, which is essential for
the content of the concept of the world, assumes a new meaning. The
finiteness of existing things . . . is interpreted with the view that things are and
to what extent they are possible objects of finite cognition, i.e., a cognition
which is such that things must first be *given* to it as already existing."[22] For
Rosenzweig, in contrast, the world is finite because the thing-in-itself actively
seizes thinking and thereby brings it to a conclusion from the other side, the
side of its origin. The finiteness of the world is due not to the activity of
cognition that limits itself, but to the activity of the finite that is present in the
world. The problem that arose for idealism out of the activity of thinking,
namely, the question as to how there can still be something purely alogical in
spite of the concepts that govern everything, here appears from the other side
as the question as to how a pure logos can exist in spite of the plenitude of
phenomena that overwhelms thinking. These questions go much further

---

[17] 44.
[18] 49.
[19] 50.
[20] 43.
[21] 43.
[22] M. Heidegger, *Vom Wesen des Grundes*, p. 19.

than the previously mentioned difficulties, shared by idealism and realism, of relating logical and alogical thinking to each other. These questions concern the claim to absoluteness made by both idealism and realism. They provide the stimulus for idealism to develop into panlogism as well as the stimulus for realism to evolve into absolute realism. Rosenzweig offers a solution to this problem that points beyond the world-formula only in the second part of his system.

The third formula, $B = B$, is the formula of man. The Yea again affirms something infinite – with regard to man, his peculiarity. The Nay negates something finite – his freedom, and the union results from the movement between two opposites that have already modified each other. Free will, with respect to its object, becomes defiant will, and the peculiarity, which "comes to lie. . .across the path of free will,"[23] becomes character. In this way the human self originates in the "encroachment by free will upon peculiarity as the And of defiance and character."[24] This time also Yea and Nay can be designated as peculiarity and freedom only with the help of the previous experience of human factuality. Only as the Yea of man can something infinite, an essence, be called peculiarity and only as the Nay of man can something finite, active, be called free will. Rosenzweig thereby once again makes use of the significance of the Yea as archetypal word for the designation of the right side of the equation. The Yea establishes essential distinctiveness here and thus again helps to make the construction concrete. In this way the formula $B = B$ comes into existence as the simultaneous expression of the rational form $y = x$ and the absolute distinctiveness of content. Since the peculiarity is infinite according to its concrete manifestation, it appears on the *right side* as *predicate, universality, essence*; since it is infinite, distinctive according to its *content*, it must be designated as B. In that freedom is finite according to its *concrete manifestation*, it appears on the *left side* as *subject, particularity, activity*; furthermore, in that according to *content* it is finite, it is designated by B. Human freedom consists, then, "not merely of such finiteness, . . . as God's freedom also possesses. The finiteness of human freedom, rather, is a finiteness which, apart from its emergence, is inherent in freedom itself."[25] As is the case with God, the And as copula again appears on the left side, because the human Nay, free will, has not only activity but also direction.

The human self, symbolized thus in the rational-non-rational formula $B = B$, is something totally different from the moral personality. It signifies

23 68.
24 68.
25 66.

man not as a fragment of the world, not "from without,"[26] but as personal life existing independently of universality. Precisely by making ethos *qua* character part of man's being, the human self is secured against any fusion with the moral personality.[27] And while man as part of the world belongs to the orbit of individual and species – there he is the distinct, B – here he bears within himself not merely the B of the world, but his own genuine individuality. For both man and world there is "a similar occurrence . . . of an aimless, absolute distinctiveness: B. Of course this B occurs as 'Nay' in the case of the world, as 'Yea' in that of man, as the ever new miracle of individuality with the world, as the permanent essence of character with man."[28] This partial equality of world and man according to content means for man, in any case, that the distinctiveness within the world is for him merely something universal. By means of something distinct belonging to man alone this universal becomes subjugated to him actively as well as according to direction. Only in this way does he arise as a self absolutely closed towards the outside and looking only into itself. The curriculum vitae of the self cuts the orbit of individual and species as "a straight line leading from one unknown to another."[29]

The moment at which "the individual dies the death of entering the genus"[30] therefore means the birth of the self. "It is inconceivable, precisely from the side of individuality, that individual life should endure beyond the generation of progeny."[31] Human life is certainly more than a part of something universal. Precisely where man was supposed to have dissolved himself into individuality, he emerges as self. "The self . . . assaults man first in the guise of *Eros*, and thence accompanies him through life until the moment when he removes his disguise and reveals himself as *Thanatos*."[32] The self completes itself in death. The death of entering the genus is "the second . . . more secret birthday of the self, just as it is the second . . . patent day of death for individuality."[33] In death "the self awakes to an ultimate individuation and solitude: there is no greater solitude than in the eyes of a dying man, and no more defiant, proud isolation than that which appears on the frozen countenance of the deceased."[34]

Thus the third formula $B = B$ leads back, as it were, to the root of the

---

[26] 70.
[27] Cf. 10.
[28] 65.
[29] 72.
[30] 71.
[31] 70.
[32] 71.
[33] 71.
[34] 71–72.

construction. Man and his death had been the cause of the destruction of the All and thereby of the inversion of the presuppositions of the all. The construction, whose point of departure and at the same time justification had been the inverted presupposition, now turns its attention to the question of human existence. Philosophical method, as pursued in the first part of *The Star*, the thesis, can only serve, according to Rosenzweig, to make the individual elements of the All comprehensible. It does this by presenting each fragment as irreducible, but thereby it deprives each element of an outward relationship to the others. Rosenzweig repeatedly emphasizes that the philosophical construction of the elements only deals with their inner constitution and not with their outward relationship.[35] With respect to man this type of fragmented conceptualization is analogous to the defiant self-enclosure of self that bears the All within itself and therefore fails to see anything beyond itself. It is the solitary man, the egoist, who reaches his zenith in death. Hence the themes egoism and death accompany thinking, as may be noted in both the purely rational philosophy, that is, in Schelling's terms idealism or negative philosophy in its fullest sense, as well as the negative-positive philosophy of Rosenzweig as formulated in the first part of the system.

Idealistic philosophy "joins death's retinue." Death is its "Musaget,"[36] and is therefore understood by idealistic philosophy as Nought. Here, too, death is only the completion of egoism just as "indeed all 'idealism,' though ostensibly too good for reality, is in fact most often but a flight from the all-too-common reality into the dream-world of selfishness."[37] One could at this point be reminded of the saying of Schelling that only the man who flees into the meditative life, into contemplation, and avoids acting in reality can find satisfaction in the idea of God. – Rosenzweig's theory of elements, however, which, exactly like Schelling's theory of potentials explains non-rational actuated being on the level of thinking and therefore must be rational, also participates in the human-existential meaning of the formula $B = B$. It, too, in so far as it is thinking, leads to egoism and death. Nevertheless a different attitude to death is manifested in positive thinking than in idealism. This thinking is associated with death not as its denial but as its acknowledgment, an acknowledgment that prepares the overcoming of thinking by faith. Egoism and death assume centrality. In place of idealism's method of conceptualization, which is intoxicated with the sense of creativity and which, certain of victory, overlooks death, appears a new thinking that admits the tragedy, bitterness and transitoriness of the human condition and by con-

[35] 25–26.
[36] 5.
[37] 355.

fronting this condition truly overcomes it. The moral personality dissolves in universality which at the same time implies for it immortality. The solitary man, however, dies and completes himself in death, and precisely because of this he longs for immortality. Death is taken seriously. It is a Nought which is also an Aught.

If egoism and death are thus imprinted upon idealism by means of the formula of the human self and then also upon positive thinking, which brought forth the formula, the significance of egoism extends to yet another area, art. – Art is the speech of the solitary self. It is the "subjective speech, the 'speaking' of that speechless world, as it were."[38] It participates with mathematics, with the construction, in this role of pre-verbal speech. "Mathematics is the objective language, the 'sense' of that silence."[39] Thus art does not belong to the world of faith. Its place is next to thinking, in the realm of abstraction. "Art is not a real world, for the threads which are drawn from man to man in it run only for moments. . . In the make- believe world of art the self ever remains self, never becomes – soul."[40] The foundation of the position of art in the second part of the system is thereby provided, just as – with respect to speech thinking – the first part had the task of laying the basis for that which was to follow. Art is regarded by faith as something counterfeit. Like Islam, it enters into the sphere of revelation without a change of its sign, without reversal. Next to creation, revelation and redemption, art appears as a reality of the second order, as something that, although it is necessary, "is real only as member."[41] Accordingly, art becomes dependent upon the empirical realities of faith as its categories of self-reference. In the third part it finally receives its justification as applied art.

Perhaps the only other philosopher who has rejected pure art with such decisiveness is Plato, who in his *Republic* took a stance against Homer. In Rosenzweig's case, however, the verdict is not based on educational grounds. The servitude of art, like that of thinking, results from the same existential motive. Art leads man not beyond himself, but only into himself. It helps him to flee from reality and eliminates his responsibility to God and to his neighbor. "Thus the arts spare man the hard labor of implanting freedom and form in the world, discipline and life in the soul."[42] Music is an especially dangerous rival of reality because it re-creates the framework of this reality – time. "For in his enjoyment, the devotee of the fine arts forgets, in the end,

---

[38] 125.
[39] 125.
[40] 81.
[41] 190.
[42] 360.

only the world. But the musical enthusiast forgets himself in his music. The former only excludes himself from productive life, and eventually can find his way back again; but the latter spoils himself, he debilitates his own soul."[43] The egoistic character of art is also clearly expressed in the Christian aesthetics of the system's third part. Art competes there with the cross of the soul, but it only shows everyone his own cross.[44] Behind this almost passionate rejection of art, above all of music – "the dog who grieved inconsolably because his mistress played the piano is more truly alive, nay, if the expression be permitted, more 'humanly' alive than the 'musical' devotee"[45] – one might be tempted to see the traces of Rosenzweig's own inner struggle with his artistic powers. He who speaks like this may himself have tasted and overcome the dangers of such intoxication.

d) The Significance of the Construction for the System

If we ask ourselves what could have moved Rosenzweig to prefer the construction to the dialectics applied by Schelling in the theory of potentials – Rosenzweig himself speaks of the "difficult construction passages"[1] – we can find the reason in part in that the point of departure, the differential, offers a connection with the "Noughts" of Kant and thereby with idealism. It corresponds to the overall design of Rosenzweig's thought, which is negatively oriented to idealism. Just as in the system in its entirety the idealistic All reappears as the realistic All through the overturning of the presuppositions, so here the idea as Nought is attached to presupposed factuality. By this means a positive idea is brought about with the aid of the construction.

One could also answer this question, however, with a view to the difference in that which is achieved by construction and by dialectics. The designation of Yea and Nay as logically older and younger, as well as the reciprocal modification of Yea and Nay approach a dialectic relationship. Nevertheless what matters to Rosenzweig is that Yea and Nay are to be equally primordial. He seeks to avoid "the reduction of the antithesis to mediation."[2] Nor does he want to permit the And to be considered as a *creative* synthesis. The reason for this is that with the scheme of construction he is at the same time preparing the inner structure of the second as well as the third part of the system. If at this

[43] 360.
[44] 377.
[45] 360.

[1] *Kl. Sch.*, p. 379.
[2] 229.

point we once more take a preview of the system as a whole, we have to note
that although the succeeding stage of the system always stands in a dialectic
relationship to its predecessor, the stage itself is arranged within according to
the scheme of the construction. Thus within the second part creation, revelation and redemption are to stand in the same relation to each other as
Yea, Nay and And. That is to say, creation and revelation are to be equally
primordial, even if they come one after another in time – the logical "youth"
of the Nay is transformed here into the temporal "youth" of revelation.
Redemption is indebted to the activity of the Nay on the Yea, that is, of
revelation on creation, as well as to a factor that is subsequently added and
which is independent of these two: God's redeeming act. – Rosenzweig's
intention becomes even clearer in the third part, where by means of the
construction he secures the same primordiality for Judaism and Christianity.
They are no longer to be regarded as having emerged from each other,
although they are successive in time. They vouch for each other's truth and
beyond that are united in God who is truth. Rosenzweig says that his
presentation of Judaism and Christianity on a sociological basis is determined
by general systematic considerations and that he is willing to put up with the
not entirely fair assessment of the two that is connected with this as the price
for avoiding apologetics and polemics.[3] Conversely, one might also say that
the interest in the avoidance of fruitless polemics also determined his systematic structure. By placing Judaism and Christianity as equals he removes the
danger of attaching a value judgment to the relationship of premise and
consequence. He thereby blocks the possibility of seeing Christianity *merely*
as something derived as well as Schelling's view that Judaism is *merely* a
precondition for Christianity.

If, then, the construction has great advantages as opposed to dialectics for
the inner arrangement of the system's individual parts, it nevertheless is also
at a disadvantage vis-à-vis dialectics. Its weakness lies in that it accomplishes
nothing for the further movement of the completed elements, i.e., for the
progress of the system. This could only have been the case if the experience of
factuality and the believing experience of the second part had been identical,
and if the construction had thereby been directly linked to revelation, that is,
to the question: "How must God, world and man be constituted in order to be
able to reveal themselves?" This was not the case, however. The construction
remained without a relationship to revelation. It therefore was not by itself
the hidden presupposition of revelation – it becomes this only by the transformation of thinking into belief, independent of the construction. The task of

---

[3] Cf. *Kl. Sch.*, pp. 392–393.

the construction is precisely to clarify the experienced factuality through its conceptualization. "A God who did not reveal Himself would not permanently hide His essence from us, for nothing remains concealed from man's far-reaching learning, his capacity for conceptualization, his inquisitive intellect. But God pours forth over us in revelation;...thereby He forges the fetters of love around our free intellect."[4] The construction thus merely reproduces conceptually the general experience of factuality, that which was called inverse transcendence by Schelling. It does this not by proving the existence of God, world and man from their concepts, as pre-Kantian rationalism did, but precisely by undertaking the derivation of the concepts, "being from existence."[5]

These conceived configurations, as they can be called like Schelling's potentials on account of their rational-non-rational character, no longer point beyond themselves. Rosenzweig speaks of "the conclusiveness of this concept of God," of its "product-like but not productive nature."[6] "Synthesis, the And...is the keystone of an arch which after all rests on its own pillars. Nor can it thus become thesis again. The keystone cannot, as with Hegel it must, transform itself back into a cornerstone. No dialectic process is arrived at."[7] In that the construction does not take us beyond this And of the completed configuration it is inferior to dialectics.

Searching, investigating, separating Schelling moves dialectically from possibility to reality until at the end of his path God's non-rational actuated being remains. The dialectic method, however, does not incorporate God's non-rational being into its premises; rather it renders God's being visible by the process of separation. Rosenzweig, in contrast, does not separate God from the dialectics. For Rosenzweig God is not a postulate articulated negatively through conceptual deduction and the dialectic method. The experience of God is introduced by him positively, that is, as a fact that philosophical construction is to include in its purview. The first part of his system certainly contains indications of problems that the construction has in comprehending the autonomous configurations of God, world and man. Rosenzweig speaks, for instance, of Aristotle's difficulties in relating the metalogical world of paganism to God as "reason's...claims to universality and unity"[8] and of the Sophists' revolt against the "metalogical view of

[4] 381.
[5] 18.
[6] 35.
[7] 230.
[8] 54.

communal life."[9] The way out is finally intimated: "The Sophists' concept of man with its deficient activity is just as incapable of a new solution to the problems of the metalogical microcosm as the philosophical concept of God, with its inactivity, [is] of a solution of the macrocosmic problem."[10] The characterization of the constructed configurations as possibilities is also found in the transition from the first to the second parts of *The Star*. "In mere existence everything is possible and no more than possible."[11] It is not clear, however, how reality can be reached from the construction. The sole motivating factor lies in the triad of the elements. Since each element carried within itself the All, it must claim to hold the two others also within itself. "What erupts here side by side are after all *three* monisms, three one-and-all consciousnesses. Three wholes were still possible; three Alls are unthinkable. And so the question of their relationship must be asked after all."[12] Not the construction, then, but the triad owed to experience makes the elements stand in need of completion. They necessitate a continuation not because they themselves are hypothetical but because their relationship is. Thus the assumption of a threefold factuality that is experienced primordially permits, on the one hand, the perception of reality as the origin of *relationship*, while on the other hand it also allows one to demand this relationship.

The demand is answered by the dialectics of the system, which thereby compensates for the weakness of the construction. Reality becomes capable of realization in the system's advance from the thesis of thinking to the antithesis of faith. "What we have found so far has been pure existence. . .a major matter vis-à-vis the pure incertitude of doubt, a trifle compared to the claim of belief. Belief can not be satisfied with a mere factuality of existence . . .it demands unambiguous certainty."[13] In this progress from thinking to faith the second half of Schelling's notion concerning the transcendence of being to all thinking is also set into action, namely, that being, since it is not congruent with thinking, can only be experienced by faith. Thinking establishes essence, but only essence.

Rosenzweig speaks of God, world and man as essences not only in his commentary article on *The Star*[14] but also, for instance, in the metalogic, where he speaks of the cyclical process between individual and species as a

---

[9] 57.

[10] 57–58.

[11] 85.

[12] 84.

[13] 85.

[14] *Kl. Sch.*, p. 380.

description of the world's essence.[15] With this designation of the positive concepts as essences we arrive at the unique quality which distinguishes them from the reality of the system's second part: the juxtaposition *in space*, as opposed to the succession *in time*. All essence is in space, something which becomes quite evident in the structure of the configurations themselves, where essence always signifies one component. While the Nay, which is finite according to its emergence, was always a one-time occurrence that continuously renews itself and was measured against the infinity of time, the Yea, which is infinite according to its form, was always something static, spread out in space. Thus the "infinitely static essence"[16] of God as well as the "infinite applicability of the worldly logos"[17] are infinities in space. Even man's essence, though finite and individual according to its content, is "an individual in the boundless void of space," something that is "everywhere."[18] As essence God, world and man are things. The spatial form belongs to their objectivity just as the temporal form belongs to the objectivity of events.[19] Thus Rosenzweig can later call this ideal space in which the world is located the space of the mathematicians, a space that is associated with that which is conceived and not that which is created. "As a result those who, like mathematicians and physicists, regard the created world under the aspect of space, necessarily strip it of its utter factuality which, exalted above all possibilities, it enjoys as creation, and relativize it into a football of possibilities."[20] From the perspective of speech thinking, Hans Ehrenberg also attributes "typification" to thinking, because it has to embrace both anterior and posterior time within the present and thus make it, the present, space, because it requires situations. The tension between old and new philosophy is to him the tension between space and time.[21]

e) Rational Philosophy, Paganism and Creation

The equation of rational philosophy, paganism and creation is present in Rosenzweig as well as in Schelling, although in Rosenzweig's case their order is reversed and there are also some differences in content. The difference in order once more clearly shows Schelling's tendency to philosophize from

[15] 49.
[16] 43.
[17] 44.
[18] 64.
[19] 152.
[20] 355.
[21] Cf. H. Ehrenberg, *Hegel* (Muenchen: Drei Masken Verlag, 1925), pp. 132, 138 ff.

God. God's absolute act, His act of creation, comes first. It introduces the process of creation from which man carries out the falling away through the elevation of his own will. In rational philosophy man's I wants itself to be a creator. Paganism is the historical parallel to this spiritual process and because it is a real process, paganism is merely the repetition of the process of creation in human consciousness. – In the case of Rosenzweig the construction of the elements comes first, representing, as it were, the role of rational philosophy. Its historical parallel is paganism and both together are posited as creation from the perspective of the system's second part.*

Thinking, in the service of experienced factuality, had shaped this factuality inwardly as living unity of polar opposites and thereby had shaped it outwardly as indissoluble. And because the experienced factuality was three-fold, its isolation from the outside at the same time meant an absence of relation, a separation from the other two elements. The historical realization of these rational-non-rational configurations that were established by thinking is paganism.

The god of paganism was a god that lived by himself and isolated himself toward man and world. The mythical god "leads a life purely unto itself. The law of this life is the inner harmony of caprice and fate, a harmony that does not resound beyond itself, that constantly returns into itself."[1] The gods do not reign over "the living" and do not know any nature outside their own. They hold within themselves merely their own nature. This inner vitality** along with outward self-containment also belongs to the plastic cosmos. It characterizes not so much the macrocosm, which was already involved by the Platonic theory of ideas in the problematics of the possibility of relating the world to an extra-worldly principle,[2] as it does the microcosm, the ancient polis. While inwardly it has unity of individual and community – "the ancient state knows only the immediate relationship of citizen and state, . . . [because it] is simply the whole whose configuration absorbs its parts,"[3] outwardly it has "no drive to progress to higher wholes."[4] This is embodied most clearly in the empire of Augustus "which was always precisely . . . a self-contained

---

[1] 34.
[2] Cf. 53–54.
[3] 55.
[4] 56.

* Hugo Bergmann rightly points to the difficulty that arises here. By the transposition of the term creation to the entire first part of the system all three elements, including the pagan god, are designated as creation. Cf. H. Bergmann, *Dialogical Philosophy from Kierkegaard to Buber* [Hebrew] (Jerusalem: Akademon, 1973), p. 164.

** If in his commentary article on *The Star* Rosenzweig denies vitality to the god, world and man of paganism, he is referring to external vitality, the outward relationship that comes into being only in faith. *Kl. Sch.*, p. 381.

whole, a world both pacified...and appeased within itself, with no urge to
carry its peace beyond its borders. What lay beyond, remained beyond; with
clearest conscience the world of Augustus identified itself with the world as –
oecumene."[5] The ancient states are "outwardly exclusive and inwardly unconditional and for just this reason become those configured individual
beings which, upon profound reflection, quite automatically evoked the
comparison with a work of art."[6] The historical form of the metaethical self is
the hero of antiquity. In Attic tragedy man exhibits "the interlacing of
volition and essence into the established unity of defiance."[7] Here, too he is
outwardly silent. "The tragic hero has only one language which completely
corresponds to him: precisely keeping silent...By keeping silent, the hero
breaks down the bridges which connect him with God and the world, and
elevates himself...into the icy solitude of the self."[8] Thus death and demise
are to him "the supreme 'heroization,' to wit, the most closed-off 'selfication'
of his self."[9]

With respect to Schelling the third potential, which here corresponds to the
formula A = A, had been monotheism's concept of God, whose separation
into individual factors produced the pagan gods. Even more than Schelling,
Rosenzweig emphasizes the distinction between monotheism and paganism.
Every concept of a god is pagan; even the concept of the *one* God, since it is
still a concept, designates the remote God. Thus to him A = A means only the
pagan god, that subsequently becomes by means of revelation the God of
monotheism who is also outwardly alive. This point is significant for the
different views held by Schelling and Rosenzweig concerning the relationship
between paganism and monotheism. In Schelling's case paganism and revelation counterbalanced each other. Monotheism contained the concept of
God and *in addition* revelation. It was exactly the relationship between
negative and positive philosophy, between thinking and faith, that is, a
relation of identity. In Rosenzweig's case the stress in monotheism lies on
revelation as opposed to the concept. Monotheism is *primarily and exclusively*
revelation. The relationship of revelation to the concept of God, and therewith of monotheism to paganism is merely dialectic, in accordance with the
systematic relationship between faith and thinking, a relationship that deviates from Schelling's. Paganism, the historical form of thinking, is both

[5] 56.
[6] 55.
[7] 76.
[8] 77.
[9] 78.

negated and preserved by monotheism, that is, by revelation. It is the basis upon which revelation is built.*

Since the completed concept of God characterized only the pagan god, Rosenzweig understands indifference to the world as the distinctive mark of paganism. Schelling characterized paganism merely as self-enclosure. Rosenzweig's view is in consonance with his affirmation of the threefold experience of reality. Schelling, on the other hand, is concerned only with God's being; his potentialities are modalities of this one and universal being. He is not yet faced with the problem of the connection with man and world at this point. Man and world emerge only through God's absolute act. Thus a separation as pagan preliminary stage to revelation can only be a division of God Himself. Rosenzweig, on the other hand, had from the very beginning three separate factualities: the universal being of God, the particular being of man and the universal-particular being of the world. Thus he could turn this already existing separation into the distinguishing mark of paganism. (If we direct our attention to the fact that God, world and man signify modes of being – and the modern ontology that is linked to Schelling is based precisely on the insight that the mode of the human "to be" is different from the modes of being of nature and God – then the three elements in their completed form can also be juxtaposed to Schelling's potentials. God, world and man would then each be a potential and we would arrive at the same concept of separation as Schelling's.) By positing outer division and paganism as equal Rosenzweig gains the possibility of still claiming the inner separation for preliminary stages of paganism.

India and China are two "historic forms"[10] which though they do not produce paganism through a process, nevertheless in relation to the unity and vitality of paganism realize in each case only one factor of this unity and therefore remain in the realm of abstraction. They are "spiritual religions"[11] without the living God and their world and man are also one-sided. – India always knows only the Yea. Its god is not alive but rather is a "deity"[12] and it

---

[10] *Kl. Sch.*, p. 382.

[11] *Ibid.*, p. 382.

[12] 35.

* Cf. F. Rosenzweig, "'Der Ewige' – Mendelssohn und der Gottesname," *Kl. Sch.*, p. 192: "The distinctiveness of the biblical faith in God lies in the fact that though it indeed presupposes this 'pagan' unity...it nevertheless recognizes this spirit in its oneness with that which is experienced personally and directly. The 'pagan unity,' however, is not something incidental. A god that has remained a part (such as a god of a group) while claiming to be 'the whole' would be an idol, incapable of entering into a unity with the 'God of Abraham';...but the monotheistic nuance, as it were, is given to this pagan unity only by the Jewish fusion of the God that is remote with the God that is near, of the 'complete' with the 'particular' God. This fusion alone is the 'essence of Judaism' and...also the essence of Christianity." Cf. also above, p. 62.

is exhausted "on the road between the Nought and the pure, all-pervasive silence of essence."[13] – The world of India is a world of essence. It becomes "a system of concepts. . .a system of world, it is true, of reality, but without any of the independent right of the particular, which is ascribed only to 'illusion.'"[14] – Man also does not attain full vitality here. "Indian man remains mixed in character. . .Nor is there an ideal of humanity that remains as intimately tied to every organization of natural character as the Indian."[15]

China, in turn, merely develops the opposite, the Nay, that is to say: God only as power, the world only as the plenitude of individuality, man only as will "which was not privileged to materialize in a character"[16] and who therefore becomes "purity of feeling."[17] – Since India and China do not arrive at a unity of form, their God, world and man are not secured against being reshaped into the Nought. India and China demonstrate the two possibilities for negating God, world and man. They "must be twofold, for the living gods will not be denied, nor the world of configuration negated, nor the defiant self extinguished. The powers of annihilation. . .are masters only of. . .the halves which have not yet coalesced into the unity of configuration."[18]

In the historical realization of antiquity's configurations there also lies a hint of what is to follow. The historical fact that paganism was subdued by Christianity is a concrete indication of the overcoming of thinking by faith. It provides important support for the notion of the system which in other respects could not make use of the construction. In that antiquity is the ground upon which revelation spread, i.e., the historical presupposition which was both accepted and negated by Christianity, paganism assumes the features of creation in relation to revelation. – Schelling had also seen something prophetic in paganism, especially in its mysteries. At the same time this suggests the transfer of revelation's import as a presupposition to thinking as well, to whose constructed forms paganism had corresponded as its "historical analogy."[19] The transposition of the concepts creation and revelation to the Yea and Nay of construction, as we have seen, approximates the dialectic method. Now, however, this transposition of these concepts to the relationship of thinking to faith, i.e., the relationship of the first part of the system to the second part, actually employs the dialectic method. This

[13] 35.
[14] 58.
[15] 74.
[16] 75.
[17] 75.
[18] 75.
[19] 147.

relationship of thinking to faith, which the construction was to have facili-
tated, thereby enters into an exact correspondence with the dialectic relationship between the parts of the system, in which thinking explicitly
remains present in faith as a basis and a presupposition.

Just as paganism can be designated as a preliminary stage of Christianity
only from the perspective of Christianity, so too is the designation of thinking
as creation, which is suggested by this, possible only from the perspective of
faith. The transfer of this theological term to the thinking of the first part is
possible only because on the level of faith knowledge is presented as creation.
In the transition to the second part Rosenzweig still says "it...can not be
manifest, that this everlasting birth out of the depth is – creation."[20] Only in
theology does thinking have its place as creation and hence as past, and only
in faith does it become possible in such a way to transform the logical *a priori*
into a temporal *a priori*. Thus it is said in the second part: "creation is...the
gate through which philosophy enters into the house of theology."[21] Further,
"the connection between knowledge and the concept of the past shows itself
in this relationship to creation. Truth is always that which has been, whether
as 'a priori,' or 'towering in ancient sacred might' as with Plato, or as 'object
of experience.'"[22] Knowledge has the "characteristic of being – just as the
past alone can be – unalterable."[23] It is knowledge "which itself lays its
foundations on a fundamental concept of belief."[24] And so finally the
conceptuality of the world, its designation with the character of the past, of
that which is already in existence, is traced to God's past act of creation. "God
has already created it on the basis of His eternal creative power. And only for
this reason it 'exists' and is yet renewed with each morning."[25]

[20] 90.
[21] 103.
[22] 103.
[23] 103.
[24] 103.
[25] 132.

II. Faith or the Antithesis

a) The Act

The second part of the system stands under the sign of revelation, which as free act highlights the nature of being and which is experienced in faith. Here we enter the realm of theology; that which had been problematic for thinking becomes within the precincts of the heart a source of creativity.[1] Being lies beyond all reason and can be fulfilled only in creation, revelation and redemption. "Injected into the reality of revelation, everything gains that freedom which it had forfeited when subjected to the slavery of the concepts."[2] Only here can man experience God's existence in a real act of God and thereby at the same time attest to his own existence. Only in faith is responsible intervention by man in the world possible, an intervention by means of which man and the world become aware of each other's reality. "God dwells beyond all our knowledge. Before our ignorance begins, however, 'your God' gives Himself to you, to your call, . . . to your preparedness."[3] The God of thinking had been equally indifferent to man and the world. He was the pagan god, only inwardly alive while outwardly closed. Therefore He had been unreal and unconditioned. In faith, however, man experiences the acting and hence the real and determined God. Obeying Him, he himself acts and is real.

The experience of factuality, which could not be entirely satisfied by the conceptual construction, now finds complete fulfilment in the experience of revelation. This justifies Rosenzweig's designation of his method as "absolute empiricism."[4] The experience of the reality that precedes thought, which had already made thinking a thinking that knows "nothing of the terrestrial that it has not experienced"[5] now becomes an "attitude that . . . knows nothing more of the divine than what it has experienced."[6] Or to use Schelling's terminology: since Rosenzweig's philosophy from the beginning is not idealism, i.e., "apriority of the empirical," this empirical, which is liberated from the *a priori* of thinking and on account of this is also not entirely comprehended by thinking, invests its surplus, as it were, in an "empiricism of the *a priori*."

---

[1] Cf. F. Rosenzweig, *Anmerkungen zu Jehuda Halevi. 92 Hymnen und Gedichte* (Berlin: 1927), p. 174.

[2] 189.

[3] *Anmerkungen zu Jehuda Halevi*, p. 184.

[4] *Kl. Sch.*, p. 398.

[5] *Ibid.*

[6] *Ibid.*

For Rosenzweig there are two dimensions to believing experience and hence also to its content, being – "the word of revelation is: I am there as whoever I am there. . . That which has being is there, nothing more."[7] Believing experience is a question, on the one hand, of the uniform becoming manifest (*Offenbarwerden*) of God, world and man, which act on each other in creation, revelation and redemption. On the other hand, it is a question of revelation, and with it creation and redemption, as absolute actions of God alone. The first view establishes a correlative theology and is linked to the antithesis, that is, to the second part in the system. The second view gives God the primacy within the correlation and utilizes the construction scheme of Yea, Nay and And, through which each stage of the system receives its inner structure. Attention should always be paid to the fact that the stages of the system stand in a dialectic relationship to one another, while the second and third stages are arranged within themselves according to the construction scheme. Both dimensions of revelation will first be expounded separately and then their coming to terms with each other in creation, revelation and redemption will be traced in detail.

Revelation in its broader sense, by which the second part of the system is distinguished as antithesis, is "the authentic idea of revelation [in which] the three 'actual' elements of the All – God, world, man – emerge from themselves, belong to one another, and meet another."[8] Inasmuch as all three elements act upon each other in deeds and experience these deeds from each other, they all arrive at being in the same manner. God, world and man, arranged as completely equal, obtain the freedom which transcends their conceptualization and which helps them to procure reality. Each of the three experiences the action of the other. As a result the equilibrium between active and passive is established in each individual element as well as in their reciprocal relationships. Being signifies a correlation of acting and experiencing in which both members occupy the same rank.

This reciprocal becoming manifest occurs through negation of the configurations, each of whose distinctiveness had been constructed in the thesis, that is, in thinking. In that these configurations are subsumed under the antithesis, faith, the And that had been employed to elucidate their protocosmic identity is shattered. The fragmented elements that had originated in Yea and Nay become a negative sign. "All revelation begins with a great Nay. All concepts of the protocosmos undergo a conversion as they enter into

---

[7] M. Buber, *I and Thou*, p. 160. Cf. also *Anmerkungen zu Jehuda Halevi*, p. 174: "God always reveals. . .only Himself to man; to man He reveals Himself. This accusative and this dative in their union are the sole content of revelation."

[8] 115.

the light of the real world, and this conversion is none other than that Nay."[9] What had been a Yea in thinking becomes in faith a Nay, and conversely a Nay of the construction is always a Yea of believing experience. The order also is reversed. The Nay, which with regard to the construction had been the second, the logically younger, is, following its conversion into a Yea in faith, the first, namely the first in time. Consequently faith, too, in every becoming manifest of an element, has something positive "at the beginning." (To be sure, this conversion of the order is not possible with respect to one of the three elements, viz., the world, precisely on account of the conception of revelation as a relation between an active Nay and a passive Yea. For if in every manifestation two elements act *simultaneously* the first expression of at least one of them must be a Nay. Thus God's Yea of creation is answered by a Nay of the world in its first act in revealing. Later, inasmuch as in faith the logical sequence becomes a temporal one, the mode of time of the future offers the justification for this special position of the world.)

Revelation as a stage of the system does not stand *next to* thinking but rather is the Nay *of* thinking. In accordance with this antithetical character of revelation every expression of the elements maintains their relation to their origin in thinking. What the reciprocal modification of the Yea and the Nay had accomplished for the inner structure of the elements, here is accomplished by the dialectic anchoring of the revealed in the concealed. Thus in the case of creation God expresses Himself by a Yea, that is, by an attribute. The power of the concealed act penetrates this attribute and thus God's ability, expressed in creation, remains grounded in His essence. "God, He who is visible in creation, is capable of all that He wills, but He wills only what He must will out of His essence."[10] By designating God's creator-ness (*Schoepfertum*) as an active attribute, Rosenzweig resolves the theological paradox resulting from the fact that, on the one hand, God must create from caprice – otherwise He would be dependent upon the world – while, on the other hand, He also needs the world, in order not to be "removed to a height that is foreign to the world."[11] In affirming the world in creation God enters a relationship (which posits a need), without forfeiting His power (which assumes His absolute freedom).

These same dialectics can be traced in all manifestations of the elements. They will merely be shown here, without investigating in greater detail the resulting theological problems. In creation the world manifests itself as creature. Its logos, having entered the world as Yea, expresses itself as Nay, as

[9] 173.
[10] 114.
[11] 114.

momentary distinctiveness. Accordingly, something distinctive is formed, something that is in need of renewal at every moment, but that is nevertheless universal, namely existence. "Existence in contrast to Being means the universal which is full of the distinctive and which is not always and everywhere, but, herein infected by the distinctive, must continually become new in order to maintain itself."[12] The problem of divine providence is thereby determined so that it is directed toward the universal, toward existence, and concerns the distinctive only by way of the universal. – Vis-à-vis man, God reveals Himself as He who loves, as a Nay that is grounded in the concealed Yea. God's love is "fate [that] bursts forth eventfully with the whole force of the moment. It is not destined from of yore. On the contrary, it is precisely the negation of everything valid from of yore...not 'destined' but suddenly there and as yet as inescapable in its suddenness as though it were destined from of yore."[13] – The humble faithfulness of being loved, in which man turns to God in revelation, stems from the defiant will of man's concealed configuration. Schelling's view of human freedom as falling away and as sin is suggested in the following passage: "Defiance is the arch-evil in man, bubbling up darkly; it is the subterranean root whence the juices of faithfulness rise into the soul beloved of God."[14] – Man opens himself towards the world in the love of his neighbor, a love that again is the Yea of a concealed Nay: "This volition, ever capable of renewal and really renewing itself knows nothing of short-lived caprice; in every one of its individual acts, rather, it applies the whole force of the firmly directed character which has merged in it."[15] – And finally the world, to which man extends his act of love, turns toward him as constant, enduring life which nevertheless is momentary on account of its rootedness in individuality. Life is "an enduring content, an individuality which contains something imperishable, something which remains in existence once it exists."[16]

With respect to this dialectic conversion of the fragmented elements Rosenzweig always gives Islam as the example of a false religion of revelation, thereby continuing the religio-historical construction of the first part. "Mohammed came upon the idea of revelation and took it over as such a find is wont to be taken over, that is, without generating it out of its presuppositions."[17] The conversion that faith works upon thinking is thus lacking here. Islam's God, world and man enter into revelation without the transfor-

[12] 120–121.
[13] 159–160.
[14] 170.
[15] 213.
[16] 222.
[17] 116.

mation of their signs and therefore remain on the level of the concept. "They retained their mute, introspective stare even while they trained it outwardly on each other. Here the Yea remained Yea and the Nay Nay."[18] To be sure, Islam accepts revelation externally. It is indeed a genuine religion, since it was "consciously established"[19] by human hands. Precisely on account of this, however, it is "the religion of reason"[20] as opposed to real religions of revelation. The Moslem God creates out of caprice a world of essence, in which He intervenes anew at every moment. He reveals Himself to man in essential, universal love and expects in vain an ever new act of love as requital. "The idea that man's shortcomings are more powerful to arouse divine love than his merits – the conceptual nucleus of belief – is an inconceivable paradox for Islam."[21] Islam's man fulfils his duty to the world in quiet obedience and not from an ever new love for his neighbor. The world does not come to meet him as something "growing gradually."[22] Rather, its life is forever streaming toward him; life progresses by itself toward infinity. Rosenzweig's remoteness from all formalistic ethics is nowhere as evident as in his rejection of Islam's concept of progress in favor of the Kingdom of God, whose quiet growth is waiting for man's act of love. Rosenzweig's theology is directed towards an act full of content, which is a free act because it can change the world. This theology is explicitly differentiated from every practical intellectual faith that is nourished on trust in the progress of culture.

In addition to this acting and experiencing, which take place equally among all the elements, there is the other view of creation, revelation and redemption as absolute actions of God. If one could call that revelation which expresses itself in the antithesis "relative act," then these actions of God would have to be designated – entirely in Schelling's sense – "absolute act." In that they are addressed by this act man and world are no longer equivalent but rather subordinate to this act. Creation, revelation and redemption are thereby related to each other according to the construction scheme of Yea, Nay and And. Creation is God's essential action – with Schelling, too, the act of creation was linked to essence inasmuch as God found the possibility for carrying out the act in His essence. Revelation is God's manifest action; redemption is His unifying action, which augments and completes the influence of revelation upon creation. This sequence of creation, revelation and

---

[18] 117.
[19] *Kl. Sch.*, p. 391.
[20] 116.
[21] 166.
[22] 225.

redemption, as God's divine actions, signifies for God His self-creation, self-revelation and self-redemption. This is because redemption, as the union of creation and revelation, also contains – in accordance with the concepts of unity and object posited by the construction in the system's first part – the completion of God into configuration. This configuration, however, is no longer merely a conceived, essential All and neither is it one All among three. Rather, God, having demonstrated His existence in creation, revelation and redemption, is the really existing unitary One who assimilates world and man.

By means of this application of Yea, Nay and And to God's absolute act Rosenzweig thus takes the decisive step from the triad of God, world and man towards God as the unity of the three. He thereby moves towards the viewpoint of Schelling, who already at the stage of thinking had known only one universal concept of God, just as the act, too, was for Schelling only a question of the one absolute being of God. For Rosenzweig the arrangement of Yea, Nay and And as the structure of the system's second part at the same time signifies this structure's augmentation. The antithesis, which was supposed to have brought creation, revelation and redemption merely as the uniform relation of the action and experience of the three configurations – just as the thesis brings the uniform construction and the absence of relation – thereby ends in a position where God is elevated above man and world.

In this sequence of creation, revelation and redemption, which progresses according to the principle of construction, the fluctuation between construction and dialectics already dealt with in the context of the formation of the elements can again be ascertained. In the relation between creation and revelation – redemption is a synthesis also according to the construction scheme – the distinction between primordiality and mutual dependence is again blurred. Creation and revelation, as absolute acts, on the one hand, are to occur in complete freedom and only subsequently to enter into a relationship. On the other hand, they also require each other in order to be creation and revelation. Rosenzweig emphasizes the necessity of referring revelation back to creation and conversely of grounding creation in revelation. This necessity also determines the relation of *The Star*'s first part to the second part, in which the relation is unequivocally dialectic. Within theology, where the logical relation is turned into a temporal one, the connection between creation and revelation expresses itself as a connection between promise and fulfilment. "Truth is and remains the only soil in which the truthfulness of experience can grow, the only firm foundation on which the ideal can be verified."[23] "And theology itself conceives of its content as

---

[23] 107.

event...As a result its preconditions are not conceptual elements, but rather immanent reality. For this reason the concept of creation supersedes the philosophical concept of truth...Revelation is providentially 'foreseen' in creation – revelation in its entire contents...But thereby revelation regains...the character of authentic miracle – authentic because it becomes wholly and solely the fulfilment of the promise made in creation."[24] In the believing soul's experience of revelation creation once more fulfils the function of foundation, albeit not the creation of the world, but rather a restricted creation – the historical factuality of revelation. "The presentness of the miracle of revelation is and remains its content; its historicity, however, is its ground and its warrant. Individually experienced belief had already found within itself the highest bliss destined for it. Now it also finds the highest certainty possible for it, but only in this its historicity, its 'positivity.'"[25] Conversely, with respect to revelation, creation is not independent. "The past creation is demonstrated from out of the living present revelation – demonstrated, that is: pointed out."[26] The "experiential and presentive character of revelation"[27] identifies creation as creation. "It is not possible to believe creation because it provides an adequate explanation of the world riddle. He who has not yet been reached by the voice of revelation has no right to accept the idea of creation as if it were a scientific hypothesis."[28]

b) The Realities – Creation, Revelation and Redemption

The tension between relative act and absolute act does not affect each of Rosenzweig's theological basic concepts of creation, revelation and redemption in the same manner. In creation the absolute act opposes the relative act and finally overthrows it; in revelation the two coincide, and in redemption the absolute act surmounts the relative act.

With respect to *creation* the relationship between God and world from the perspective of the uniform revelation of all three elements would be on the part of the world an act – to be sure, an act limited by a concealed essence – and on the part of God an essence that is merely rooted in an act. It must be kept in mind, however, that in the case of the world the manifestation of this relationship would have to be active, while in the case of God it would have to be passive. God experiences the creatureliness of the world that is pressing

[24] 108.
[25] 183.
[26] 182.
[27] 183.
[28] 134–135.

toward Him. Accordingly, the movement proceeds from the act of the world to the essence of God. Similarly, in revelation, for example, where the opening up of the soul also is an "attributive act,"[1] the emphasis is on the attributive and the soul therefore is passive recipient. It is obvious that a theory of creation in which divine passivity and worldly activity come together would be impossible. Thus with a view to God's absolute act – and creation can of course only be understood as an act of God – the relationship between God and the world is reversed. Here Rosenzweig stresses the *act* as opposed to the attributive, while with respect to the world he stresses *essence* as opposed to activity. As a result, in the case of God as well as in the case of the world the concealed primordialities, which are supposed to be merely "foundation-stones,"[2] are operative principles. Further, a creation is produced which "as a movement of God towards the world is distinguished by the nature of divine activity, not of worldly passivity, in short by the Yea."[3] In this sentence the character of creation as divine activity and worldly passivity is clearly expressed, while with respect to God the Yea is merely to express the *manner* of creation.

In the case of creation the absolute act thus once more reverses the relative act, which for its part had been founded on the reversal of the fragmented elements. As a result, the system's point of view, which holds that thinking is preserved in faith only as hidden presupposition, is damaged. It is precisely God's absolute transcendent freedom that helps thinking receive a stronger emphasis.

To be sure, in this victory of the absolute act, another feature peculiar to the relative act remains, namely the relationship between two independent elements. It is only the action that passes over to the realm of God under the compulsion of the absolute act. The world, even if not equivalent to God, is nevertheless independent. The uniform relationship between God, man and world, which is inherent in the triad of experienced factuality and which is brought about by means of faith, lets creation still remain a correlation and thus burdens it with a new difficulty. Here, too, as previously with the dialectic conversion of the fragmented elements, we can only point to specific theological problems without going into the details. A correlative creation would seem to be theologically very questionable. Further, the "paradox"[4] that Rosenzweig himself felt concerning a creation that creates from the Aught

[1] 208.
[2] 115.
[3] 126.
[4] 119.

rather than from the Nought would not be cancelled by granting redemption, as the completion of the world's creation, the meaning of creation *ex nihilo*. Creation "in the beginning," in any event, remains a creation by means of the completed configuration – not to mention the fact that in redemption, inasmuch as it occurs between man and the world, the metalogical world by all means is not Nought. This suggests that correlative creation grew out of its equality with revelation – an equality which of course is based on the system's structure – and that the theory of revelation gave birth to this notion of creation.

Even creation as a scientific concept of the world, as Rosenzweig describes it through comparison with idealism's concept of generation, would not be creation *ex nihilo*. The creation taking place in a world whose formula is $B = A$ certainly contains the renunciation of chaos, the disjunctive multiplicity of contingent phenomena (B) bereft of a unifying principle (A). "The predicate sentence always becomes intelligible only if the predicate has been known 'for longer already' than its subject."[5] The universal A consequently is the presupposition for the chaotic B – unlike idealistic generation where the chaos B is the presupposition for A. A, however, also is not the Nought, but rather "the 'given' vessels placed there by the creator, into which the distinctive is funnelled as it bubbles forth freely in creation."[6]

The relative roles of God and man in revelation are compositely identified with the absolute act. Due to the inversion of these elements, God and man, as well as to their alignment within God's actions, in revelation the active aspect of the absolute act is associated with God and the passive aspect with man. It is clearly the case that God's love takes hold of the man who experiences it. Especially conspicuous here is the deviation from Spinoza. Spinoza's concept of *amor dei intellectualis*, in which man may not demand that God love him in return, is turned into precisely its opposite. On account of the select position of revelation in the sequence of God's absolute actions, His act of love receives special emphasis. It is not an essential act, but rather is only act. In relation to creation it is "the emergence of a...revelation which is nothing more than revelation, a revelation in the narrower – nay, in the narrowest – sense."[7] Only its coinciding with the relative becoming manifest gives God's love a relationship to a concealed essence, to a fate in which it originates. With respect to God, however, manifestation is nothing but act. "Thus love is not an attribute, but an event, and no attribute has any place in it. 'God loves'

5 138.
6 139.
7 161.

does not mean that love befits Him like an attribute, as does, say, the power to create...Nor does it proceed into the breadth of infinity, like an attribute...love is no all-love. Revelation knows of no 'all-loving' father; God's love is ever wholly of the moment and to the point at which it is directed...[it] roams the world with an ever-fresh drive."[8]

In spite of the fact that the activity remains wholly with God, revelation is also a relationship between two elements, as was the case previously with creation. God's act does not obliterate man. Though passive and subordinate to God, man remains independent. The structure of Rosenzweig's theology can thus be seen in the complete coinciding of the absolute and relative acts in revelation, just as with respect to the metalogical formula of the world the coinciding of the rational-formal stratum and the non-rational-content-laden stratum had provided an example for Rosenzweig's theory of cognition. We shall only be concerned with the structure itself, and not with the problems arising from it.

To begin with, revelation makes possible the free encounter between God and man. "The separation of their 'being' is presupposed here, for if they were not separate they could not act upon one another...If God were 'within me,' or 'only my higher self' then this would be no more than an unnecessarily obscure formulation of an otherwise clear relationship. Above all, this God would hardly have anything to tell me since I know anyhow what my higher self wishes to tell me. And if there were such a thing as a 'godly' man...this man would find himself barred from the path to God that is open to every truly human being."[9]

In revelation this correlative And of God and man has overcome the "inability" of Spinozism, and, one might add, also of idealism. "Once to say 'and' instead of always saying only '*sive*'."[10] The correlative And must be carefully differentiated from the synthetic And of the configuration of the elements. This synthetic And did not designate by itself a correlation in the configuration. Rather, in the formula of the world it formed together with the Yea one part of the correlation between Yea and Nay, namely that part which ever again joined this correlation to the object. The decisive difference between that theoretical And and this theological And lies in the fact that the former was in the service of the cognition of the object. Even if the theoretical And had embodied the entire correlation, as in Rickert's heterothesis, the object nevertheless is always possible only if the correlative tension is suspended at least momentarily. Object always signifies unity, a unity even of

[8] 164.
[9] *Kl. Sch.*, p. 86.
[10] *Ibid.*, p. 352.

fundamentally separate components. Object is always something closed and the difference between correlation and synthesis with respect to it concerns only the manner of unification. In the case of correlation the unification is momentary and full of tension, while in the case of synthesis it is final and satisfied with itself.

No unification takes place in revelation, however. God and man together do not constitute an object. They stand in true correlation to each other, a correlation that never closes itself into a unity in which both God and man would be contained as parts. "The gap between the human-worldly and the divine is indicated precisely in the ineradicability of personal names. It is beyond the power, ascetic or mystic, of man and the world to leap over. It is deeper and more real than any ascetic's arrogance, any mystic's conceit will ever admit in his despisal of the 'sound and haze' of names earthly and heavenly."[11] Correlation so conceived is an interrelationship of ever new actions of God and ever new experiences of man, a process in which man recurrently approaches God without merging with Him even for a moment. This interrelationship can be expressed as follows: the full import of the concealed objectivity of God and man depends on God's act of revelation as well as upon man's experience of revelation, and this deters God and man from union. God acts and believing man experiences this act with the readiness to receive it; he meets God as His trusting child.

In this conception of faith Rosenzweig touches upon the views of both Martin Buber as well as Herman Cohen.[12] To be sure, Cohen's concepts of creation and revelation are far removed from any absolute act. A creation in which God is the only being and therefore at the same time an infinitely private origin from which the world's becoming emerges,[13] and a revelation which signifies the precondition for the cause of the formation of moral reason,[14] can certainly be called rationalistic. Cohen explicitly seeks to dispel the semblance of miracle from revelation,[15] asking "how is it possible to love an idea?"[16] The love of man for God is love of the moral ideal.[17] Cohen nevertheless arrives at a correlative theology by way of the individual's sin and repentance and his longing for forgiveness. "Only nearness to God, not union with God can be the object of my longing...Sin alienates me from God; forgiveness brings me near again. And thus is formed an unceasing two-

---

[11] 39.
[12] Cf. above, pp. 62–63.
[13] Cf. Cohen, *Religion of Reason* pp. 59 ff.
[14] *Ibid.*, pp. 71–73.
[15] *Ibid.*, p. 71.
[16] *Ibid.*, p. 160.
[17] *Ibid.*, p. 161.

way communication between God and the human soul: longing and the bliss, consisting in trust."[18]

This divine-human encounter is not an emotional one. Where all is volition and activity, event and experience, feeling remains secondary. According to Buber, relation means "some action on what confronts us...feelings accompany the metaphysical and metapsychical fact of love, but they do not consist of it;...love is a cosmic force."[19] This "theology of experience (*Erlebnistheologie*)"[20] thus does not signify the non-rationalism of life, as is the case with Bergson, for example, where life as absolute is posited as something ultimately mystical, something of which one makes sure by means of vision and introspection. Life is merely "the surroundings in which we meet God."[21] Living (*Erleben*) means the experience of an act of the absolute, of an event coming forth from transcendence, an event that addresses man and to which he must reply.

Just as revelation, through being both active and passive, wards off every contemplative philosophy of life, its relational character excludes two other possibilities. Man can generate God neither from feeling nor from knowledge – in accordance with the approach of idealistic theology. Nor is man a nought in the face of God, as taught by the dialectic theology of Barth and Gogarten.

In idealism the difference between Schleiermacher and Hegel is merely one of degree. Both view theology as religion, that is, not as a theory of a God transcendent to man but rather God as active source of man's creative powers. God would not be, if man would not imagine Him. The difference lies in the fact that for Schleiermacher this human power of imagination is supreme: intuition and emotion lay hold of the universe. (For Rosenzweig it is important for theology to view precisely thinking as creation, as past, and in this sense attain a rational theology. He therefore rejects Schleiermacher on account of the mere presentness of the religious feeling that is central to Schleiermacher.)[22] – With respect to Hegel, on the contrary, "the creative religious phantasy" – as Richard Kroner calls it – "in which sensibility and intellect unite synthetically,"[23] is subordinated to reason as the highest authority. Hegel acknowledges religion as imagination, but it must give priority to thinking. "The concept is omnipotent, for it is not possible to think of something that itself – could not be thought."[24]

---

[18] *Ibid.*, p. 212.
[19] Buber, *I and Thou*, pp. 65–66.
[20] 107.
[21] H. Ehrenberg, *Fichte*, p. 126.
[22] Cf. 100 ff.
[23] Kroner, *Von Kant bis Hegel*, Vol. 2, p. 219.
[24] *Ibid.*, p. 269.

On the other hand, man and his reflections are not excluded in correlative theology either. God may not surpass the human capacity for comprehension to such an extent that he ultimately becomes obscure and inaccessible. It must be possible for man to attest to God and therefore preserve his independent, though passive, existence. Revelation can occur only to someone, not to a nought. In this way man's concealed objectivity protects not only God but man himself from annihilation in that which is facing him. This dialectic acceptance of the concealed configuration at the same time contains the merging of man's knowing attitude into his believing attitude. Thinking is not rejected, but rather merely serves as a basis for further development. Although its validity is limited by faith, thinking remains in faith. Thereby it makes theology rational, albeit in a totally different manner than pre-Kantian rational theology. As previously mentioned, Rosenzweig designates knowledge in the context of faith as creation and then transposes the term creation back into the first part of the system. Here in our examination of the theory of revelation, we may in a similar fashion regard the soul's concealed configuration as its creatureliness and God's configuration as His creatorness. Accordingly, we may characterize the rationalism of this theology as knowledge that signifies a creatureliness which can coexist with faith. Man need not deny his thinking; it is an innate part of him. He can fully pursue the possibilities inherent therein up to the limits imposed by his very creatureliness, that is, as long as with this thinking he remains dependent on an absolute that ultimately transcends him. "If all culture, including religion as it is practised, merely represents human expedients or subterfuges, as today's radical theology tells us, if all that is possible for man is not also God's will and hence a force in reality, then man is not the child of the Father, but merely something incidental that happened to the creator, the consequences of which He is now trying to come to terms with as best as He can."[25]

With respect to *redemption* relative act and absolute act are clearly differentiated. Redemption is, to begin with, only the act of man that is experienced by the world, the activity of the love that is rooted in man's character upon the quietly growing life of the world, the life in which the plenitude of the world's individuality is revealed. The absolute action of God is added separately. Redemption thus supplies a vivid example of what the relative act signifies when it is detached from its association with the absolute act. The acting component of the correlation no longer takes precedence over the passive component, as was the case with creation and revelation. The action does not

[25] H. Ehrenberg, "Gottesreich und organisches Leben," *Die Kreatur*, Vol. I (1926–1927), p. 383.

occur in complete freedom as something unconditioned. Rather, it needs the world, exactly as the worlds needs it. It is a correlation of two factors that are also qualitatively equivalent. "Here, then, man and world act and react upon each other in indissoluble reciprocity... Action delivers the act out of man, but it also delivers the newly delivered act back into the world. And waiting delivers the kingdom out of this world... but this waiting also delivers the delivered kingdom into the action of man."[26]

And so the absoluteness, which is not present in the correlation itself, must be added from the outside. Two levels of redemption are thereby created. God's act of redemption signifies an enhancement; it is the essence of redemption. From the standpoint of the absolute act, man's act of redemption in the world is tantamount to God's revelation to the world or creation. Redemption by God is the And that joins this activity of the Nay in the Yea in order to complete it. Man's act is thus viewed as the fulfilment of revelation's commandment of love. "Love of neighbor originated in the mystery of the directed volition; it is distinguished from all ethical acts by the presupposition of being loved by God, a presupposition which becomes visible behind this origin only through the form of the commandment."[27] And the life of the world that faced man in his need becomes the ground for creation upon which revelation works. "The law of growth is instituted in the world by its Creator just as much as the overflowing drive of its love is instituted in love itself by the Revealer, and this law determines, without man himself being conscious of it, the way and object of love... Thus redemption originates with God, and man knows neither the day nor the hour."[28]

In redemption, God's third absolute act in which man and world merge with God, God completes Himself into actual configuration just as in the And of thinking He had closed Himself into a conceptual configuration. This is the only place where the synthetic And of the construction appears in faith. It appears not *in* creation and revelation, and also not *in* redemption, but *as* redemption vis-à-vis creation and revelation, whenever these are arranged among themselves so as to designate God's absolute acts. This new unity, stemming as it does from the first part of the system, signifies the transition from the antithesis of faith to the synthesis of the third part of the system that again unites faith with thinking. "Thus redemption has, as its final result, something which lifts it above and beyond the comparison with creation and redemption, namely God Himself... He is Redeemer in a much graver sense than He is Creator or Revealer. For He is not only the One who redeems, but

[26] 228.
[27] 214.
[28] 241.

also the One who is redeemed. In the redemption of the world by man and of man by means of the world, God redeems Himself. Man and world disappear in the redemption, but God perfects Himself. Only in redemption God becomes the One and All which, from the first, human reason in its rashness has everywhere sought and everywhere asserted and yet nowhere found because it simply was nowhere to be found yet, for it did not exist yet."[29]

c) Dynamic Objectivity

With regard to the stepping forth of the elements into the manifest and their reciprocal activity in creation, revelation and redemption, only part of each configuration had been operative in each of these three relationships. Here, in the realm of faith, where God, world and man are active and hence actual, the objectivity that they had possessed in thinking has been lost. Their activity had indeed shown their "that," but it had left open the question regarding their "what." When God created, only half of His hidden unity was made visible; when He revealed Himself to man, again it was only the other half that became visible. It is exactly the same with respect to man and world. Faith, insofar as it wants to be not only confession but also cognition, must seek a new objectivity in place of the objectivity that has been lost. It seeks this in the form suitable to its character as event – in time.* "The despairing 'where' of the beginning...changes into a hopeful 'when'..."[1] While the construction of thought had had spatial character so that its object had been stationary, here the full configuration of God, world and man arises out of flowing movement. Faith aspires to a "factuality...established...on the one track of the one reality."[2] Time thus assumes the function of the synthetic And of the construction. It joins together into unity fragments which had split asunder in two different directions. The flow of time, proceeding from the past through the present to the future and including creation, revelation and redemption each in its own tense, forms the course along which the elements grow together. Creation is past, revelation present and redemption future. By living through this "real course of the cosmic day"[3] God, world and man obtain objectivity. Their existence, manifest in *actio* and *passio*, is objectified by means of time joining the correlation. It can thus be said of them: *they* are.

---

[29] 238.
[1] *Anmerkungen zu Jehuda Halevi*, p. 230.
[2] 158.
[3] 189.
* Reference should be made here to Heidegger for whom being also means event from out of transcendence and is therefore linked to time.

This "they" is something that flows. *They* are, inasmuch as they are coming to be.

A twofold becoming is thereby to be discerned, corresponding entirely to the twofold act. Each of the three configurations originates in two tenses and each enjoys an equal status within the process of becoming. Moreover, a special becoming which comprises yet the third tense belongs to God. As a result, God unifies all the modes of time and the history of God can become eternity. Thus, to begin with, God fashions Himself in creation and revelation. He is primordial and completes Himself in the present. "To regain it [the 'factuality' of God], it is not enough that He becomes manifest a first time in an infinity full of creative acts. There God threatened . . . to become . . . once more the concealed God after all, just what He had ceased to be by virtue of creation."[4] "Revelation is thus the means for confirming creation structurally. The creator could still retreat behind creation into darkness . . . But the revealer in his all-time presentness can at every moment transfix him in the Bright, the Manifest, the Unconcealed, in short in the present. And by doing so, he lets God's concealedness sink into the past once and for all."[5]

Although God's becoming in creation and revelation fully replaces the individuated factuality of the elements, the concealed, objective And nevertheless is not entirely eliminated. In a similar manner, the hidden origin of each of the elements, rendered manifest in creation and revelation, is dialectically retained. The And acts as a demand for a new unity and therewith as a demand for progress. "The elements of the All . . . must open up out of their occlusion and turn to face each other. In this rapprochement, however, it becomes clear that the entire content of the elements cannot join in a single concept such as the concept of creation is in and of itself. As they open up both elements retain contents which can only go into effect in other directions, in God's case His revealing Himself, in the world's case its being redeemed."[6] The necessity for dynamic relation among the elements is thus based precisely on the hidden, static unity.

Just as God's becoming lies between past and present, so man's becoming lies between present and future. Man awakens to be man in revelation and completes himself in redemption. "For God had, as long as He appeared to be merely creator, really become more amorphous than He had previously been in paganism . . . Just so the soul, too, as long as she is only beloved soul, is now likewise still invisible and amorphous, more amorphous than the self once

---

[4] 160.
[5] 161–162.
[6] 139.

was."[7] Only man's act of love towards the world* brings about its full
factuality. The hero of antiquity finds his parallel in the world of faith in a
man "whose waiting for God would grow up into a walking before God."[8]
"The secluded man is rounded out into a wholly disclosed man by waiting and
walking, by the experience of the soul and by soulful act. Thereby he assumes
a configuration...of the saint."[9] Such growth of the configuration takes
place in so far as "the hand of the world-clock moves forward";[10] it takes
place only in the future. To Rosenzweig, however, future is not that which is
always only imminent and therefore never comes. Rather, in accordance with
the Jewish conception of messianism, that is, the hope for the coming of the
redeemer already in our days, future is that time which must be anticipated in
order to be truly future and which, by being drawn into the present, establishes the consciousness of time. "For the future is first and foremost a matter
of anticipating, that is, the end must be expected at every moment...For just
as the tenses in general are mutually distinguished by their relation to the
present, so too the present moment obtains the gift of eternity only here: from
the past it receives the gift of ever-lasting, of duration, from the present itself
that of ever-being. Every moment can be the last. That is what makes it
eternal."[11] "The future is no future without this anticipation and the inner
compulsion for it; without this 'wish to bring the Messiah before his
time'...it is only past distended endlessly and projected forward."[12]

This characterization of the future demonstrates once again the extent to
which Rosenzweig's interest is entirely directed to the act, that is, to the act
performed in the present. His concern expresses something restlessly urgent,
something revolutionary, an attitude that can not wait for an unsatisfactory
present to change by gradual progress into a better future. Rather, it is an
attitude that seeks to make this better future present by means of its own good
act, so that "the end is for the time being represented by the just present
moment, the universal and highest by the approximately proximate. The
bond of the consummate and redemptive binding of man and the world is to
begin with the neighbor and ever more only the neighbor,the well-nigh
nighest."[13] Redemptive future – the messianic future – is a time that is really

[7] 206.
[8] 208.
[9] 209.
[10] 211.
[11] 226.
[12] 227.
[13] 234–235.
* Rosenzweig calls this human act of love "messianic socialism." "Einleitung in die Aka-
demie-Ausgabe der juedischen Schriften H. Cohens," Kl. Sch., p. 309.

coming, a time that is to be realized actively. These views touch upon those of
Hermann Cohen, who sees in the longing for God the power of anticipation of
the future and therefore the power of the consciousness of time.[14] The
drawing near of the future, which is a matter of acting and not merely of
yearning, has already been mentioned in reference to Cohen.[15] Martin Heidegger similarly establishes time from the perspective of the future, in that for
him the ethical decision anticipates the end and thus forms time.[16]

Faith, for its part, now supplies information regarding the meaning of
human existence in the type of the saint. Man, who in revelation and redemption is standing between present and future, is no longer the introspective, closed self; rather he suffers and acts. By opening himself towards two
sides – as recipient towards God and as giver towards the world – that is, by
his twofold stance in reality, man attains his full development and his whole
humanity. He must have both relationships, for it is not only the one track
running between God and man that is decisive for him. "Loved only by God,
man is closed off to the world and closes himself off."[17] One-sided disclosure
would make him a mystic, whose relationship to the world, which he forgets
because of God, is "thoroughly immoral."[18] – Rosenzweig would be in
agreement with Schelling in this view of the personal experience of God as
mysticism. Unlike Schelling, however, he avoids this mysticism not by applying the categories of thinking to revelation, but by linking revelation to man's
worldly act. Moreover, in accordance with his correlative concept of revelation, that which Rosenzweig calls mysticism here is not a mystical
becoming one with God, in the sense of Meister Eckhart and Jacob Boehme,
for example, in whose theories Richard Kroner can therefore see the embodi-
ment of a spiritual position akin to idealism.[19] In Rosenzweig's sense mysticism is the disclosure of the soul towards God only and not towards the
world, that is, it is a question not of union but of one-sided relationship.[20]

The resumption of the motif of death – previously the concern of the
solitary self – is in accord with the nature of the human, existential sphere.
Man, whose growth into configuration begins in revelation, is he who awakens into life, he who has overcome death, overcome, that is, the self-
completion of the self-enclosed egoist. The solitary one, who is without

[14] Cf. Cohen, *Religion of Reason*, p. 375.
[15] Cf. above, pp. 84–85.
[16] Cf. M. Heidegger, *Sein und Zeit*, p. 301 ff.
[17] 207.
[18] 208.
[19] Cf. Kroner, *Von Kant bis Hegel*, Vol. 1, p. 10 ff.
[20] The designation of mysticism as becoming one with God, that is, its more limited meaning,
is also found in *The Star*, p. 39, as cited above, p. 125.

relationship, as the construction of thought had visualized him, i.e., the creature in the realm of faith – the man whose humanness fulfils itself in his creatureliness – has fallen into the hands of death. "Death as the capstone of creation first stamps every created thing with the ineradicable stamp of creatureliness, the word 'has been.'. . .[But] love which knows solely the present, which lives on the present. . .challenges death. The keystone of the sombre arch of creation becomes the cornerstone of the bright house of revelation."[21] And just as the man of revelation leaves death behind him, so he nevertheless only conquers death finally not by opening himself to God's love but by redeeming the created world into life and making the "other" his "neighbor" through his own act of love. From the perspective of the fully disclosed existence of the believer death is thus the boundary between the modifications of human existence that express themselves in creation, revelation and redemption. It separates the creatureliness, which is the presupposition for the configuration of man, from this configuration itself, which moves from present to future. Death also marks off the two stages of becoming against each other within the movement of the configuration – just as in creation and redemption faith once more embraces the modes of human existence, which in thinking had been represented as solitary self and in faith thinking as man in community. The second part of the system, the antithesis, can thus be regarded as the epitome of the human, existential viewpoint and accordingly as the heart of Rosenzweig's philosophy of existence.

God's becoming and man's becoming together include all three tenses in one straight line. The becoming, then, of the third configuration, the world, unites beginning and end into the cycle of the course by combining past and future. The world is formed in creation and attains its full configuration only in redemption. The double relation – the one of the past to God and the one of the future to man – gives the world its unity. "Only in the kingdom would the world be configuration as visible as had been the plastic world of paganism, the cosmos."[22]

To begin with, what does it mean to the world that it was created? The logos of the world had revealed itself in faith under the sign of the Nay. It could therefore be designated as existence, that is, as something only momentarily universal, something that must be renewed at every moment. The conception of existence, as it is taught by faith, thus also contains the state of being in need, the creatureliness, that demands the creator exactly as the applied logic of the metalogical formula of the world had demanded the unity of pure logic.

[21] 156–157.
[22] 219.

Faith carries out the equation of the sought-for unity with the act of creation, with God's essential act. It does so in such a way that "the infinite unity of divine being [which] expressly precedes any identity of reasoning and being and thereby precedes both the reasoning which is valid for being and the being which can be reasoned out,"[23] serves as support for the logos dwelling within the world. The realistic world-formula's logic of the objective world completes itself here in a *realism of freedom*, a realism of the act, which is experienced in faith. This believing realism is thereby classified with the designation "absolute empiricism." Between God's act of creation as "point of unity"and the logos of the world as that which is "to be unified" there is no "rationally conceivable connection."[24] Creation, as absolutely free act of God, is something that happens to the world from the outside. As an act extending to nature as well as to man,* creation can be comprehended only in faith. Reason, namely natural law as well as moral law, is thereby clearly designated as created reason,whose absolute is beyond its scope. – Through the comparison that Rosenzweig makes between creation and the concepts of emanation and idealistic generation, respectively – both of which seek to derive the world *logically* from God or from the I and therefore must set up a formula of the world as $A = B$ – it becomes clear that faith, for its part, is directed towards the realistic formula of the world, $B = A$. Only in this formula can the impossibility of comparing God with the world, that is, of comparing $A = A$ with $B = A$, be shown and only in it is God's free act thereby made understandable.[25]

The creation of the world, however, does not yet bring about the world's full factuality. "With the mere creature it is much the same. . .as previously with the divinely beloved soul, with God in his creative potential: it is in danger of vanishing. . ."[26] From the perspective of creation the plastic cosmos appears as something "at rest in itself, wanting nothing," as "an enchanted world."[27] By disenchanting this world creation at the same time deprives it of its support. In order for the world "to become structure, to be of the kingdom and not merely apparent existence tied to the moment, it must acquire essence, it must acquire durability for its essence."[28] The redemptive

[23] 43.
[24] 135.
[25] 135 ff.
[26] 219.
[27] 220.
[28] 221.

* Cf. above, p. 121, where the biblical concept of creation, which is cosmological as well as anthropological, is discussed. The ground is prepared for this concept of creation by the integration of nature and moral law into the formula of the world, which was already indicated above, pp. 99–100, with reference to the influence of the Marburg school.

future thus turns the world into a world that is entirely configurative. Thereby the world attains infinite life, which supports the world's creatureliness through man's act of love. That life which sustains itself in opposition to death and which is already in the world, merely hints to the infinite enduring life of the kingdom of God, just as the human act, from its side, actively anticipated the kingdom of God. Both members of the relation, man as well as the world, complete themselves in the messianic future which is advanced into the present actively by man and passively by the world.

The designation of the passive manifestation of the world in redemption as essence makes it clear why Rosenzweig could designate redemption as creation. He transfers creation and revelation, the essential and manifest (*tathaften*) actions of God, not only in a wider sense to the first and second parts of the system, but also in a narrower sense to the formation of each of the two configurations that are distinct from God. The becoming of man and world that passes through two tenses is for them also a becoming from creation to revelation. With respect to man his essential passive manifestation – being loved by God – signifies his creation and the act in the world signifies his revelation. With respect to the world its essential manifestation – enduring life – likewise is its creation while its momentary existence is its revelation.

A reversal of the sequence of tenses for the world's two manifestations is connected therewith to the world's becoming. This reversal leads to a new concept of becoming. While for God and man their creation had preceded their revelation, here the revelation of the world, i.e., its being created by God, already occurred in the past, and hence its creation, i.e., its becoming redeemed, can only follow thereon. "Identification must begin with the self-denying appearance and end with the simple and wholly affirmed essence."[29] The world is thus that which truly becomes. The two other configurations become by advancing from their creation to their revelation, whereby God's creation falls into the past and man's creation into the present. The world becomes, however, when that which lays its foundation comes later, namely in the future. Rosenzweig finds an indication of the special position of the world with reference to becoming in antiquity.[30] This reversal of becoming finds its substantiation in the distinct peculiarity of the future. Future is distinguished not only as that time which must be anticipated, but also as that time which anticipates itself by turning the last into the first. "The future is experienced solely in expectation. 'The last' must be here 'the first in thought.'"[31]

[29] 219.
[30] 89–90.
[31] 219.

Parallel to this temporalization of the relative act Rosenzweig conceives an absolute becoming of God. The latter process comprises all three tenses and thus transforms the movement of the configurations into integral movement with an unambiguous direction. In the case of God the cycle of the course becomes a straight line. For this absoluteness of the temporal sequence, however, the two tenses do not suffice – as they hitherto had been made equal use of by each element for its becoming. Nor can the beginning intertwine with the end – as was the case with the world's becoming. God's absolute history combines with the absolute act and adds the universally temporal (*Allzeitigkeit*) to God's existence, so that God absolutely comprises both being and time. Rosenzweig thereby adopts and expands the motif of divine becoming that Schelling touched upon in his *Freiheitslehre* and elaborated upon in *Die Weltalter*. Schelling freed this becoming of its character as process in his positive philosophy, thus making it into a real history motivated by freedom and act. In the case of Rosenzweig God posits Himself as He who becomes not only through creation, as was the case with Schelling, but through His three acts of creation, revelation and redemption. God thereby creates not only a beginning of time but a complete organism of times that is clearly arranged within itself and that encompasses present, past and future. The category of time, that is, time in Kant's sense as the form of intuition, appears merely to be derived from this absolute world time. "The time in which the events of the world ensue is...merely 'ideal,' merely 'cognitive' and thus without beginning, middle, end; the present as marker of the standpoint of cognition is perpetually shifting. Only revelation fixes its marker in the middle of time, and now there is a Prior and a Posterior which will not be shifted."[32] It might be pointed out here that other twentieth century thinkers also take into consideration time as quality in addition to time as category – for example Henry Bergson with his conception of the time of experience and Richard Hoenigswald with his conception of the time of presence. Above all, however, the positing of qualitative time as absolute and the conception of absolute time is found in Martin Heidegger who thereby, like Rosenzweig, associates himself with the heritage of Schelling.[33] – A further difference between Rosenzweig and Schelling lies in the fact that with the latter the past was something prior to the world and the future something subsequent to the world, while world-time was equated only with the present and conjointly with the category of time. With Rosenzweig the world-time that passes through the three tenses coincides entirely with reality; God's creation,

[32] 361.
[33] Cf. Heidegger, *Sein und Zeit*, pp. 330–331.

revelation and redemption are all in "this world." Within this world-day God becomes through present, past and future the eternal God. "Eternal is to us mortals...the last word of our 'song of the earth'...Even the biblical word that is usually translated 'eternity' truly means our world time until its turning point, until 'that day.'"[34] Only the concept of eternity itself as the convergence of the three tenses produces the transition to "that world," only it leads life into the life to come and the movement of time beyond itself, into a state of rest.

Thus God also becomes, as do man and world, through the connection of creation with revelation; but it is not a complete becoming. "Now God is present...and therewith He proceeds to become a 'matter of fact' – something which as creator He had not yet truly been and which even now He only begins to become – like the gods of the heathen behind the ramparts of their mythology."[35] God's becoming is completed only in the future. This consummation, because it is a conclusion, constitutes, in turn, the formation of a new being. God's becoming in three tenses, His world-day, is for God Himself contemporaneous. "The times of that [world-]day are indeed experiences of His own for God; for Him, the creation of the world means becoming the Creator; revelation means becoming the Revealer, redemption means becoming the Redeemer. Thus He is becoming to the very end. Whatever happens is, for Him, a becoming. And everything that happens happens simultaneously, and in truth revelation is no more recent than creation and for this reason, if for no other, redemption too is no more recent than either. Accordingly this Becoming of God, is, for Him, not a changing, growing, augmenting. Rather, He is from the beginning, and He is at every moment, and He is ever a-coming. His Being is simultaneously everlasting and at all times, and eternal, and only this is the reason that the whole has to be designated a Becoming."[36] The world-day thus turns into God's own day through the addition of the future for God. The classification of the world-day into three tenses can be derived only from eternity's day of God, which is the unity of those tenses and which encompasses all of them simultaneously. "The world-day of the Lord must already bear within itself the predisposition to eternity's day of God. For God, redemption provides this assurance of eternity despite the temporality of self-revelation. Redemption connects creation with revelation; it is not only the assurance of eternity but also itself the fulfilling realization of eternity and thus for God, His world-day becomes, without more ado, His own day."[37]

[34] *Kl. Sch.*, p. 197.
[35] 162.
[36] 258.
[37] 259.

The gathering of the three tenses into eternity, in which their following upon one another, their movement, comes to rest is already a surpassing of time, "a point...far beyond the 'route'"[38] and thereby the transition to the third part of the system. God's unity as He who exists, which arose through His absolute actions and was completed through redemption as unification, acquires the character of a *becoming* unity through the temporal invariable. By being added as the third tense, future turns this becoming into a becoming in all time. It thus turns it into eternity, into a full convergence of the tenses which can be connected with that becoming and unity. "Unity is, then, in truth but Becoming-unity; it is – only as it becomes. And it becomes – only as unity of God. Only God is – nay, precisely: only God becomes the unity which consummates everything."[39]

d) Speech Thinking

1) Rosenzweig's Historical Precursors and Contemporaries

The sequence of divine actions, which through their temporalization became the divine history in which God had completed Himself, is depicted by Rosenzweig in a manner decisively different from Schelling. They are depicted not in the dialectic movement of the potentials or in the construction, but by a method which, inasmuch as it is a method, can still be regarded as a theory. It is a theory, however, in which primacy is given to the non-rational that is testified to within faith. It thus imprints the term method with a new meaning. This believing theory is speech thinking. Its three forms – narrative, dialogue and choral speech – are the means by which creation, revelation and redemption are made comprehensible. It is no longer thinking that becomes the organon of theology but speech, for which thinking forms an immanent residuum.

Schelling began his book *Die Weltalter* with the striking sentences: "The past is known, the present is perceived, the future is surmised. That which is known is told, that which is perceived is described, that which is surmised is predicted." The terse rhythm of the three steps of time itself, the steps toward the truly powerful time that by itself determines the manner of its rendering, resounds in these sentences. These sentences thus provide the theme of *Die Weltalter*, but only in so far as they refer to the past, for in the published

[38] 258.
[39] 258.

fragment of this work Schelling dealt only with the past. He had in mind a philosophy that no longer dialectically develops "the divinity's eternal life in its entirety"[1] – a life that comprises the past, the "primordial beginnings of life"[2] but rather a philosophy which, after overcoming dialectics, resigns itself to the absolute that surpasses the human capacity for thought and merely seeks to render this absolute in narrative form. "All science, then, must pass through dialectics. It is another question, however, whether science will ever reach the point where it will become free and living, as with the historian, whose image of the times becomes so vivid that in his description of them he no longer remembers his research. Can the memory of the primordial beginning of things ever again become so alive that science, which is history according to its subject and its semantic meaning in Greek, could also be alive according to its external form? Can this memory become so alive that it would be possible for the philosopher to return to the simplicity of history, like the divine Plato who though dialectical throughout all his books became historical at their zenith, at the ultimate point of effulgence?"[3] Schelling nevertheless did not yet offer this narrative philosophy in *Die Weltalter*. The book was merely to be "a preparation for the objective presentation of science that was to come."[4] Schelling maintained that the time was not yet ripe for this philosophy. "The light of science must dawn through inward separation and liberation before it can shine."[5] He thus regarded his own dialectics merely as a means for bringing about the fulfilment of that philosophy. Later, in his positive philosophy, Schelling perceived the absolute act as that which is distinctive in divine history, thus moving beyond the merely essential development of God presented in *Die Weltalter*. Here too, however, he did not venture to give a solely narrative rendering of God's absolute actions but rather explained creation and revelation by the same potentials which had formed the *concept* of God. Even in his most mature period Schelling is thus merely a forerunner of the believing philosophy of the future. "Perhaps he who is to sing the greatest heroic epic is still to come, he who, as extolled by the seers of ancient times, encompasses in his spirit what was, what is and what will be."[6]

Rosenzweig tries, as he says,* to offer this narrative philosophy which

---

[1] Schelling, *Werke*, I, 8, p. 197.

[2] *Ibid.*, I, 8, p. 207.

[3] *Ibid.*, I, 8, p. 205.

[4] *Ibid.*, I, 8, p. 206.

[5] *Ibid.*, I, 8, p. 201.

[6] *Ibid.*, I, 8, p. 206.

* Cf. *Kl. Sch.*, p. 383. Cf. also Rosenzweig's *Briefe*, p. 399, where he writes that if Schelling would have completed *Die Weltalter The Star*, aside from the appeal it obviously has for Jews, would not have deserved any attention at all.

refers to the past. The construction of the first part of the system having been left behind, he now, at the stage of faith, attains a manner of presentation that no longer violates God's absolute freedom by rational principles – and faith can rightly take offence at the application of the theory of potentials to revelation.* Rather, Rosenzweig expresses believing experience through means suitable to it, speech, which itself has the character of revelation. It may be that Schelling liked the use of the potentials for the description of revelation so much because the threefold tempo of the dialectics offered him the opportunity of rediscovering the Christian trinity in revelation and in this way carrying out the equation between philosophy and Christianity. To be sure, Rosenzweig also accepts the construction's tripartite division for theology. In accordance with the division of the entire system into thesis, antithesis and synthesis, each of which in turn is arranged into three parts, he elevates tripartition as the ordering principle among God's three absolute actions – actions in which at the end of days, when man and world merge into Him, God consummates Himself into the unitary All. On the other hand, within these acts themselves no construction is to prevail and therefore there is also no tripartition that could be interpreted as an article of faith. The acts are directly symbolized in grammatical categories, whereby the speech of revelation – the dialogue between I and Thou – is truly the pillar that supports the entire method.

Direct indications of the use of language as organon are also found in Schelling aside from his previously cited words that pointed to the future. In *Philosophie der Kunst* Schelling had placed rhetoric above the plastic arts, in so far as the aesthetic idea appears in the book not as something material but through a means which itself is ideal, even if – and this is what leads beyond idealism – there is something real in speech itself. Speech "is the most appropriate symbol of the absolute or infinite affirmation of God because it presents itself through something real without ceasing on that account to be ideal."[7] This explains why reason and speech are frequently designated with the same word [logos], a word which is also God's word of creation, "God's spoken word."[8] Schelling, exactly like Rosenzweig, had a predilection for linking theoretical considerations to the literal meaning of words and thus verifying logical arguments by means of the logic of language (*Sprachver-*

---

[7] *Ibid.*, I, 5, p. 483.

[8] *Ibid.*, I, 5, p. 483.

* Cf. Knittermeyer on this point, who stresses the fruitfulness of Schelling's later philosophy for the present, but is of the opinion that a philosophy which receives its authority from a supreme principle outside itself should not participate in the characterization of this supreme principle to such an extent that it can no longer be authorized by it. H. Knittermeyer, *Schelling und die romantische Schule*, pp. 434, 456–458.

nunft). In addition to this, Schelling later in his positive philosophy also expresses thoughts that directly approach speech thinking. "Since not only philosophical consciousness but also human consciousness in general would be inconceivable without language, it follows that consciousness can not lay the basis for language. Yet the deeper we penetrate in language, the more decisively we discover that its depth is far greater than that of even the most conscious product. The same holds true for language as for organic creatures: we think we see them arise blindly, yet we can not deny the unfathomable purposefulness of their formation up to the smallest detail."[9] "Language...can...be used and expanded with the greatest freedom; within certain limits it can be continually enriched with new inventions,...but its foundation is something that extends beyond human invention and human caprice, something that is not made by man."[10] Schelling speaks of the "unavoidable assumption of a primordial language common to the human race"[11] and the riddle of its origin repeatedly occupies him. "Whence this power that creates this tool not *prior* to its application but directly *during* its application, the tool which I wield neither with my hands nor with external organs but directly through the spirit, the tool in which, properly speaking, *I dwell*, which I animate, in which I move freely and without hindrance?"[12]

If Hegel says in the *Phenomenology of Spirit*: "the power of the spirit is only as great as its expression, its depth is only as deep as it dares to expand and lose itself in its exposition"[13] then this sentence is directed against the intellectual intuition of Schelling. This power of the spirit that is identical with its expressions, however, refers not to language but to the concept, to which language is merely a subordinate tool freely controlled by the concept. Until the present all idealistic philosophy of language has viewed language as something subjugated to thinking or something that should be subjugated to it – in Rosenzweig's words, it saw "in language a means...and consequently in words signs."[14] Karl Vossler[15] and Benedetto Croce[16] regard language as a creation of the human spirit which finds its norm in aesthetics. Ernst Cassirer's great work, *The Philosophy of Symbolic Forms*,[17] which differen-

[9] *Ibid.*, II, 1, p. 52.

[10] *Ibid.*, II, 1, p. 222.

[11] *Ibid.*, II, 3, p. 4.

[12] *Ibid.*, II, 3, p. 4.

[13] Hegel, Introduction to *Phaenomenologie des Geistes, Vollstaendige Werke*, Vol. 2, p. 9.

[14] Rosenzweig, *Anmerkungen zu Jehuda Halevi*, p. 226.

[15] K. Vossler. "Das Verhältnis von Sprachgeschichte und Literaturgeschichte," *Logos*, Vol. 2 (1912), p. 167.

[16] B. Croce, *Aesthetic as Science of Expression and General Linguistic*, translated by Douglas Ainslie (London: P. Owen, 1967).

[17] E. Cassirer, *Philosophy of Symbolic Forms*, Vol. 1–3, translated by Ralph Manheim (New Haven: Yale University Press, 1953–1965).

tiates between three stages of symbolic form: gesture, language and conceptual thinking, sees language as a form between mythos and logos and examines it according to its capacity for conceptual thinking. And thus Richard Kroner differentiates Schelling's position with regard to language from the position of idealism when he says that for Schelling language is a given tool "whose inherent constitution and self-conditioned manner of employment places certain insurmountable boundaries for thinking and prescribes a fixed course for it."[18]

It is no accident that Schelling's friend Franz von Baader, who also strove toward an existential form of thinking, encountered one of the main problems of speech thinking, just as Schelling had encountered speech thinking as such. Baader already anticipated the concept of I-Thou* that is found later in Ludwig Feuerbach. His conception of I-Thou, however, demonstrates a closer proximity to Rosenzweig's than it does to the materialistic anthropology of Feuerbach. Baader repudiates the isolated idealistic I which he wants to see limited by both God as well as by a human counterpart. Thus among his theories on the philosophy of nature, which often stray into the realm of mysticism, we find sentences such as the following: "I . . . am removing myself more and more from that egoistic philosophy which calls the law an activity of my I and . . . which places me in danger . . . of losing sight of the lawgiver above me . . . just as I find a Thou *facing* my I, so I find something *above* me and something *below* me, without my being able to place opposite me either the one or the other or to explain them away as something emerging from my I."[19] "The need for unity (self-preservation) of consciousness makes it a law for that soul-forming force to always keep itself facing a similar unity (a Thou) and to be in reciprocal activity with it . . . we lose ourselves (our I) at that very moment when we lose this leading and supporting Thou."[20] "To the extent to which man truly binds himself to true human beings (persons), he will also see that true being thrives in himself and in others, that being of which the idle speculator, of whatever kind, speaks only in his dreams."[21]

---

[18] R. Kroner, *Von Kant bis Hegel*, Vol. 2, p. 210.

[19] F. von Baader, *Saemtliche Werke* (Leipzig: H. Bethmann, 1850–1860), Vol. 15, p. 178.

[20] *Ibid.*, Vol. 3, pp. 227–228.

[21] *Ibid.*, Vol. 3, p. 245.

* In his lecture "Der Mensch in der Philosophie Schellings" at the Schelling conference in Ragaz, Herman Zeltner pointed to the fact that beginnings of the I-Thou are found precisely in the thought of the young Schelling. (Cf. *Studia Philosophica*, Jahrbuch der Schweizerischen Philosophischen Gesellschaft, Vol. 14 (1954), pp. 219–220.) Similarly, Paul Tillich is of the opinion that in his positive philosophy Schelling discovered "the category of encounter that is existentially so important." (Paul Tillich, "Schelling und die Anfaenge des existenzialistischen Protestes," *Zeitschrift fuer Philosophische Forschung*, Vol. 9, (1955), p. 206).

While in the case of Baader the I-Thou is theologically grounded, in the case of Feuerbach it has entirely sensate-materialist features, in keeping with the struggle he waged against theology. The love between I and Thou is not the love of the neighbor which grows from the obedience to a divine Thou but rather sexual love deprived of all relation to anything divine. To be sure, Hans Ehrenberg thinks that Feuerbach was more of a theologian than he cared to admit and that he rejected theology because it had allied itself with the idealism against which he was fighting. Thus, in Ehrenberg's opinion, Feuerbach's faith in God stands behind his faith in love.[22] But in Feuerbach's sentence: "the unity of I and Thou is God"[23] God has the meaning not of the subject but only of the predicate. God constitutes the more precise definition of the I-Thou unity as it is understood from the standpoint of the senses. Ehrenberg's interpretation, which would be appropriate if the position of subject and predicate were reversed, seeks to give the primacy to God. It springs from Ehrenberg's own viewpoint and is understandable in its context. As Ehrenberg himself declares, "love without faith is an absurdity."[24] While it is thus difficult to place Feuerbach's materialistic existentialism and Rosenzweig's believing existentialism on the same plane, both nevertheless have in common the limitation of the idealistic I by a Thou, whatever the nature of that Thou may be. If the different structure of this Thou, and thereby also of the I that is founded upon it, is disregarded, it is possible to discover a historical preliminary stage to speech thinking in Feuerbach when he says, for instance: "The true dialectics is not a monologue of the solitary thinker with himself; it is a dialogue between I and Thou."[25] Elsewhere, Feuerbach states: "I maintain that the I which is the idealist's point of departure, the I that cancels the existence of sensate things, does not itself have existence. It is merely a conceived, not a real I. The real I is only that I which faces a Thou and which itself is a Thou, an object, vis-à-vis another I. For the idealistic I, however, there exists neither I nor object...I am not only a creature that is separate from the other; I also think only as a creature separate from the other."[26]

In the more recent past these historical precursors of speech thinking are joined by Hermann Cohen, with whose concept of correlation between God and man and its orientation to I and Thou we already dealt in the course of

[22] Cf. H. Ehrenberg, *Fichte*, pp. 167–168.

[23] L. Feuerbach, *Grundsätze der Philosophie der Zukunft*, 60, *Saemtliche Werke* (Leipzig: O. Wigand, 1846–1866) Vol. 2, p. 344.

[24] Ehrenberg, *Fichte*, p. 168.

[25] Feuerbach, *Grundsätze*, 62, *Saemtliche Werke*, Vol. 2, p. 345.

[26] Feuerbach, *Kritik des Idealismus*, *Saemtliche Werke*, Vol. 10, pp. 186–187.

considering Rosenzweig's complete works.[27] We must also mention a group of thinkers from Rosenzweig's own surroundings that includes the names Eugen Rosenstock, Hans Ehrenberg, Victor von Weizsaecker and Rudolf Ehrenberg alongside of Martin Buber, Ferdinand Ebner and Florens Christian Rang.[28] Between the end of the First World War and the beginning of the 1930's, additional works on the new thinking were produced, for the most part idependently of Rosenzweig and his *Star of Redemption*.* Karl Heim deals with the I-Thou theme from the standpoint of faith.[29] Dialectic theology[30] also accepts the I-Thou, albeit with special accent on the divine Thou in the face of which the I, man, can not detach himself from sin and guilt, so that he does not meet God freely. In an anthology called, like Rosenzweig's important essay on speech thinking, *Das neue Denken*,[31] Hermann Herrigel offers a penetrating, nearly passionate critique of idealism, but only gropes hesitatingly toward a positive new thinking that finds its completion in theology. The spiritual situation of this period, which witnessed the shattering of the old values and which demanded better, stronger views that would give man and his actions support and content, is given expression in Herrigel's work. Philosophy "carries on its sharp-witted art in a vacuum which does not require any decisions. It leaves untouched exactly the one burning question for us: what do its formal sentences mean for the man of action?"[32] Thinking therefore has to ally itself with faith: "faith and knowledge belong together like core and peel. All knowledge has a core of faith and all faith has a peel of knowledge. It is faith that establishes knowledge, for behind all knowledge lies the faith in an ordered reality. At the same time faith also cancels (*aufhebt*) knowledge, for no knowledge can exhaust this reality."[33] Karl Loewith published his book *Das Individuum in der Rolle des Mitmenschen*,[34] the principal part of which represents a significant contribution to the new

---

[27] Cf. above, pp.

[28] *Kl. Sch.*, p. 388.

[29] Karl Heim, *Glaube und Denken* (Berlin: Furche Verlag, 1931).

[30] Cf. Friedrich Gogarten, *Glaube und Wirklichkeit* (Jena: E. Diederichs, 1928).

[31] H. Herrigel, *Das neue Denken* (Berlin: Verlag Lambert Schneider, 1928).

[32] *Ibid.*, p. 107.

[33] *Ibid.*, p. 185.

[34] K. Loewith, *Das Individuum in der Rolle des Mitmenschen* (Muenchen: Drei Masken Verlag, 1928).

* Although *The Star of Redemption* was written in 1918–1919 and published in 1921, Rosenzweig remarks about Buber (*Briefe*, p. 462) that in 1921, at the time of the composition of *I and Thou* (first published in 1923) Buber did not yet know *The Star*. Similarly, in 1928 he writes of Herrigel (*Briefe*, p. 619) that he had indeed read his "Das neue Denken" but not *The Star*. Also, Loewith says in his introductory remarks to "Martin Heidegger and Franz Rosenzweig" (*Philosophy and Phenomenological Research*, Vol. 3, no. 1 (1942)) that in 1928 neither he nor his teacher Heidegger had known *The Star of Redemption*.

thinking, at the same time as Herrigel. Taking Feuerbach's sensate I as a point of departure, he offers a structural analysis of being-with-one-another (*Miteinanderseins*) and pursues the question of the extent to which the individual is constituted by his fellow man (*Mitmensch*), that is, the extent to which the I is constituted by the Thou. Dilthey's reflections on world and life as "companion-world" (*Mitwelt*) and on man's historicity as a being-together are thereby amplified. Loewith's penetrating investigations, which make extensive use of the semantic content of language, explain according to Heidegger's phenomenological method the I-Thou relationship as a true and unique relationship that is essentially different from any relation of a person to a third person or to an object. "It is not by chance that the conjugation of 'to be' for the so-called second person, its 'is' (*ist*) which is conjugated as 'are' (*bist*), shares the same linguistic root as the first person, which is conjugated as 'am' (*bin*). And both differ radically from the third person, which is conjugated 'impersonally' with the 'is' (*ist*). . . In that 'I' am the one and 'thou' are the other, we both directly belong to one another. Only 'thou' can be 'mine' just as only 'I' can be 'thine'. . . Thou forever determines me as I."* The structures of being-with-one-another repeat themselves in the speech with one another. Here, according to Loewith, Wilhelm von Humboldt's approach to language becomes fruitful, an approach in which language is "not an intellectual structure formed by science and lacking real existence, but the individual craving for reciprocal conversation."[35] All true speaking is conversation – address and response. It is not so much the theme that connects the speaker to the listener as it is the reciprocity of the I and Thou. Only "speaking-with-*one-another* is *responsible* thinking."[36] Loewith also knows an absolute relationship, from which the mutual autonomy of the one and the other can be explained and for whose proof he utilizes Kant's principle of the practical reason – by which it is made clear, however, that the Thou of the absolute relationship can not be a divine Thou.** The most important con-

---

[35] *Ibid.*, p. 109.

[36] *Ibid.*, p. 112.

* K. Loewith, *Das Individuum in der Rolle des Mitmenschen*, pp. 54–55. In connection with this truly belonging to one another, Loewith cites here Jasper's "communication," which also represents an I-Thou relationship.

** W. Schulz calls the I-Thou relationship a completely meaningless reflexive relationship of pure reciprocal cancellation, a relationship that proves precisely the *loss* of the world consummated by idealism. Further, he says that K. Loewith indirectly demonstrated this dependence upon idealistic thought. (W. Schulz, *Die Vollendung des deutschen Idealismus in der Spaetphilosophie Schellings* (Stuttgart: Kohlhammer, 1955), p. 236.) This "cancellation" (*Aufhebung*), however, is refuted by the relationship's anthropological foundation referring back to Feuerbach's sensate I-Thou. Moreover, one can not speak of the loss of the world as long as the I-It relationship continues to exist at the side of the I-Thou relationship and takes the place of the idealistic subject-object relationship. To be sure, the I-It relationship does not constitute the

temporary representative of existential thinking is Martin Heidegger, whose book *Sein und Zeit*[37] offers many possibilities for comparison with *The Star of Redemption*. In his essay "M. Heidegger und F. Rosenzweig"* Karl Loewith[38] compares the two thinkers with respect to their point of departure and their aim, that is, from the perspective of temporality and eternity. Both take their point of departure in the real, solitary man, who is determined by death and who lives in the fear of death. But while human existence in the case of Heidegger remains closed in finiteness and temporality and has no relationship to a human Thou, to the world and to God, Rosenzweig's philosophy advances through creation, revelation and redemption to the eternity of God and finds its ultimate expression in the Star of David, which symbolizes eternal truth.

2. Speech, Faith and Thinking

What is it that enables speech to become organon of faith, which is so crucial for existence, so that speech stands in a relationship of identity** to faith, paralleling the relationship of thinking to being?[39] This question can be answered by referring to the differences between speech and thinking. It is precisely the peculiarities which differentiate speech from thinking that make speech acceptable to faith. Speech is not an abstract kind of reproduction whose origins can be surveyed and which dominates its object. It manifests itself in something real, in the spoken word. Its origin is mysterious and it

[37] M. Heidegger, *Sein und Zeit.*

[38] For Heidegger's later philosophy, which removes him from Rosenzweig, reference should also be made to K. Loewith, *Heidegger Denker in duerftiger Zeit* (Frankfurt a. M: S. Fischer, 1953).

[39] 147–148.

subject of Loewith's investigation. He mentions the relationship of man to objects and to nature only incidentally and by way of contrast to the I-Thou relationship.

* K. Loewith, "M. Heidegger und F. Rosenzweig" (Revised German version), *Zeitschrift fuer philosophische Forschung*, Vol. 12, no. 2. – Nathan Rotenstreich offers a brief comparison of Rosenzweig and Jaspers concerning the latter's theory of transcendence. Rotenstreich is of the opinion that Rosenzweig can be more easily compared with Jaspers than with Heidegger. *Jewish Philosophy in Modern Times* (New York: Holt, Rinehart and Winston, 1968), pp. 183–184. On Rosenzweig's relation to other representatives of "speech thinking" see: Michael Theunissen, *Der Andere. Studien zur Sozialontologie der Gegenwart* (Berlin: Walter de Gruyter, 1965); Bernhard Casper, *Das dialogische Denken. Eine Untersuchung der religionsphilosophischen Bedeutung Franz Rosenzweigs, Ferdinand Ebners und Martin Bubers* (Wien, Freiburg: Herder, 1967); Harold Stahmer, *"Speak That I May See." The Religious Significance of Language* (New York: Macmillan Co., 1968).

** It is clear from speech's role as a means of *presenting* the experienced reality of faith that this identity between speech and faith does not signify a *complete* identification. If speech and revelation were one and the same, speech thinking would do in its own way exactly that which panlogism did with the total identification of thinking and being. Rosenzweig speaks elsewhere simply of a *"sense* of identity." (*The Star*, p. 150.)

merely designates its objects without wanting ro create them. Speech has "self-evidentness" and is "a growth amidst all growing life; it nourishes itself on life as life nourishes itself on it."[40] Rosenzweig thus says of idealism's "'pure' logic...that is foreign to language and beyond man"[41] that it is its "own creature."[42] To speech, on the other hand, which does not stem from within us, simple trust is due. "Idealism was not of a mind to listen and respond to this voice, which resounds in man without apparent reason but the more realistically for that. It demanded reasons, accountability, calculability – everything that language was unable to offer it – and invented for itself logic, which offered all this."[43] Since speech, then, is rational neither in its appearance nor in its origin and application it allows faith to label it creation. Philosophy is to trust in "its own wisdom" no more than "in the creative power of God which encompasses it visibly."[44] To be sure, the objection could be raised at this point that the *ratio* should also be seen as something created. The difference is to be seen, however, in the fact that reason is something created within man of which he is therefore free, within certain limits, to dispose. Speech, in contrast, is something created *next to* man, something which he certainly uses and the use of which indeed makes him truly man, but which at the same time endows his person with a new quality.

It becomes clear from Rosenzweig's comparison of language and art that language's independence from man and his *ratio* is of paricular importance for the preference given to language over thinking. Art, which in the system's first part had been the language of the solitary self, is accordingly designated in the second part as idealism's substitute for real language. As a result, that which holds for the role of art in relation to idealism also holds for the role of language with regard to Rosenzweig. Art, which idealism "apotheosizes,"[45] was thus something which man did not consciously create and which he did not control. Rather, it was a garden "that surrounded man though he knew not whence. Man would have to have planted it, but he could not himself know this. It had to be his work, but unconsciously so. It had to bear all the marks of purposive labor and yet have originated aimlessly. It had to be effected work, and yet plant-like growth."[46] And precisely because idealism had found in art something that in spite of its compatibility with pure thinking possessed its own mystery-laden life, art could be for it "an Ultimate, at once

[40] 145–156.
[41] 141.
[42] 146.
[43] 145.
[44] 146.
[45] 146.
[46] 146.

confirmation of the method of reasoning – 'organon,' that is – and visible manifestation of an 'absolute.'"[47] It may be inferred from this that language is all the more suitable as organon of faith; for if in the case of a work of art, which "stands there like a part of nature in its unconscious becoming and unquestionable being,"[48] the human author must still be taken into consideration, then language is not the work of man and can thus be regarded as the work of God. – To be sure, Rosenzweig goes on to say: "Thus art became for idealism the great justification of its procedure. If doubts haunted it about the inadmissibility of its method – that of the 'panlogistically' pure generator – it had only to regard the work of art, produced by mind and yet nature-like reality, to clear its conscience."[49] With reference to this justification of the idealistic method Rosenzweig's views on the function of art in idealism can be utilized for his own attitude to language. Rosenzweig's theology also makes use of speech as justification for faith. Speech offers in creation the opportunity of experiencing miracle. "In the sphere of creation" speech is "the creature...the 'subject' which bears the visible seal of revelation on its countenance."[50] In speech, which develops the richness of its forms beyond the root-words of logic, faith, coming upon thinking as miracle, finds, as it were, the immediate reality of such a miracle. Speech as miracle confirms the miracle of revelation in the visible.

Aside from the fact that its reality has a basis beyond thought, the fact that it can be represented as extending over world time in its entirety makes speech suitable for faith. "Speech is truly mankind's morning gift from the creator...It is entire from the beginning: man became man when he first spoke."[51] Speech just as much comprises the middle, the present, in that it is the "visible criterion" of man today. Finally, it is also the end, future, for it is "dominated by the ideal of . . . perfect understanding."[52] As a result the three grammatical tenses in which speech thinking renders the absolute times of creation, revelation and redemption are already inherent in speech's unversal temporality.

The advantage of speech over abstract thinking thus lies in its reality as well as its temporality. Ferdinand Ebner's book, *Das Wort und die geistigen Realitaeten*,[53] can be epitomized precisely by the title: the word *is* spiritual

---

[47] 147.

[48] 147.

[49] 147.

[50] 109.

[51] 110.

[52] 110.

[53] F. Ebner, *Das Wort und die geistigen Realitaeten* (Innsbruck: Brenner Verlag, 1921).

reality. Speech nevertheless does not remain without thinking but stands in dialectic relationship to it.

In exact correspondence to the system's thesis and antithesis, in which faith negates thinking in order to carry it within itself as presupposition, speech is built upon the "archetypal words" of logic: Yea, Nay and And. They are speech's "secret bases," even though the language which is really spoken knows logical affirmation more than the ideational possibilities of arriving at an understanding. . . Reasoning is mute in each individual by himself, yet common to all, and thereby the basis of speaking which is common to all."[54] What Rosenzweig says here with reference to hidden thinking is that which Hans Ehrenberg terms the mystery of the unity of speech. "Two men, thoroughly different, each one, as it were, engrossed in his words. . . each one invisible and alien to the other. And yet they can speak with one another! The words already bore within themselves the hidden kernel of mutual understanding."[55] A logical principle must thus be assumed to be inherent in speech, namely, the unity of all languages. This unity allows us to consider the multiplicity of living languages as divisions within one coherent structure. It is the presupposition for all understanding as well as for all translation. Rosenzweig's work as translator in his later years clearly expresses how important the concealed *ratio* of speech was for him.[56] Only this principle of unity that is inherent in speech can justify speech thinking as a scientific method, but only if this unity can be arrived at through deduction and only if it can be raised from a concealed presupposition to a manifest condition of speech. In the long run, however, the connection between thinking and speech remains something that is visible only in faith. Speech thinking is not a method in the strict sense of the term but as Eugen Rosenstock says "a road that accompanies [life's] events (*Mitweg der Ereignisse*)."[57] It draws its justification from its usefulness in elucidating these events – be they events of a social or political nature, or as in the case of Rosenzweig, of an absolute nature.

Conversely, logical thinking for its part appears to be in need of speech thinking – and this because of the dialectic connection between the two. Speech is the paradise out of which philosophy was "driven," the garden "in which it had lived without the distrust and the mental reservation of logic, and it had to leave it because of its own fault."[58] In a similar fashion, Eugen

---

[54] 109.
[55] Ehrenberg, *Fichte*, p. 182.
[56] Cf. above pp. 65 ff.
[57] E. Rosenstock, *Angewandte Seelenkunde*, p. 77.
[58] 146.

Rosenstock says: "It is only in its second step that the soul limits its speech and conversation, full of trust, to a more and more mistrustful thinking and reflection upon spiritual riches."[59] And Hans Ehrenberg compares the solitary thinker to Robinson Crusoe, who was able to think only in so far as he was part of "a plurality, that is, through his memory."[60] Logical thinking, then, is a form of recollection derivative of speech thinking. Hence, the object of recollection, the original moment of speech, enjoys, entirely in Plato's sense, preeminence. Cassirer's philosophy of language does not share this understanding of logical thinking. To be sure, Cassirer also views logical thinking as an abandonment of language's meaningful contents, but he considers language, as something material, to be an inferior form, opposed to which the functionalistic represents progress.

Speech thinking in its position vis-à-vis thinking is thus the appropriate method for a theology that elevates itself above the foundations of thinking. Still another motive for the choice of speech can be inferred aside from the dialectic connection between thinking and faith, namely, that the historical testimony of revelation, the Bible, serves as a model for speech thinking. The word of God in the Bible, just as it offers the basis of certainty for the dialogue between God and man in the present, also constitutes the support for speech thinking in its entirety. To be sure, when Rosenzweig speaks of the word of God, to which the word of man is the answer,[61] or of the "vitally confident unity"[62] of the word of God and the word of man, he always means only the mutuality of the word spoken in the present. The word is peculiar to God as well as to man. It was created by God as the means by which God and man could communicate with each other. It is spirit, in which both God and man have part. Only in this sense, to begin with, are the word of God and the word of man the same. "The word as heard and as spoken is one and the same. The ways of God are different from the ways of man, but the word of God and the word of man are the same. What man hears in his heart as his own human speech is the very word which comes out of God's mouth."[63] In connection with this, however, Rosenzweig carries out the equation of God's spoken word with His written word. He finds in the biblical narrative of creation the grammatical categories in which speech thinking expresses objectivity, suggesting thereby to us that his use of the root-word "good" was inspired by the biblical account of Genesis.

---

[59] Rosenstock, *op. cit.*, p. 75.
[60] Ehrenberg, *Fichte*, p. 185.
[61] Cf. 146.
[62] 200.
[63] 151.

Precisely with respect to creation, however, the equation of the biblical word of God and the living, spoken word of God leads to the paradox that God creates *with* the word, even though he also creates *the* word. Rosenzweig solves this difficulty by transferring the real speaking of God to revelation. To him God's word of creation is thus not yet a word. Rather "it too is but another creative *act* of the creator."[64] "God speaks, but His word is still as if something inside of Him, not He Himself, were speaking."[65] The distinction between the real and unreal word of God, which makes it possible to grant revelation the favored position with respect to speech, parallels Rosenzweig's peculiar uncertainty with respect to God's *created* word. Speech indeed is the "creature,"[66] but on the other hand God merely "ordained"[67] that the fountain of speech would flow forth from the rock of creation. Consequently not only the word of God but speech itself emerges only in revelation. Here too, therefore, two levels of speech must be assumed: the speech of the created self, which still is really silence – Rosenzweig also speaks in the metalogical world of the "personality delimiting and individualizing itself from others *in speech*"[68] by which he means the indifferent speech of men who are of no concern to one another – and the speech of the soul. "Language, for all it is all there, all created from the beginning, nevertheless awakes to real vitality only in revelation."[69] In a similar fashion Eugen Rosenstock also distinguishes between two levels of language: "the ability to speak and the compulsion to speak,"[70] that is, speech as the language of the intellect through which the things of the world enter into us[71] and "currents of speech that burst open in the soul with primordial force."[72]

Speech thinking's orientation to the word of the Bible is even more clear with respect to the speech of revelation. Again, the biblical Song of Songs is but the confirmation of the living dialogue between man and God.[73] This dialogue itself, however, as presented by Rosenzweig, uses the words of the Bible, from the "Where art Thou?" of the Fall and the commandment "Thou shalt love the Lord thy God" to the conclusion of revelation in Job's cry for redemption "Oh that you would." So it is that in his commentary essay on *The Star* Rosenzweig declares with great awe and hence as the most profound

[64] 155.
[65] 154.
[66] 109.
[67] 145.
[68] 77.
[69] 111.
[70] Rosenstock, *op. cit.*, p. 28.
[71] Cf. *ibid.*, p. 29.
[72] *Ibid.*, p. 28.
[73] Cf. 198.

truth, that he "has received the new thinking in these old words" and therefore "has reproduced and transmitted it in them."[74]

3. Speech Thinking in Its Existential Character (The Other - Time)

Speech thinking, in exact conformity with the theology which it is to serve as method, wants to encompass all possibilities of human existence: man in so far as he is object and similar to things, true man who is awakened into soul, and man in community. Consequently, speech thinking divides itself into three basic forms – narrative, dialogue and choral speech. This breadth of scope is to its great advantage as opposed to pure thinking, which could know man only as part of the whole and hence could not evaluate him properly. "To understand someone and to understand something...are...two utterly incomparable matters."[75] Speech thinking is to accomplish both. "Totality is ...the real verification of the new thinking. Its problems are for the most part hidden from the old thinking and if they do crowd into its horizon they are not recognized as scientific problems...In contrast, the entire realm of the old thinking remains perceptible and tangible from the position of the new thinking. The problems of the old logic of Aristotle and Kant by all means remain as problems of the It for speech thinking."[76] "Language is ...the thread running through everything human that steps into revelation's miraculous splendour and into its ever renewed presentness of experience."[77] This same totality is expressed by Martin Buber in the duality of the basic words – the I-It next to the I-Thou. Eugen Rosenstock expresses this totality by characterizing the soul as a total process that appears in the "modification of its grammatical form"[78] from the It by way of the Thou to the I.

Speech thinking "knows about man and ...does not allow this knowledge to slip through its fingers in idealistic self-deception."[79] This existential character of speech thinking is expressed in all of its three basic forms " in the need for the other and ...in taking time seriously,"[80] – this again being analogous to theology's correlative concept of existence, a concept that is dependent on time.

Let us, then, consider first of all the speech of cognition, the I-It, the speech which is to describe creation. The categories of grammar in speech thinking

---

[74] *Kl. Sch.*, p. 391.
[75] V. von Weiszaecker, "Der Arzt und der Kranke, Stuecke einer medizinischen Anthropologie," *Die Kreatur*, Vol. 1 (1926–1927), p. 80.
[76] *Kl. Sch.*, p. 389.
[77] 110.
[78] Rosenstock, *op. cit.*, p. 27.
[79] *Kl. Sch.*, p. 295.
[80] *Ibid.*, p. 387.

correspond to the categories of logic. Like the logical categories, they too can not be deduced from one another but rather presuppose one another. With the help of the root words, which themselves grow out of the background of the archetypal words – the logical Yea, Nay and And – the grammatical categories are clearly arranged in tabular form. Their arrangement is a product of the reality that they are to categorize. The tabulation is thus merely an *a posteriori* arrangement of material "which does not emerge here as the material of an independent subordinate science of language, but which appears as the original symbolism of reality itself and accordingly in the closest sense of 'identity' with this reality. Language here is no independent content which would have to develop according to an inner system. Rather it describes the daily cosmic orbit of our planet along the zenith of world history."[81] We have seen that speech is by means of its own nature adapted to this sense of identity with a reality experienced in faith and that it can be "simile in its essence."[82] The grammar that serves as symbol of creation is thus not a grammar that is verified by science and tradition. This can be seen quite clearly with respect to Eugen Rosenstock, who designates grammar as the inner structure of the soul. Instead of traditional grammar, however, he posits a new grammar based on experience in which the Thou, and not the I, is the first person.[83]

The root-word of creation, from which the coherence of the remaining word forms is established and which corresponds to the logical Yea that is prior to speech, is the predicative adjective that contains a positive evaluation, namely, the word "good."[84] From its perspective the adjective in general, the demonstrative pronoun, the indefinite and definite articles, and finally the plural and the positioning as object, which together designate objectivity, are made visible. Afterwards we return again to the root-word as illustration of the reality of the object by means of the verb, which completes the "that" of the things in the infinitive, indicative, third person and past tense, just as the first group of grammatical forms had described their "what." This "selection from the grammatical categories"[85] is in part already represented in the work of Eugen Rosenstock, as is the selection which later serves revelation and redemption.[86] It can be summarized as follows: speech renders objectivity in

---

[81] 150.
[82] 201.
[83] Rosenstock, *op. cit.*, p. 24 ff.
[84] 127 ff.
[85] 141.
[86] Cf. Rosenstock, *op. cit.*, pp. 29–31, 50 ff. Though Rosenstock's *Angewandte Seelenkunde* was not published until 1924, it was already available in draft form to Rosenzweig during the composition of *The Star of Redemption*. Cf. *Kl. Sch.*, p. 388.

the form of narrative, that is, in a form which leaves to things the independence due to them by virtue of creation and simply adopts them as they are. Narration does not create the object, but gives an account of it; in this way it can make God's creation comprehensible. In the case of objective thinking the "need for the other" thus lies in the fact that speech thinking remains dependent on the object, like naive realism, but recognizes the creator behind the object. Moreover, narrative also requires a human listener.

Hans Ehrenberg, who of all the speech thinkers was most concerned with the problems of the It, gives the being bound to that which confronts us a new, less theological formulation. While in the case of Rosenzweig speech thinking does not go beyond the task of making creation, revelation and redemption comprehensible, Ehrenberg constructs a theory of cognition based on the conversation between I and Thou. As a result the "other," outside of the object, is not God and also not the listener of a narrative, but rather the interlocutor. Here, too, the It is not produced from the I and Thou but is just as primordial as they are. The It stands between I and Thou as an object independent of them, as something that in conversation the I and Thou make into *their* object by means of a number of "partial and insignificant decisions." "I, Thou and It unite into our object."[87] "A common love"[88] must take hold of the two speakers. Each must immerse himself in the other in order to reach agreement on the object through the medium of speech. "The word is the milieu of disputation. It belongs to you and to me and no less to – it."[89] Ehrenberg meets the relativistic objection, which he himself raises here, by seeing truth with respect to conversation as lying in the acknowledgment and in the personal responsibility of the speaker that is behind his word. "Without acknowledgment there is no cognition that could be given recognition."[90]

The difference between this conversation of cognition and the Platonic dialogues is to be seen in the much stronger human, existential tone of the former. In the case of Plato two men who abstract themselves from their full humanness and want to be merely thinkers speak to each other. For that reason neither one of them can bring the full weight of his own particularity into play vis-à-vis the other. "The other [in the Platonic dialogue]...makes only those objections which I really should have made myself."[91] Thus it is not the Socrates of the Platonic dialogues who is to be juxtaposed to the

---

[87]   Ehrenberg, *Fichte*, p. 175.
[88]   *Ibid.*, p. 176.
[89]   *Ibid.*, p. 177.
[90]   *Ibid.*, p. 180.
[91]   *Kl. Sch.*, p. 387.

thinking speaker in the dialogue between I and Thou, but the real Socrates. This is the Socrates "who loves the truth, but for the sake of man,"[92] who sacrificed his life for it and thereby turned it from mere theory that does not concern man inwardly into a truth that is tied to his own existence and attested to within this existence.

Rosenzweig assigns dialogue its place only within revelation. Dialogue is no longer a question of simultaneously understanding an It through the understanding of a Thou, but rather entirely and solely a question of understanding the Thou. As bearer of a proper name the Thou can not be reduced to a concept. The problems of conceptual definition must here turn into problems of nomenclature. Dialogue is the speech of love between God and man. It symbolizes the relationship of active and passive that exists between them. – The root-word of revelation, which grows out of the archetypal word Nay, is "I." To begin with, grammatical categories do not yet ensue from this I; they merely form the "appendix."[93] The present, which includes the categories of the imperative, the nominative case of the substantive, the singular and the proper name, certainly illustrates revelation. These categories, however, function not as species or types but entirely as definite, individual words. The dialogue between God and man moves "from real word to real word."[94] In His question "Where art Thou?" God discloses Himself as I. The I is His name with which He enters revelation. By calling man by his proper name He awakens the human Thou, which testifies to itself in the answer "Here I am." God continues the conversation with the commandment "Love me." He is answered by the soul's admission of love, the shame of "I have sinned." The answer culminates in the confession of faith and ends in the prayer for redemption.

This dialogue is one of the most beautiful and profound portrayals of man's encounter with the living God that is possible to express in words. It locates speech in its most innate realm as "vital back-and-forth interconnection of address passing to and fro."[95] Further, it is the basis for speech thinking per se inasmuch as it demonstrates speech thinking's character as existential thinking by the inclusion of the "other." In dialogue God's existence as well as man's awakening into full existence are depicted. Human existence thereby makes itself clear in its response to God's call – not *cogito ergo sum*, but "God has called me , therefore I am."[96] That is to say, man's

---

[92] Ehrenberg, *Fichte*, p. 134. Cf. also Buber, *I and Thou*, pp. 113–115.
[93] 185.
[94] 174.
[95] 81.
[96] Rosenstock, *op. cit.*, p. 36.

dependence on the word of an absolute Thou provides the explanation for his dependence on the words of a human Thou and the concrete realities of the objective world. God's dialogue with man is the absolute dialogue in comparison with which all other possible speech and response must appear derived. God is the absolute "Other".

From the vey start Rosenzweig knows only this dialogue between God and man, which serves him as a means to depict revelation just as previously narrative had served to render creation. Here too we find with the other speech thinkers amplifications extending beyond theology. With them the absolute dialogue between God and man is reached only indirectly by way of the dialogue between man and man. In response to the call of a human Thou it is first of all man's full being that demonstrates itself. By understanding his fellow-man, having an effect on him and bearing responsibility for him, man shows himself as a complete human being. Martin Buber points to the priority of the basic word I-Thou over the isolated I as a temporal becoming in the life of peoples and in the life of children.[97] The divine call can be heard only through the human call. The eternal I-Thou completes and fulfils all inter-human experience of speaking and responding. Eugen Rosenstock also bases man's self-consciousness on the encounter with a human Thou. The child awakens to the I only by being addressed from the outside. "We acquire self-consciousness through receiving orders from the outside and through being judged from the outside."[98] This "outside," however, is from the beginning only the world surrounding us. The call by God signifies the highest enhancement of the conversation between I and Thou, for all philosophy of the Thou ultimately must continually push on towards an absolute Thou.*

The speech of redemption, man's acting on the world and God's acting on man and world, is the song of the community united in praise and gratitude, a song which augments itself stanza by stanza. The archetypal word is voiced here in an entire sentence which brings together the "I" of revelation and the "good" of creation: "God is good." This sentence contains the highest truth of speech thinking not in the sense of theoretical objectivity but as the greatest possible concentration of existentially verified truths. It is "the sentence true in itself,"[99] which means that it is true for *everyone* who utters it because it

[97] Cf. Buber, *I and Thou*, pp. 69–73.
[98] Rosenstock, *op. cit.*, p. 26. See also H. Ehrenberg, *Hegel*, pp. 120 ff.
[99] 231.

* Cf. Karl Heim, "Ontologie und Theologie," *Zeitschrift fuer Theologie und Kirche*, Vol. 11, no. 5 (1930), pp. 336–338. Concerning Buber's conception of I and Thou, he remarks that this must lead either to an infinite series – since each Thou is again the I of another Thou the I-Thou relationship would thus ultimately be living according to a fictional presupposition – or it must presuppose an absolute Thou that exists by its own means and through which everything else becomes I.

concerns everyone. "That two times is four can become untrue, for example, if one has taught it to a parrot and he now 'says' so; for what is mathematics to a parrot? But the sentence 'God is good' can not become an untruth even in this most scurrilous of all possible vocalizations. For even the parrot was created by God, and even he is in the end reached by God's love."[100] – It is characteristic of speech's role in depicting reality that this root sentence can undertake the same combination of "I" and "good" that Rosenzweig had considered to be foreign to speech in the case of idealism. If the idealistic logic of objects is measured according to linguistic requirements and the objection is made that the idealistic positing as adjective does not have a grammatical connection to the pronoun "I" that founds it, but only a dialectic one,[101] then it is even less possible within a grammatical method for "I" and "good" to be united into one sentence by the copula "is." This irregularity can be eliminated only by the decree of the reality of redemption. As man and world pronounce the divine I in redemption it becomes in their mouths a He. God as He then joins the declaration "good" without any difficulty.

This time the grammatical categories follow the root sentence as explanation of its meaning. The sentence is the content of the common song. The song opens with the exhortatory "let us thank"; this is joined by the dative, which represents the recipient of the gratitude, and then by the future as time of anticipation. In the song's second stanza the form of exhortation is heightened to the formation of the dual, which designates the relation of man to his neighbor and which is joined by the verb, the act. This dual thus occupies the place at which the dialogue between man and man , which is the point of departure for the other speech thinkers, could also come into play in the case of Rosenzweig. The need for the "other" is here directed to a human "Thou." The dual attains its highest elevation in the "We" through which the world of redemption receives its full determination and factuality. The unity of all language, which was the hidden presupposition in speech thinking, is manifestly fulfilled in the "We." The plural "You" arises out of the "We" as the judgment separating the holy and the profane. Finally the "They" arises out of the "We," the "They" which God Himself speaks as the real redeemer and which he not only speaks but turns into action, thereby consummating all speech.

Among the grammatical categories in which the three basic forms of speech thinking are arranged, the tenses have a special significance. They are represented not selectively, but completely. Further, they appear not in groups, but

---

[100] 231.
[101] 141.

individually, each one in connection with one form of speech thinking. Together they thus form a closed and unequivocally determined organism that directly undertakes the arrangement of the three absolute times. Just as the depicted reality of creation, revelation and redemption proceeds through past, present and future, so too the depicting method is linked to past, present and future. Its three basic forms are modes of expression of the three tenses. It is not only speech that needs time for its execution – and this, above all, is what Rosenzweig means when he says: "Speech is tied to time, nourished on time."[102] Speech thinking as method is also dominated by time and its modalities. It perceives differently in the past than in the present and differently in the present than in the future. "At every moment cognition is thus also tied to this very moment. It can not make its past into a non-past or its future into a non-future."[103] Time is not the object of speech thinking, but rather directly and actively participates in it. "And thus a truly new thinking results, a new thinking that does not merely 'relate' to life but whose relation to life or to existence is embodied in its thinking."[104]

The temporalization of thinking, which one also encounters in Martin Heidegger,[105] signifies a complete reversal of the manner of observation. The new method no longer seeks to subjugate time to thinking but rather wants to make thinking dependent on time. This change is analogous to the change in the image of the physical world brought about by the theory of relativity.[106] It turns the objectivity of thinking from something timelessly valid into something guaranteed precisely by time. In the case of conceptual cognition, for example, whose objectivity is guaranteed by the past, this signifies the transformation of a logical *a priori* to a temporal *a priori*.[107] "Correct...means ...in the 'fullness of time,' with regard to the occurrence of organic development as well as the history of the soul."[108] Speech thinking turns "the 'method' of common sense into the method of scientific thinking... Common sense can wait, continue to live; it has no "*idée fixe*." It knows: all in good time. This secret contains the entire wisdom of the new philosophy. It teaches, to use Goethe's phrase, 'understanding at the right time.'"[109] The question of speech thinking's methodological character again suggests itself here: it can

[102] *Kl. Sch.*, p. 387.

[103] *Ibid.*, p. 385.

[104] Ehrenberg, *Hegel*, p. 134.

[105] Cf. S. Marck, *Die Dialektik in der Philosophie der Gegenwart* Vol. 1, pp. 155–160.

[106] Cf. Herrigel, *Die Kreatur* Vol. 1 (1926–1927), p. 137.

[107] Cf. above, p. 114.

[108] Ehrenberg, "Gottesreich und organisches Leben," *Die Kreatur*, Vol. 1 (1926–1927), p. 391.

[109] *Kl. Sch.*, p. 384.

be method in the old sense only at the point where it reaches the end of the temporal movement, that is, the point where it absorbs time in its entirety. As the consummation of time redemption once more gathers time into one point and thereby brings it to a standstill, so that movement again becomes being. Just so is speech thinking method only as biography, in which it can survey from death the time that has passed. Accordingly, we were entitled to regard Dilthey's views and the method of Rosenzweig's *Hegel und der Staat* as a preliminary stage to existential thinking. Speech thinking, in its basic pre-supposition – the unity of speech – had found itself for the first time on the border of a scientific method. Its characterization by a temporal quality, in which its existentiality is consummated, brings speech thinking for the second time into the proximity of a theory – to be sure into proximity alone. The advantage that scientific theory, in its universality, possesses, namely the possibility of being transmitted, taught and studied, must be renounced by speech thinking. The speech thinker can teach only through his own personal example. Hans Ehrenberg says that his teaching would be unfaithful to itself as systematic teaching; only in biography can it become systematic and offer positive contents.[110] "As theory of cognition it evaporates and is diminished to a directive of an ever-provisional teaching that can become final only if the life of mankind would be consummated and fulfilled. And thus thinking really does belong within reality."[111]

[110] Cf. also E. Rosenstock, *op. cit.*, p. 45 and V. von Weiszaecker, "Der Arzt und der Kranke," *Die Kreatur*, Vol. 1 (1926–1927), pp. 85 ff.
[111] H. Ehrenberg, *Hegel*, p. 134.

III. Faith Thinking or the Synthesis

a) Eternity

The third part of the system draws the conclusion from the two previous ones. The elements that had been constructed in thinking – God, world and man – combine with the experienced realities of faith – creation, revelation and redemption – to form the configurations Judaism, Christianity and All. These configurations lie beyond the disjunction of the non-rational objects as well as beyond the correlation of believing experience. Hence, they are perceived in a way that can absorb unity and multiplicity equally, that is, in vision. The synthesis of thinking and faith is envisioned in the illumination of communal prayer.

Rosenzweig symbolizes the synthesis in an image, the image of the hexagonal Star of David which as the star of redemption gives his book its name. This imagery makes it clear that in the third part of the system we find ourselves in a realm beyond ordinary experience. In the second part redemption was ever yet reality that could be experienced, that is as Rosenzweig declares in *Anmerkungen zu Jehuda Halevi*, an essay which remains entirely in the realm of the theology of experience, we found ourselves in that world that is "known as equally real"[1] with this world. The star of redemption, however, symbolizes something *beyond* ordinary experience, something holy that can be grasped only in the vision of prayer and that, from the standpoint of faith, is to be designated in a figurative way as messianic future and redemption. The star signifies configuration, not in the sense in which we hitherto met configuration, as secondary expression of the objective unity of the system's first part or of the historical presentation of a conceptual form, as was the case with paganism or Islam, but rather configuration as such. The star as configuration is constituted by the logic of the system, which can only present itself clearly as a simultaneous embrace of thinking and faith. Opposed to it the proneness to historical configuration of Judaism and Christianity, which these religions certainly also possess, appears in turn only as something secondary.

Concerning Judaism and Christianity as historical configurations, the religio-historical construction reaches its conclusion in them inasmuch as through their position in the system they represent the genuine religions of revelation. They take the place of paganism in a way different from Islam by

---

[1] *Anmerkungen zu Jehuda Halevi*, p. 211.

undertaking a complete reversal of paganism from the perspective of faith, a reversal which at the same time preserves paganism. Judaism and Christianity are the consolidation of the reality of faith. They raise faith to the level of eternity and supra-personal validity, although in doing so they must ever again renew themselves out of this reality. Judaism can be designated as the succession and abolition of paganism, however, only if one views paganism in a wider sense that goes beyond Hellenism. From the perspective of revelation, the entire third part appears as redemption and stands in the light of messianism. Accordingly, Judaism and Christianity are at the same time messianic religions, whose ultimate union in absolute eternity, in the truth of God, designates the final stage – the completion of all history of religion.

Aside from the interpretation of religio-historical associations Rosenzweig offers in the introduction to the third part another special construction of Christian ecclesiastical history according to creation, revelation and redemption, a construction that closely follows that of Schelling.[2] The Roman church, that is, the Petrine church, conquers the paganism that is external through love and creates thereby the world body of Christianity. The Pauline church of the Reformation conquers the paganism that is internal through faith; it is the "Christianization of the soul, the belated conversion of a pagan spirit never wholly deceased."[3] The church of Johannine fulfilment, which comes only in the future, conquers both pagan body and pagan soul in hope. It is not a church that is especially constituted. Rather, just as hope becomes void when it dissociates itself from faith and love and seeks to be on its own, so is this future church of John merely a revival and renewal of the other extant churches.

Such a historical configuration, however, is not initially intended by the image of the star. The star forms the synthesis of thinking and faith in quite general terms as that which is "more than elemental, more than real; it is directly subject to perception."[4] God, world and man, the constructed elements, are the points of departure for the lines of an equilateral triangle. Creation, revelation and redemption, which are experienced in the course of reality, are symbolized in the lines of this first triangle, and in addition form the lines and corners of a second equilateral triangle – which thereby also expresses the superiority of the antithesis. This second triangle intersects the first and joins with it into the image of the star.

The synthesis of contents at the same time contains the synthesis of the perspectives upon which these contents are founded. If thinking was de-

2 Cf. above, p. 61.
3 281.
4 295.

termined by the I and faith by the Thou, then faith thinking unites these in the We, which is beyond I and Thou and yet encompasses them. Judaism, Christianity and All are communities, as people, as communion and as absolute community of the All, respectively. This synthetic We explains the "sociological basis"[5] for the presentation of the two religions. Moreover, the ultimate solution of existential problems facing man follows from this. The community of faith signifies "the immediacy of each single individual to God, realized in the pefect community of all with God"[6] and creates "the harmony precisely of men of the most diverse countenances."[7] In joining this community man, in the solitude of his I as well as in his openness to God and to the surrounding world, is completely satisfied.

Linked to this existential "We" is the main concept of the system's third part, namely, the concept of eternity as the synthesis of space and time. This concept had arisen in the second part with the fulfilment of time in the movement from creation to redemption. Having grown entirely in temporal experience as the eternity of God, eternity now signifies a being of becoming (*ein Sein des Werdens*). To be sure, "life must become wholly temporal ...before it can become eternal life,"[8] but the eternal itself "has no history, at most a prehistory."[9] Thus God's absolute eternity had been the complete congruence of the three tenses. "Time and the hour...are powerless before God...any conception of a development in time such as mystical impertinence or disbelieving arrogance may impute to Him, bounces off His eternity. It is not for Himself that He Himself needs time, it is He as Redeemer of world and man, and not because He needs it but because world and man need it...He is eternal, He alone is eternal, He is the Eternal per se. In His mouth, "I am" is like "I shall be" and finds his explanation only in it."[10]

This concept of eternity, as it is transmitted from the perspective of the eternity of God, is the concept that sustains the new stage of the system, exactly as the non-rational object had sustained the stage of the thesis and the act had sustained the stage of the antithesis. Again it is possible to point to two strata within the concept. One stratum corresponds to the relative act and coincides in general with the synthesis, the third, final stage of the system, while the other stratum, like the absolute act, takes up the scheme of the construction Yea, Nay and And and effects the augmentation within this

[5] *Kl. Sch.*, pp. 392–393.
[6] 331.
[7] 345.
[8] 288.
[9] 353.
[10] 272.

stage of the system. For, like the relation of the second part to the first part, the new part of the system stands in a dialectic relationship to its predecessor, whereas within itself it is arranged according to the construction.

The first stratum, relative eternity, signifies a decline from the absoluteness that had already been attained at the conclusion of the second part. To be sure, it resembles the absolute eternity of God in that, just as absolute eternity had bound itself to absolute existence, it also binds itself to existence, namely to the We. However, just as this existential We represents merely relative existence in relation to God's existence, so too relative eternity is merely a diminution of God's eternity. It signifies not the total convergence of the tenses, but merely a spatialization of time, a relative overcoming of temporal succession by means of making it visible in juxtaposition.

In addition to this relative eternity, which becomes the pillar of the rest of the synthesis, the absolute eternity of God is to be discerned, an eternity that can be considered as the direct and undiminished acceptance of the system's second part. Absolute eternity is arranged according to the scheme of the construction. In its consummation it signifies the unification of the relative eternities Judaism and Christianity in a supreme unity. This unification signifies therewith the zenith of this stage of the system as well as of the system in its entirety.

b) The Configurations – Judaism, Christianity and the All

The relative existing eternity, i.e., the communion in its connection with the spatialization of time, shows itself to be the supporter of the rest of the synthesis lying at this stage of the system. It does this by making visible the unity of God, world and man with creation, revelation and redemption. Judaism, Christianity and the All are such relative, "existent eternities." A completely new and original illumination of Jewish and Christian doctrines of faith results from this, opening up thereby a wide field for theological investigations. Here the new view will merely be presented briefly in its main features.

From the viewpoint of the "We" and of relative eternity Judaism, Christianity and the All thus present themselves equally as communions whose contents God, world and man as well as creation, revelation and redemption come into view in an eternity. With reference to Judaism and Christianity Rosenzweig says: "The question touches on the formative element in this community...In the preceding book we raised the question of the formative element in the communion of Judaism, which Jewish dogma might have answered with 'the Torah.' But we were not entitled to be satisfied with that answer, and the dogmatic answer 'Christ' would avail us no more here. Rather, it is precisely the manner in which a communion founded on dogma gives itself reality which we wish to fathom. More exactly still – for we know it has to be an eternal communion – we asked . . . how a communion can found itself for eternity."[1]

In the case of Judaism this question is answered by the fact that Judaism attests to itself as eternal communion through the *eternity of life*, through the eternal rootedness in itself. This may be expressed symbolically by saying that in Judaism eternity burns like a fire within the star of redemption, a fire that neither sends its rays outward nor receives its nourishment from the outside. The Jewish people is the eternal people, for whom past, present and future coincide in the succession of its generations. The eternity embodied within this people is "the covenant between scion and ancestor. By virtue of this covenant the people becomes an eternal people. For in catching sight of each other, scion and ancestor catch sight in each other at the same moment of the last descendant and the first ancestor. Descendant and ancestor are thus the true incarnation of the eternal people, both of them for each other and both together for him who stands between them."[2] The current of time becomes insignificant for this eternity. "Time has no power over it and must roll past. It must produce its own time and reproduce itself forever . . . Elsewhere, past and future are divorced, the one sinking back, the other coming on; here they grow into one. The bearing of the future is a direct bearing witness to the past."[3] And since Judaism sees the guarantee for its eternity in the propagation of its blood, it renounces its own land and its own language, two possessions which, in addition to peoplehood, have guaranteed other nations their durability. The land of the Jewish people is for it the holy land; its language also became holy from that which is living and hence transitory. Custom and law, in which the life of other peoples is shaped, is regarded by the Jews as a holy form of life that is eternally valid and immutable.

This eternal life can bear within itself the elements of the All. God, world and man – experienced in the course of reality only in flow of time – now become visible in their entirety.[4] As was the case in thinking, they are formed as unities of polar opposites. The Jewish God is creator and revealer, He is "simultaneously the God of retribution and the God of love."[5] Jewish man is

---

[1] 341.
[2] 346.
[3] 298.
[4] *Kl. Sch.*, p. 392.
[5] 306.

both child of God and redeemer of the world: "Over against Israel, eternally loved by God and faithful and perfect in eternity, stands he who is eternally to come, he who waits and wanders, and grows eternally – the Messiah."[6] The Jewish world is this world as well as the world to come. Certainly here, too, no less than in the experience of the second part, the unity can not be called static. For life, which reconciles the opposites, itself is in flux and effects the unity only in "unexpected reversals...quick as lightning."[7] As *eternal*, however, life places creation, revelation and redemption in juxtaposition. In this fashion, eternal life renews the dynamic of its temporal expression.

Just as the people's eternal life makes God, world and man evident, so Judaism possesses in the believing congregation a mirror-image of the national community and in its spiritual year a mirror-image of eternity. Creation divides the uniform flow of time through the course of the stars into days, weeks, months and years. By means of the cult, of the prayer of the congregation – which thus assumes here at the same time the role of the depicting method – these divisions become like hours established by themselves, hours which in the unbroken repetition of that same moment are eternity in miniature. "The cycles of the cultic prayer are repeated every day, every week, every year and in this repetition faith turns the moment into an 'hour,' it prepares time to accept eternity, and eternity, by finding acceptance in time itself becomes – like time."[8] "The year becomes representative of eternity, in complete representation,"[9] and accordingly the congregation becomes the representative of the people.

The Sabbath is the creation of the year. "The very regularity in the sequence of Sabbaths...makes them the cornerstones of the year. The year as a spiritual year is created only through them. They precede everything that may still come, and imperturbably go side by side with all else, following their even course amid the splendors of feast days."[10] Each Sabbath in turn comprises within itself creation, revelation and redemption. – The three pilgrimage festivals reveal the year. Since they themselves are arranged according to creation, revelation and redemption they paint a picture of the eternal history of the people, which in these feasts "grows aware of its vocation to be the recipient of revelation."[11] In the festival of deliverance from Egypt, in the festival of the revelation of the Ten Commandments and in the festival of

[6] 307.
[7] 350.
[8] 292.
[9] 324.
[10] 310–311.
[11] 316–317.

booths the people celebrates "three stages: the people are created into a people; this people is endowed with the words of revelation; and, with the Torah it has received, this people wanders through the wilderness of the world."[12] – The festival of booths, however, is the festival of redemption only at the stage of revelation. The true redemption of the year occurs on New Year's Day and the Day of Atonement. The "Days of Awe"[13] place "the eternity of redemption into time."[14] In these days, when the Jew faces God in his shroud in order to confess his sin, "the one sin in the unchanging human heart,"[15] and to implore for atonement, he experiences the end of days, the day of judgement, in the today.

The annual cycle of creation, revelation and redemption is at the same time a "curriculum of communal silence"[16] that gives rise to the perfect congregation of the faithful. The communal listening, in which the congregation is created, the communal meal, which signifies its renewal and its revelation, and the communal kneeling in silence, in which it completes itself as absolute congregation – "for union occurs in silence only; the word unites, but those who are united fall silent"[17] – are associated with the annual festivals of creation, revelation and redemption as cultic act and liturgical forms.

The manner in which Christianity is founded as eternal communion is not the eternity of life closed within itself, but the *eternity of the way*. This may be expressed in the symbol of the star: "The rays go forth . . . from this fire and flow unresisted to the outside."[18] The eternity of the way must also bring the flow of time to a standstill. Since Christianity can not "create its own time, and thus liberate itself from time, after the fashion of the eternal people, continually reproducing itself in itself,"[19] it makes itself master of time. It does this by being based on an event which comes from beyond time and leads beyond time,[20] to wit, the birth and second coming of Christ, which turns time into "this temporality,"[21] into a mere epoch between eternity and eternity. "As such it can be surveyed in its entirety from any one of its points, for beginning and end are equidistant from each of its points. Time has become a single way, but a way whose beginning and end lie beyond time and

[12] 317.
[13] 323 ff.
[14] 324.
[15] 325.
[16] 353.
[17] 308.
[18] 298.
[19] 337.
[20] 337.
[21] 338.

thus an eternal way."[22] The Christian stands always in the middle. "Since it stays and does not perish, this world-time consists of...'midpoints.' Every event stands midway between beginning and end of the eternal path and by virtue of this central position in the temporal middle-realm of eternity, every event is itself eternal."[23]

The Christian community is the communal witnessing of faith in this eternal way. As faith in something that is, i.e., as dogmatic faith, Christianity can pave this way further and further in the world by means of the mission as well as join together all those who are united in it, in Christianity, into an ecclesiastical community. In Judaism the people had through its life united later generations with earlier generations. In Christianity a similar function is performed by the *ecclesia*, the church, which through brotherhood establishes a bond between men.

Since "diffusion throughout all that is outside – ...is the secret of the eternity of the way,"[24] the elements God, world and man become visible in the eternal way in a different manner than in the eternal people. They are not configurations whose polar opposites are united in the life of the people, as had been the case with Judaism. Rather, they signify two contrasting paths which Christianity traverses. "Beneath Christianity's footsteps into each of the countries God, man, world there must bloom respectively two different sorts of flowers. Indeed, these steps themselves must diverge in time, and two forms of Christianity must traverse those three countries, each along its own path, hopeful of reuniting again one day, but not within time. Within time they march their separate ways and only by marching separately are they certain of traversing the entire All without losing themselves in it."[25] God is thus divided into Father and Son, and "Christian piety...follows different paths according as it is with the Father or with the Son."[26] The contrast in man is embodied in the two separate configurations of priest and saint, "going their separate ways, separate even when they meet in a single person as is always possible."[27] The Christian world is "organized into the great dualism of state and church."[28]

The ecclesiastical year is again the mirror-image of the eternity of the way and the believing congregation, which envisions eternity in prayer, is the

[22] 338–339.
[23] 340.
[24] 348.
[25] 348–349.
[26] 350.
[27] 351.
[28] 352.

mirror-image of the Christian community, the *ecclesia*. In its regular succession Sunday, the "festival of creation,"[29] established the year. – The three
major festivals are "an annually recurring celebration of revelation."[30] Within this revelation Christmas has the meaning of creation, but creation,
revelation and redemption are once more contained within it. Easter, the real
festival of revelation, also encompasses the entire sequence of the three times.
As "the one great central event in Christian life" it "thus undergoes one single
re-presentation in the entire festival season, from Lent through Good Friday,
to the day of the resurrection."[31] Pentecost celebrates the redemption within
revelation, that is, the beginning of redemption, in which the disciples receive
the Holy Spirit in order to bring it to the peoples of the world. – The
ecclesiastical year lacks real festivals of redemption. Christianity sees redemption as having already occurred in the life and death of Christ. The
church, only by participating in the world's historical festivals, "by casting its
light of glorification over the branches of national life, . . . renders a service on
the path of redemption, for redemption is never other than the sowing of
eternity into the living."[32]

The Christian year also educates the community to the highest form of
communion, silent prayer. It does this by preparing and attuning the individual soul for the communal listening, communal meal and communal
kneeling. This task of preparation is undertaken by art, which is thereby
enlisted into the service of the cult and thus receives its justification. In its pure
form art remained behind, like thinking, in the position of creatureliness, of
the egoistic I. In its applied form, however, art participates in eternity. Thus
the plastic arts attune the believer to the first stage of communion, to
communal listening, in the architecture of the church and the decoration of its
space with paintings and sculptures. Music prepares the soul for the sacra-
ment of the meal. The participatory arts, namely the art of mere gesture,
folkpageant and dance, the "self-expositions. . .[that have] no spectators
. . .only participants,"[33] were to have introduced the believers into the final
communion of silence. Christianity, however, did not know such a communion, while in redemption Christianity thrust back to life in the world. Just
as the cycle of the ecclesiastical year, Christian liturgy and therewith the
congregation also lack the ultimate consummation; the circle opens up for
them into a spiral.

[29] 359.
[30] 359.
[31] 365.
[32] 369.
[33] 372.

This supporting scaffolding of communion and eternity, into which the elements God, world and man and the experienced realities of creation, revelation and redemption are built, is also present in the third configuration at this stage of the system. The All also signifies an eternal communion in which God, world and man as well as creation, revelation and redemption exist next to one another. If it was said previously about the symbol of the star that it is illumined by light, with reference to the relative eternity of the All, this can only mean that all the elements become visible here in ultimate clarity. It is not an All that "is without content even if it be also without limits or contradictions. . .[but rather] the living All that surrounds us, the All of life, the All composed of God, man and world,"[34] that is, a positive All that preserves all its components and exhibits them next to each other. And so the All can not be something universal that comprehends the particular as *subordinate* to it. Rather, it is a community *in* itself, in which God, world and man come together no longer in a Jewish or Christian formulation, but in a form completely detached from all specific admixtures, as *the* God, *the* world and *the* man. This All of life, which corresponds to this stage of the system and for that reason must include the configurations of thinking and the experiences of faith in a manner that is clearly discernible, is not depicted separately, as were Judaism and Christianity. This is due to the twofold gradation of the concept of eternity and to the concurrence of these two grades or eternity in the concept of the All.

We must now occupy ourselves with absolute eternity and its interlacing with the relative eternity embodied in Judaism, Christianity and All. Absolute eternity, as it arose in the consummation of reality and as it is now admitted into the level of vision, is complete oneness, the contemporaneity of the three tenses. In the presence of God the movement of time expires. This absolute eternity of God is constructed in the system's third part out of the Yea and Nay as an And, in accordance with the overall scheme of construction. Its confrontation with relative eternity, which is tied to the synthesis, that is, to the third stage of the system, occurs here in a different way than the confrontation between form and content in the first part and between relative and absolute act in the second part. One can not speak of a total coincidence of both strata, as we could observe in the case of the formula of the world and of revelation. This is because here the synthesis already contains all the factors and relative eternity must therefore always be broader than absolute eternity. Rather, the tension between both views of eternity, that is, the tension

[34] 349.

between the stage of the system and the construction, is expressed by the fact that with respect to Judaism and Christianity absolute eternity gives special emphasis in each case to one factor. In its relation to the living All absolute· eternity appears as enhancement of this All, as synthesis within the synthesis. In this sense as concurrence of the two syntheses – for absolute eternity in its consummation as the And of Yea and Nay is itself a synthesis – there is in the case of the All a concurrence of both strata of eternity. Absolute eternity, as such a synthesis within the synthesis, is called truth.

From the perspective of God's absolute eternity Judaism and Christianity, each of which had comprised a complete synthesis in its eternity, again become individual components of this new synthesis. Thus Judaism becomes world and Christianity man; again Judaism becomes space and Christianity time; and yet again, Judaism becomes creation and Christianity revelation. This happens in such a way that absolute eternity is always adding the And to these factors that are divided into Yea and Nay. In so far as Judaism and Christianity are equally eternal, they are so from the perspective of relative eternity; in so far as they are nevertheless different, as life and way, they are so from the perspective of the eternity of God.

Judaism is essential eternity, eternity that is *at rest*, "world of the law, . . . law of the world."[35] It has its own *world*, which is complete, while the rest of the world is growing. "It is this very growth that the eternal people denies itself. Its nationality has reached the point to which the nations of the world still aspire. Its world has reached the goal."[36] It thus turns away from world history and from the wars with which the state creates in the uniform lapse of time epochs of growth. – Jewish life, then, is something at rest *in space*. "The differences of space did not mean a separation that first had to be overcome. For . . . these differences had already been overcome from the start, in the innate communion of the people."[37] The Jewish act thus has only to preserve the communion throughout time. – Above all, however, Judaism differs from Christianity as the difference of passive from active, of *creation* from revelation. The Jewish community is "a common structure, a common result, a common existence."[38] Eternity of life is self-rootedness, self-enclosement, the infinity of a point that "is never erased; thus it preserves itself in the eternal self-preservation of the procreative blood."[39]

[35] *Kl. Sch.*, p. 396.
[36] 329.
[37] 346.
[38] 354.
[39] 341.

Christianity, in contrast, is eternity *in action*. As eternal way it unites men in faith. Embodied in it is "faith of men . . . and men of faith."[40] The accent lies on the *individual soul*. It alone experiences the redemption that the congregation and the ecclesiastical year lack. Only in it does the eternal way become the way of the cross, a way that shapes the contrasts between creation and revelation and can thereby overcome them. And since Christianity stresses the believing soul, for whom preservation and renewal are embodied in the cross, in suffering, and for whom art as form of suffering signifies a rival power, Rosenzweig can establish from this "a Christian aesthetics, that is, a theory of suffering."[41] In like fashion, he had been able to deduce "a messianic politics, that is, a theory of war"[42] from the worldliness of the eternal people and its isolation from the rest of the world. By this means the idealistic deities state and art find their final delimitation in eternal life and eternal way.[43] – Furthermore, Christianity is the overcoming of *time* through brotherhood, which turns every moment into a midpoint in time. Man can thus simultaneously behold himself and his neighbor. The Christian act, before which time "already overcome is placed at its feet," still has only to "traverse the separating space."[44] – Finally, the Christian way is act and thus conveys the features of *revelation* – and therein lies the principal opposition to Jewish life. The Christian congregation in "a common going, doing, becoming."[45] The way vanquishes time is "contest"[46] with this temporality. It is "ever in the event, ever *au courant*,"[47] and has the infinity of a line which, dissatisfied with itself, always presses towards elongation. "The infinity of a line . . . ceases where it would be impossible to extend it . . . Christianity, as the eternal way, has to spread even further, . . . Christianity must proselytize, . . . proselytizing is the veritable form of its self-preservation for Christianity. It propagates by spreading."[48]

With this last application of the scheme of the construction in view, we shall now direct our glance once more to the distinction between construction and dialectics and thereupon consider whether in the relationship between Judaism and Christianity the Yea and Nay are unequivocally part of the construction or whether this relationship moves into the realm of dialectics.

---

[40] *Kl. Sch.*, p. 396.
[41] *Ibid.*, p. 393.
[42] *Ibid.*
[43] 346.
[44] 346.
[45] 354.
[46] 339.
[47] 340.
[48] 341.

In consequence of this inquiry it can be ascertained that the distinction between construction and dialectics is nowhere as sharply made as it is in this case. (This distinction is especially important with respect to Yea and Nay, for the And in any case has a synthetic character.) Yea and Nay are here set free of all dialectical admixtures, which had not been the case with respect to the construction of the elements and also with respect to the relationship between creation and revelation. Judaism and Christianity are not contained in one another; neither are they cause and effect. Rather, they are equally primeval and equally independent. Later, when he once more takes up the Yea and Nay with reference to the verification of truth, Rosenzweig speaks of Judaism and Christianity as laborers working at the same task, which they serve in different ways. To be sure, they are dependent on one another, and this reciprocal need is emphasized even on the part of the act, that is, in Christianity. Christianity, i.e., revelation, which as a rule was always that which was propagating, needs Judaism in order not to lose itself on the way "in the outermost distance of feeling."[49] The existence of the Jews guarantees Christianity its own truth.[50] This need, however, says nothing about the formation of Judaism and Christianity and their purity and independence of each other. The need is not something *by which* they become Judaism and Christianity, something that stipulates their character as Yea and Nay. Rather, it is something they possess *after* they already are Judaism and Christianity, something that is of no inportance for their formation and for their character as Yea and Nay. The two religions do not identify each other as Judaism or Christianity, as was still the case with creation and revelation in the system's second part.

Absolute eternity as synthesis of these different kinds of eternity represented by Judaism and Christianity, as synthesis of life and way, is called truth. "The truth lies behind the way... For though its end lies in eternity, and it is thus eternal, it [the way] is at the same time finite, since eternity is its end... In this ocean of light every way is submerged like vanity. But thou, o God, art truth."[51] This direct identification of absolute eternity with truth is expressed even more clearly in the following sentences: "God is truth. Truth is His signet. By it He is known. And will be even when one day all has come to an end by which He used to make His eternity known within Time – all eternal life, all eternal way – there where even the eternal comes to an end: in eternity. For not the way alone ends here, but life too... In truth, *in the truth*, life too disappears."[52]

[49] 413.
[50] 415.
[51] 379.
[52] 380.

Absolute eternity also rests on the foundation of relative eternity, on the All of living matter. It obtains this basis through the elevation of the factors that exist next to one another into pure unity. To phrase it in the image of a star: the light in which God, world and man become visible becomes purely light, in which there is nothing other than itself. The positive All is elevated therewith to a theoretical All, to the truth, even before it has been described; living matter, the All of reality, becomes the "*essence* of living matter."[53] With this characterization of truth as the essence of living matter, the zenith of the structure of the system's third part, and therewith of the system as a whole, is attained. For all systematic philosophy must ultimately conclude in something theoretical, in a supreme point of unity which comprehends all else not *in* itself but *under* itself and in which all differences are therefore obliterated.

This final result, the merging of all the elements and tenses into an ultimate unity, nevertheless is not the same as Hegel's All, neither in scope nor in significance. The essence of living matter, the realistic All, is a mere dialectic appropriation of Hegel's notion of the All, just as the non-rational object – a comprehension of that which can not be thought by means of thinking – was a dialectic appropriation of the idealistic notion of the object. That which is real can not be conceived out of itself. There should be no All of the real, that is, a real in general, just as there should be no non-rational object. The real is the singular, the particular. It does not presuppose any unity and in its multiplicity can be absorbed only by experience. The All of the real thus does not find its justification, like the idealistic All, in the creative unity of thinking consciousness. It is not an All that is conceivable from the very beginning. Nevertheless the non-rational object and the realistic All are not dogmatic metaphysics. Rather, they are precisely an appropriation of the conclusions of Kant's *Critiques* and Hegel's notion of the All, and in both instances specifically a dialectic appropriation. Rosenzweig adopts idealism not through the location of objectivity and universality within the things themselves, as in pre-Kantian metaphysics, but through the recognition of thinking's power to form objects and unite the All. His divergence from idealism, however, lies in the fact that these functions of thinking are depreciated. Thinking, by carrying out its activities, is not creative. It produces an object, it also produces an All, but it only *re*-produces them. With respect to the logic of the objective world as expressed in the formula of the world, the activity of content and the passivity of form means nothing else but this limitation of the power of thinking. Similarly, the unification of the real into a

[53] 385.

final point of unity now means nothing else but this limitation. Truth is merely an *a posteriori* unification of living matter, a final abstraction on the basis of this living matter itself. 'But truth never appears before the end. The end is its locus. For us it is not the given but the result."[54]   Inherent in this character of the unity of the real is the need of the unity, since it is not justified by means of creative thinking, for a non-rational justification, i.e., a justification by means of faith. And so the significance of the realistic All, the theoretical unification of the real, also can not be identified with Hegel's All. In Hegel's case the All, truth, is the subject of Philosophy. With Rosenzweig the All, the truth, is merely an assertion about another subject. *The All is based on God.* At this point we have to take notice of the fact that the sentence that epitomizes Rosenzweig's system does not say "Truth is" but rather "God is truth." God, He who *exists* absolutely, He who in faith had arrived at the unity of actual configuration, is the subject of truth. As this subject, God is not an idea, not something conceived, but rather someone experienced in revelation and existing on the basis of this believing experience. As that which is absolutely free and transcendent to thinking God now enters into a relationship with truth, that is, with something theoretical.

Let us bring to mind once more the conclusion of the second part: in self-redemption God had perfected Himself into the unified All, in which world and man merged. If it had been said there that God is the unity that consummates everything,[55] this unity referred not to an assertion, but to nothing other than God's absolute, actual existence, to the absolute identification of God and the All by means of God's action. It should have been said: God, the One, *is.* In accordance with the temporalization of God's act, the unity of time, absolute eternity, was directly bound to God's actual unity. In the system's third part eternity is conceived as possessing two dimensions. The first, relative eternity, is linked with relative existence, that is, with the We, while the second, absolute eternity, is once more related to God's actual configuration. The All, the essence of living matter, joins God, He who exists, as *His* essence.

The sentence: "God is truth" thus links faith and thinking, act and essence; the act is posited as subject and the essence as predicate. With this, the synthesis of faith and thinking is expressed at the highest level, but with the preference given to faith.

Rosenzweig clarifies this link between faith and thinking in the last book of the third part by first of all reducing God to revelation, designating truth as

---

[54]   398.
[55]   Cf. 258.

beyond experience and then elevating God as the Lord of truth. "We learn that God loves us but not that He is love. He draws too nigh to us in love for us to yet be able to say: He is this or that. In this love we learn only that He is God, not what He is. The What, the essence, remains concealed."[56] "As such a [loving] one however, God is not the Lord. As such He is active. He is not above His deed. He is within it. He loves. Only as the Lord is God beyond that of which He is the Lord."[57] But truth lies beyond this, "our living knowledge."[58] It is beyond the name, "beyond the word,"[59] in silence. Truth is "simple existence of the Highest...unimpaired reality, omnipotent and solely potent, beyond any desire for a joy in realization."[60] "What then might be the essence of living matter...With what word...are we to designate that which would lie beyond words? The Aught is at home in the world of words. But above this world, as little apart of it as the Nought, there rests the All...And as the Lord of life God would be equal in essence to this essence: He would be the Lord of the one-and-all. And just this, this lordliness over the one-and-all, is meant by the sentence: God is Truth."[61]

c) The System and Its Relativation by Revelation

Rosenzweig's philosophy does not stop at the zenith of the system designated by the sentence "God is Truth." Rosenzweig examines the relation of God to truth as an aspect of His essence – but God is indeed more than truth, "just as every subject is more than its predicate, every thing more than the conception of it. And even if truth is really the last and the only thing one can still declare of God and His essence, still there remains to God a surplus beyond His essence."[1] In this context Rosenzweig poses the question of truth to truth itself and perceives in it too a fact of revelation. This means, in other words, that the ascendancy of faith over thinking expressed in the sentence: "God is Truth" is allowed to take effect upon thinking itself. This preference thereby negates the system as a whole, in that it leads the synthesis back to the standpoint of the antithesis. In so far as the revelation of the system in general by means of faith contains a renewed unification of thinking and faith, this last stage of *The Star*

[56] 381.
[57] 382.
[58] 383.
[59] 383.
[60] 384.
[61] 385.
[1] 386.

of Redemption also signifies a synthesis of thinking and faith. Before tracing the descent from the highest stage that was reached in the system, we shall once more turn our attention briefly to the progress of the system.

In the introduction to the first part, the system takes as its point of departure the personal experience of the threefold factuality of God, world and man, which is then reconstructed in thinking, in the thesis. God, world and man thus arise out of the hypothetical Nought as positive concepts, as essences in space, each an All in itself, a unity of polar contrasts, each outwardly without relation to the others. The existential parallel to this individuating thinking is the egoistic I, the solitary man. Although the construction does not point beyond its result, the triad of elements – each of which, since it is an All, must claim to include the other two elements – nevertheless contains the demand for an order in which all three would have their place next to each other.

This demand is fulfilled in faith. Faith brings about the relation of God, world and man to one another by means of activity and passivity, that is, by means of the realities creation, revelation and redemption, which are occurrences in time. Further, faith leads through the sequence of God's absolute actions, which are arranged according to the construction scheme, to God as He who is absolutely and eternally existing. The human mode of existence that corresponds to faith is that of acting and hence real man who is addressed by God, and in turn addresses the world. Inasmuch as the modes of human existence that correspond to thinking, i.e., the egoistic I and man in community, are also included in faith as creation and redemption, the second stage of the system unites all of man's modes of existence and therefore can be spoken of as the true philosophy of existence.

Faith proves itself to be antithesis not by appearing *next to* the Yea, as the Nay of the construction does, but by being the Nay *of* the preceding Yea. Faith thus places the elements of thinking under a negative sign. These elements thereby lose their inner unity and their contrasting components, which had been joined together in this unity, step forth inverted in their contents and in their sequence. This conversion occurs in complete freedom and remains unexplained, just as in the case of Schelling the transition from negative philosophy to positive philosophy also occurred through volition. The non-rationality of the inversion can be clearly seen in Rosenzweig's analogy of the traveler's trunk: "This transformation...can find expression only as interchange of the two first arch-words. What merged as Yea, emerges as Nay, and vice versa, much like the contents of a traveler's trunk, which are unpacked in the opposite order from that in which they were inserted."[2] This

[2] 112–113.

analogy indeed explains the independence of the Nay from the Yea within the construction, for each of the layers of contents within the trunk is by itself independent. Here, where he has his eye on the relationship between creation and revelation, Rosenzweig gives the difference between construction and dialectics special emphasis. The image of the trunk also explains the inversion of the sequence, for what was inserted last, may be removed first, but it does not explain that which truly constitutes the antithesis, that is, the inversion of the contents. That which was packed last as Nay must also be removed first as Nay. The analogy would serve as an explanation of the antithesis only if content and sequence were to be conceived as directly connected, if it were already inherent in the Yea that it must always be first and in the Nay that it must always be subsequent. This, however, is not the case. The Nay is merely "*logically* younger"; in faith it could just as well be first. Thus the antithesis is expressed only indirectly by the difference between "packing" and "unpacking." In so far as "into" and "out of" are opposites, a difference is intimated. Elsewhere Rosenzweig also speaks of the first two stages of the system as opposing contents, one of which "remains stationary" while the other "happens or better, materializes"[3] as "recondite...[and] emerging,"[4] as "thing ...and act."[5] Aside from such formulations that are present in the text, the content's antithetical character can be characterized as essence and freedom, space and time, isolation of the I and relation to the Thou. The reason for this conversion of contents, however, does not lie in the mere fact of conversation. It can be understood solely through the free act springing from faith, which indeed signifies freedom and action, solely as "an act of conversion that though based on the historical origin of the points was without foundation in and of itself."[6]

The creative, dynamic character of faith is supported by the view of the historical fact of the overcoming of paganism by revelation, more specifically, by the fact of the subjugation of ancient Greece by Christianity, by the fact that the world-time of revelation has inverted the contents of paganism. Or to speak in the language of faith, it is supported by the view of divine providence as a "plan of salvation"[7] acting in history. Islam, which does not know conversion, is "a belief in revelation derived directly from paganism, without God's will as it were."[8]   Another factor accounting for the freedom of faith

[3] Cf. 117.
[4] Cf. 117.
[5] Cf. 242, 295.
[6] 255.
[7] 116.
[8] 117.

vis-à-vis thinking and its realization of a reversal is the fact of the personal conversion of the thinker into a believer, that is, his inner reversal. This, too, is a free turning to the living God, a turning that can indeed be prepared by thinking but that ultimately occurs in complete freedom from thinking. The turning, for its part, makes itself dependent on the even higher freedom of divine love. All opposition between autonomy and heteronomy is resolved in such an encounter of divine freedom and human freedom, in which man turns "through one shining moment of grace of choice to an obligation that is beyond freedom."[9] Man's free act, the reversal which negates all that came before, is the trust with which he opens himself to God's love that appears before him as "the moving, the gripping, the searing experience,"[10] as "free gift, gracious beyond all measure of righteousness, . . . the primeval force of the divine which elects and need not be entreated."[11] This human, existential motive for the conversion of the signs and thereby of the contents of thinking is quite clearly expressed when Rosenzweig discusses the conversion with special reference to man. Man's defiant will is converted into humility and his character, the essential will, which "is already fixed once and for all in its direction,"[12] nevertheless is converted into an act of love. Rosenzweig takes this opportunity to speak of an "inner conversion" not only with respect to man but also with respect to God and world. Echoes of this can be found later where, with respect to the conversion of the world's plenitude of phenomena he says: "All emergence into the manifest must be an inner conversion."[13]

In the introduction to the second part, Rosenzweig uses theological categories to designate the transition from thinking to faith from the perspective of faith, which itself carries out the transition: thinking is the prophecy whose fulfilment occurs through the miracle of faith. In accordance with the dimension of temporality prevalent in faith, he thereby arrives at a theology of miracle that comprehends miracle as the temporal fulfilment of that which has been predicted. The miraculous aspect of the miracle does not lie in its deviation from the laws of nature. Rather, the core of the miracle is its "predictedness. . . The miracle is that a man succeeds in lifting the veil which commonly hangs over the future, not that he suspends predestination. Miracle and prophecy belong together."[14] "Prediction and its fulfilment [are] the two factors that are decisive for its miraculous nature. Prediction, the

[9] *Kl. Sch.*, p. 384.
[10] 179.
[11] 39.
[12] 213.
[13] 223.
[14] 95.

expectation of a miracle, always remains the actually constitutive factor, while the miracle itself is but the factor of realization; both together form the 'portent.' To lend the character of a portent to their miracles of revelation is, accordingly, of supreme value both to Scripture and to the New Testament. The former does so through the promise to the patriarchs, the latter through the prophecies of the prophets."[15] The thinking that takes its point of departure from the personal experience of death, that is, from the factuality that precedes thinking, and is thereby a philosophy of the standpoint, requires faith as "the lucid clarity of infinite objectivity"[16] in order to become systematic and scientific. And faith, the experience of revelation, needs the foundation of thinking, which shows it its "preconditions"[17] "for the sake of its integrity."[18] Like the relation of two stages of miracle to each other, thinking as prophecy is related to faith as fulfilment. – Further, since theology designates thinking as creation, creation is the prophecy that is realized through revelation. "As practiced by the theologian, philosophy becomes a prognostication of revelation, in a manner of speaking the 'Old Testament' of theology. But thereby revelation regains before our amazed eyes the character of authentic miracle – authentic, because it becomes wholly and solely the fulfilment of the promise made in creation. And philosophy is the Sibylline Oracle which, by predicting the miracle, turns it into a "sign,' the sign of divine providence."[19]

The designation of philosophy as creation, which is found throughout the second part, as well as the transposition of the theological concepts creation, revelation and redemption and hence of the tenses past, present and future to the stages of the system, contain the characterization of thinking from the perspective of faith, as Rosenzweig himself says here. The equation of thinking with the first stage of the miracle, however, its designation as prophecy, contains an effacement of the difference between thesis and antithesis in favor of the latter. It transforms thinking from something independent – and only as something different from faith can thinking lay the foundation for this faith – into a content of faith. The introduction to the second part thus characterizes the transition from thinking to faith from its own standpoint, that is, from the standpoint of theology.

This view of thinking from the perspective of faith is already indicated at the conclusion of the first part. There the hypothetical Nought of thinking

---

[15] 96.
[16] 106.
[17] 108.
[18] 106.
[19] 108.

becomes a "real Nought."[20] With respect to the construction Rosenzweig
had still explicitly denied that the Nought is a "somber basis"[21] or "anything
else that can be named with Ekhart's terms, or Boehme's or Schelling's."[22]
After having completed the construction, however, and with the proximity of
the second part proclaimed, the three elements are to him "births from out of
the dark depth"[23] and "creations."[24] Their components become "occult
powers"[25] and the construction becomes "prehistory,"[26] the secret of the
everlasting birth that is creation.[27]

All these fluctuations in approach imply a negation of the thesis. Without
this encroachment on the part of faith, the construction, which serves precisely to clarify the experience that precedes thinking, could not be designated
as secret. How is it possible for secrets to be constructed at all and how is it
possible to regard mathematics as history? If God, world and man were
secrets, creations whose history is narrated, the complicated manner of their
construction would be unnecessary ballast. – As presupposition of the revealed fragments as well as presupposition of correlation and of dynamic
objectivity, the construction does indeed have important significance and is to
be taken seriously. Nevertheless, within the second part it is increasingly
devaluated and from being the recognized partner of theology it sinks to a
mere analogy. The construction of the fragmented elements is "divine origin"[28] of the course of reality, while the elements "were the inner histories of
the self-creation, the self-revelation, the self-redemption of God, world and
man."[29]

Rosenzweig thus denies the dialectic relationship between thinking and
faith, even if on the other hand it is clearly evident in the entire structure of the
second part. This denial can be viewed as a consequence of the actual
character of the antithesis, which is wholly freedom and act and hence can not
recognize anything aside from itself. Only reluctantly does the antithesis join
the three steps of dialectics, in which it is a link based upon another link. It is
also possible, however, to see in this denial the sign of a dynamic cognition,
incorporating speech thinking within the logic of the system, especially since

[20] 88.
[21] 26, 29.
[22] 26.
[23] 90.
[24] 90.
[25] 88.
[26] 90.
[27] 90.
[28] 258.
[29] 257.

the synthesis leads to another shift in the appraisal of the first part. Everything is thus seen from the perspective and in the light of that stage which has been attained, while the other stages appear to be non-existent. Then, after the system has progressed, it readjusts its perspective and includes everything within this new perspective.

If vis-à-vis thinking faith is thus complete freedom which undertakes the conversion and from the perspective of the conversion gives a new interpretation of the construction as an analogy of faith, we must now investigate why this freedom is nevertheless able to enter into a dialectic relationship with thinking and unite with it into a synthesis. To be sure, faith negates thinking, but it thereby "cancels" it in the way that Hegel understood the verb *aufheben*, that is, first of all in the sense of *tollere* and *conservare*, by simultaneously negating and preserving thinking within itself. On the basis of this equality that is inherent in the difference there is yet a third sense to the "cancellation," i.e., the elevation to a higher level in which the two differences come together in unity. There is no doubt that the intermediary position of the antithesis thereby implies a mediation. The antithesis must glance backward at the thesis and forward at the synthesis. Here, where the antithesis signifies complete freedom, this leads to a difficult problem. The subjugation to faith thinking seems to be even more of a burden to freedom than the preservation of thinking. Rosenzweig speaks of this danger of mediation in another context, where he seeks to keep the dialectics away from the relation of Yea and Nay in the construction and hence away from creation and revelation.[30] By means of the construction he did indeed almost completely avoid this danger for the sequence of creation, revelation and redemption within the second part, preserving therewith the special position of revelation. He did not avoid it, however, for the system in its entirety, that is, for creation, revelation and redemption in their transmitted sense. The second part, just as it arises from the basis of the first part, is inevitably subjugated to the third part. The fear that the freedom of faith might thereby disappear once again in a higher necessity is therefore certainly justified. In spite of this fear, this does not come to pass. Rosenzweig solves the difficulty not only by securing the preeminence of faith within the synthesis itself, but also by once more juxtaposing revelation to the entire system.

But in order for faith to be able to negate thinking and at the same time hold thinking within itself as presupposition, in other words, in order for both to be able to meet in a higher unity, it is necessary that faith not be totally alien to thinking. Both thinking and faith must bear within themselves the possibility,

---

[30] Cf. 229–230.

the will of communion. Faith, even if it signifies freedom, must by its very nature be linked with thinking. We have been able to establish some of these links in the course of our discussion. The archetypal word Yea signifies in thinking more than logical affirmation; it helps concretize the construction. In the method of the second part, on the other hand, Yea and Nay were the logical basis of living speech, of "speech in general," as it were. – Death, the self-completion of the solitary self and as such that which is attached to thinking as its human, existential accompaniment, formed in faith the boundary between the modifications of human existence in creation, revelation and redemption. It thereby represented the conceptual means of negation – to be sure, not in the course of dialectics, but in the course of the construction, which did not always strictly remain distinct from dialectics. – Art, the language of the solitary self and therefore organon of idealism, formed within faith a reality of the second order that could be categorized by the unique sequence of creation, revelation and redemption. – Thesis and antithesis do not meet only in such individual instances of communion that make it clear how art can bestow upon revelation "the meaning of a sign,"[31] and how the archetypal word can be the "prognostication"[32] of real speech. In addition, the first part in its entirety has something in common with the whole of the second part, something through which they are made kindred. Thinking is reflecting on the experienced, non-rational factuality, and as such it is thinking against the background of a universal faith in a threefold reality. Faith, in turn, is faith that designates *ratio* as creation and, by including creation within its purview, establishes therewith a rational theology. In such intersections and connections we may see the justification for the antithetical relationship between faith and thinking. They prepare the ground for the ultimate union of faith and thinking in the superimposed perspective of believing thinking. Furthermore, the antithesis, in that it includes not only the thesis as creation but also the synthesis as redemption, is also directly connected to this believing thinking. From the perspective of the antithesis the entire third part of the system appears as redemption. The intermediate position of the antithesis, in which on the one hand we could see an infringement upon its freedom, proves itself on the other hand to be of exceptional scope, encompassing the entire system. Further, it provides a completeness and self-inclusiveness that makes it superior to the other parts of the system. In other words, the antithesis is truly a system in miniature.

The introduction to the third part offers a theory of genuine prayer, which allows us to envision God and the All in its enlightenment. Just as the

[31] 190.
[32] 109.

theology of miracle, which formed the transition to the second part, had subordinated the miracle to time, so too is prayer made dependent on time. In genuine prayer it is possible to draw eternity into time or, as Rosenzweig says in the course of transferring the reality of redemption to eternity, it is possible to accelerate the coming of the Kingdom. This prayer occurs in "the desirable time,"[33] in "the time of grace."[34] The transition to the third part thereby still stands entirely under the sign of the second part, just as within faith prophecy and prayer also brought about the transitions from creation to revelation and from revelation to creation. The prayer of the sinner praying for his own advantage is not sinful on account of its content. For "there is no sinful plea on the basis of content. By creating the suppliant as individual, God has already fulfilled his prayer before it is uttered, even as criminal a prayer, say, as that for the death of another; it is after all true already without any prayer that the other must die."[35] It is only the improper time of this prayer that is sinful. The suppliant "should have requested it before his creation; once created, he can only thank for his Own. If nevertheless he requests it, he misses the period of grace for entreating that which he currently needs to pray for."[36] The prayer of the fanatic also comes at an improper time, since it reaches too far ahead and seeks to bring about the coming of the Kingdom by force. The former prayer lagged behind the moment of grace, while the latter leaps over it. Thus only two kinds of prayer occur at the right time: the prayer of the creature to its own fate, as Goethe prayed, and the prayer in community. The suppliant who prays to his own fate, does not pray for his own, like the sinner, but "in his own."[37] His fate is "an hour...in the growing ages of the world."[38] By grasping his fate, his prayer always comes "in the personal hour and simply can not occur in an alien one. Accordingly it is ever in the desirable time, the 'time of grace,' and is fulfilled as fast as it is prayed. It is fulfilled from the side of the world; in it, man enters his own fate, and thus it constitutes at the same time the confident entrance of man into that which has been from eternity, into creation."[39] But this prayer to one's fate only fulfils one of the conditions necessary in order to envision eternity. It must be completed by prayer in the believing community – and it is only at this point that the connection with the third part takes place. The We must join the proper time,

[33] 273.
[34] 273.
[35] 273.
[36] 274.
[37] 276.
[38] 276.
[39] 277.

and this communal prayer, the liturgy that extends throughout the cycle of the year, can become the representative of eternity.

The third part, the synthesis, adopts the concept of existing eternity from the conclusion of the second part. There absolute eternity, the absolute convergence of the tenses, had been directly connected with God, the unified All who exists absolutely. Both these factors, in weakened form, become the support of the synthesis. Here the We takes the place of God's absolute existence, while relative eternity as spatialization of time takes the place of the absolute convergence of the three tenses. The three configurations Judaism, Christianity and All are thus three eternities that are, carrying within themselves God, world and man of thinking in conjunction with creation, revelation and redemption of faith. The parallel to the synthesis of thinking and faith in the realm of human existence is man in community, in which man's individuality (*Eigensein*) as well as his relation toward the outside are satisfied.

Within this synthesis God's absolute eternity, aside from His existence, then arises as the ordering principle among the three "existent eternities." God's absolute eternity follows the construction plan of Yea, Nay and And. It appears in its completeness as the direct adoption of the total convergence of the tenses that had been attained in the second part. But inasmuch as it is at the same time an augmentation of the relative eternity of the All, this absolute eternity here absorbs the synthesis and presents itself as "essence of living matter." That is, it presents itself as essential All, which as such is called truth and which as predicate ultimately joins the subject of that which exists absolutely. This essential All is the mainstay of the system. It is the theoretical viewpoint under which a unified gathering together of the multiplicity of all existing matter is alone possible. Inasmuch as this All is based on God, however, on He who actually exists, faith has the mastery over it. The sentence "God is truth" thus unites thesis and antithesis, thinking and faith, in a synthesis which at the same time expresses the preeminence of faith. It thereby sows the seed for a further encroachment of faith into the realm of truth itself, that is, for a relativation of the concept of the system. The fact that thinking and faith must complement each other is implied in the thesis and its rational non-rationality. It is repeated in the antithesis, where revelation is based upon creation and both enter redemption together. The synthesis now completes the unity of thinking and faith by joining both in one sentence. It is the ultimate refutation of the "dual truth, a truth of reason vis-à-vis a truth of faith."[40] If the Scholastics of the Middle Ages had made thinking into a

[40] 280.

picture, in front of which there was "a veil to open and shut at will,"[41] then the sentence "God is truth" unites faith and thinking at the most visible place in that very picture.

In this high point of the system a new shift in the evaluation of the system's first part is evident. At the stage of theology the construction had become an analogy of believing experience, and its beginning, the hypothetical Nought, had become a real Nought. But even in its result as a real Nought, the construction still has an important role to play. Here, too, it certainly is "the original institution" to which "continual return" is needed "so that by this summoning to concentration new strength could again and again be drawn from the depths of the beginning."[42] The elements of thinking are the "nought posited before life."[43] The pagan gods, the lords of death, the lords of the Nought, are themselves also Nought. "But as lords merely of the Nought they themselves become – Noughts."[44] This new conception of the construction is also proclaimed in the preceding part of the system, where from the perspective of the redeemed world the metalogical world in its entirety was equated with the Nought.[45]

If we now ask how Rosenzweig could arrive at a new, essential All – though one that is based on God – in spite of his shattering of the idealistic All, that is, how he could nevertheless philosophize systematically, we must take into consideration here, just as we did in the case of the dialectic relationship of faith and thinking, whether the completed structure is not already represented in the nature of the building blocks. It will thereby be seen that this ultimate unity of all being was already assumed from the beginning and that the conditions for the solution were given along with the posing of the problem. The concept of the All has a role to play from the very first moment, and the theoretical aspect of the unity is always present next to the realistic-empirical multiplicity. That experience of the threefold factuality which is the system's point of departure is shaped by thinking into three Alls, that is, into three unities. But how can there be three Alls? Three Alls are in themselves a paradox. The moment they are conceived they can only be valid as specifications of one imagined All of reality. The demand to advance from three Alls to one All can only be made if a unity is assumed to be contained in the triad of factualities, that is, if the triad is already seen from the viewpoint of unity. – Similarly, the fact that God is the subject of this All, that it must ultimately be

[41] 280.
[42] 315.
[43] 367.
[44] 382.
[45] 120.

He upon whom the All is based, is implied in the first experience of factuality and its reconstruction in thinking. Among the three unities God is especially emphasized. For if God is experienced and conceived as the absolutely universal, His ascendancy over the other two Alls is thereby also expressed. Strictly speaking there must be nothing *next to* an absolute universal. As a matter of course an absolute universal must claim to comprise everything else *under* itself. A compulsion to advance to one All is present not only in the juxtaposition of the three Alls but also in this claim of A = A to a special position vis-à-vis the other two factualities. Rosenzweig mentions that Kant had surmised the factuality of God as *common root* of the thing in itself and intelligible character, that is, of world and man.[46] Further, "without recourse to reasoning..." Kant had surmised "the reality of the common All which was only guessed at in the 'common root.'"[47] As a result idealism "with this surmise alone,... opens the prospect on an All in which these three elements, world, man, God, live side by side in undisturbed factuality."[48]

The elements thus contained an empirical, non-rational stratum next to the formal, constructive stratum that aimed at unity, specifically a unity not merely of each of the individual elements within itself but of the three elements together. These two strata can then be traced throughout the course of the system. Our differentiation between relative and absolute act as well as between relative and absolute eternity served the pursuance of this duality of viewpoints. With their arrangement of the three elements as equal, relative act as well as relative eternity descend from the experienced triad, while absolute act and absolute eternity, which are arranged according to the construction plan, are the bearers of the concept of unity. Accordingly, the second part unequivocally brings the one All of God, world and man, even if in temporal succession and in flowing movement. Here, too, the absoluteness of God is stressed. The absolute act rules over the relative act and ultimately leads to God, the existing All in which world and man merge. In the third part the essential All finally arises from the concept of eternity, an All which as predicate joins the existing God, the unified All, as subject and which thereby brings the system to its conclusion.

If the ascendancy of faith over thinking and of existence over essence is clearly expressed in the concept of the system, then existence finally also encroaches upon essence itself. It is possible to detect therein another sign of the activity of the antithesis vis-à-vis the thesis. Rosenzweig poses the question as to what truth, which according to the view of idealism vouches for

[46] 21.
[47] 147.
[48] 145.

itself, really is. Through discerning and profound investigation he arrives at the answer that truth is none other than a fact that in turn stands on itself as a fact demanding trust. Truth must therefore refer to the existing God who is truth. "That God is the truth, the concept with which we had to designate the essence of God, is the last thing we recognized in him as Lord of the Last, of the one life which is consummated in the All of the hypercosmos. And this last concept of his essence dissolves in our fingers. For if God is the truth – what does this tell us about his 'essence.'? Nothing but that he is the primeval ground of truth and that all truth is truth only by virtue of deriving from him."[49] Truth "is none other than God's revealing himself. Even the 'ultimate' that we know of God is none other than the innermost that we know of him, namely that he reveals himself to us. . . the apparent knowledge concerning his essence becomes the proximate, immediate experience of his activity: that he is truth tells us in the final analysis none other than that he – loves."[50]

This return to the antithesis corresponds exactly to Rosenzweig's final opinion regarding the construction. The result of the construction is no longer designated together with its beginning as a real Nought. Rather, mention is again made only of the hypothetical Nought of the beginning, a Nought that becomes "a mysterious predication,"[51] a "prophecy"[52] of revelation. This evaluation from the perspective of revelation, however, now finds its justification in the revelatory character of truth. For in the declaration "God is truth" the Nought signifies essence and therefore like truth the Nought is ultimately something non-actual and dependent, "a fact which is still seeking the ground on which it stands."[53] Thus even in the Nought of God merely a leading up to revelation may be detected. "As the answer 'God is truth' brings the mystical question concerning His hypercosmic essence, this ultimate question, back to the living discovery of His actions, so too the answer 'He is Nought' leads the abstract question concerning His protocosmic essence, this pristine question, forward to the same discovery."[54]

In the truth that does not vouch for itself but rather is based in revelation man, too, along with his experience, can find his place. Man receives the truth from God as his share, which he has to verify in the *hic et nunc* of his creaturely life, in the Here of birth and the Now of rebirth, in creatureliness of the world and creatureliness of man. These two possibilities of verifying truth that are open to man crystallize in the two eternal communities, Judaism and Chris-

[49] 388.
[50] 388–389.
[51] 389.
[52] 389.
[53] 390.
[54] 390.

tianity, which are discussed once more from the viewpoint of the verification of truth. The Jew is the man of the Here, the believer from birth, whose rebirth signifies the revelation to his people at Sinai and thus does not occur to him personally. The Christian is the man of the Now, the believer by virtue of rebirth, who personally experiences revelation and who places at the foundation of this personal experience the birth at Bethlehem. In these two, in the Jew and the Christian, world and man, rest and movement, creation and revelation – which complete each other and come only in the truth of God – are once again embodied. Rosenzweig points out the dangers that threaten both of them in their passage beyond the dynamic unity of believing experience to absolute unity which would thereby lead to a new isolation of God, world and man from each other.

This application of the notion of verification to Judaism and Christianity contains an analogy to Lessing's fable of the rings.* Rosenzweig justifies this fable in all its profundity. Nathan the Wise also teaches that truth, that is, the authenticity of the rings, is proved by the verification of their owners. There is nevertheless a questionable aspect to the fable in that of the three rings two are in fact false and their owners live in a state of illusion that is willed by God. In the case of Rosenzweig verification is merely "countersignature" to the existential character of truth. Truth is not something static that can be handed over like a ring. Rather, it *comes to be* in God's revelation and man's verification. God, He who exists, is more than truth. Truth is supported by Him and it is only as His revelation that truth is alloted to man. Man, as the recipient of this allotment, must verify it with his life. Both, God's existence and man's existence, are alone that which bestows meaning upon truth.** It is only through them that truth becomes truth, or, as Rosenzweig expresses it, that the star turns into the image of living matter. The truth is the illumination of the divine countenance in whose image man was created.

The entire antithesis finally arises therefore in the movement backwards from redemption to revelation and to creation, from God, He who exists in redemption as the unified All to the revelation of truth and to the creaturely verification by man, to that believing experience of which it was said elsewhere that it is "founded and promised."[55] "It is experience only for those who are conscious of coming from that foundation and who have determined to

---

[55] *Anmerkungen zu Jehuda Halevi*, p. 205.

   * The reference is to Gotthold Ephraim Lessing's play, *Nathan the Wise* (1779), in which the fable of three rings, each of equal value and each representing one of the three monotheistic faiths, provides the play's *leitmotif*. (editor's note)

   ** Cf. M. Heidegger, *Sein und Zeit*, p. 226: "There is truth only inasmuch as and as long as there is existence."

proceed into that promise. To the others it is invisible, but to them it is experience... This experience is not at all suited for education. In order to be made suitable it demands those who are already educated – educated by life."[56] So it is that the final word of *The Star of Redemption* is not thinking but faith; not essence, but freedom; not the system but speech thinking. And Rosenzweig makes yet another step backwards. This final word of philosophy must be verified by the philosopher who thinks it. The problem of the philosophizing man accompanied the course of the system in the introductions to each of the three parts. It began with the experience of death, where the philosopher undertakes to philosophize from the "standpoint," proceeded to the experience of revelation, where the philosopher became a theologian of experience, and ended in the unification of the experience of thinking and faith in the personal union of the philosopher and the theologian. This problem is finally solved in the personal responsibility of the philosopher to everyday life.

[56] *Ibid.*